D0071144

The New War on Drugs:
Symbolic Politics and Criminal Justice Policy

Edited by
Eric L. Jensen
University of Idaho
Jurg Gerber
Sam Houston State University

ACJS Series Editor, Joycelyn M. Pollock

Academy of Criminal Justice Sciences
Northern Kentucky University
402 Nunn Hall
Highland Heights, KY 41076

Anderson Publishing Co.
Criminal Justice Division
P.O. Box 1576
Cincinnati, OH 45201-1576

The New War on Drugs:
Symbolic Politics and Criminal Justice Policy

ISBN 0-87084-438-5
Library of Congress Catalog Number 97-80358

Gail Eccleston *Editor*
Elizabeth A. Shipp *Assistant Editor*

*Dedicated
to the memory of
Alfred Lindesmith*

Foreword

Hans Magnus Enzenberger[†] once coined the term "the heroes of withdrawal." With this expression, he had in mind historical characters who took the leading role in dissolving empires. Other formulations were "the great debuilders" or "the great demolitioners." With these expressions, he established the counterpoint to the great entrepreneurs in world history. Alexander the Great was an empire builder; so were Queen Victoria and Genghis Khan. They created large social systems—honor and fame stuck to their names.

Enzenberger was interested in the opposite characters, those who proved essential in transforming what often were aggressive empires into more modest forms. History is also filled with such personages, but often described in less heroic and celebrating terms. János Kádár of Hungary, seen by many as a traitor (also by himself, he turned insane toward the end), was also highly respected for rescuing elements of civility when Joseph Stalin brought Hungary under severe pressure. General Jaruzelski from Poland was seen as a traitor because of his opposition to Solidarity and democratic demands, but slowly built a base for those who despised him. And of course Mikhail Gorbachev, the super debuilder, created the foundation that dissolved the basic features of the former Soviet Union. The empire builders stand out as the heroes, but their accomplishments might be of no greater value than those of the demolishers.

The drug empires are interesting political entities. They have czars and servants. They have their strongholds within certain national bases, but relate to opposite numbers in other countries. They have diplomats at their disposal, reaching out to other nations and to the United Nations. They dispose armies in the form of police and customs officers. Sometimes they also use the soldiers, airplanes, boats, and surveillance systems of the ordinary military system. These are empires constructed for war.

Such empires need suitable enemies. A suitable enemy for generals is one that is strong enough to keep the machinery of war at optimum level, but not so strong that it prevents the empire builders from their war profits. The drug-control empires are strong on both counts. Drugs are dangerous for many, have strong effects, and are distributed by a system that is difficult to fight. While they are strong enemies, they are not so dangerously strong that a war against them would end easily in visible defeats. In the war against drugs, the enemy is well chosen. The enemy is not the great killers, alcohol and tobacco, with their

---

[†] Enzenberger's article was printed in several major European newspapers in early 1990. My copy is from *Information*, December 29, 1989.

well-established strong producers and users, nor is it the numerous sedatives from the pharmaceutical industry. The enemy is the much more suitable auxiliary category, the pleasure-providers, produced mostly outside the major empires, and initially introduced mostly by national newcomers or foreigners.

The drug empire reaps enormous war profits. Czars achieve honor, fame, and dignity. Hawks among politicians get their votes and the media get their stories. And, as Beckett and Sasson point out in this book, political troubles are neutralized. Drugs provide an explanation for most of what is not perfect within a society. Also, within welfare states built on a relatively egalitarian ideology, defects are visible: young people without paid employment, homeless people, and general misery. "If not for the drugs, we had lived in a paradise." In countries with less welfare and more rudely expressed class differences, the war on drugs is also useful in the direct control of the dangerous classes, those with so little to lose that they cannot be controlled into obedience by any means other than direct physical coercion. Again, drugs are exceptionally well suited, a theme developed in several chapters in this book.

But cracks exist in the frontier surrounding the control empires. Warriors need victories. In the drug war, these are few and far between. The street prices in most industrialized countries are going down. Drugs are easily available. The drug warriors' claim of success—victories—are based mostly on an hypothesis that the situation would have been even worse if not for the war. This is not unlike the claims by military headquarters that, when defeat is near, send out bulletins of "victorious retreat."

However, even highly successful wars are not without costs. In the drug wars, these costs become increasingly visible. Most important is the death toll. In most Western countries, a number of long-term heroin users live in miserable conditions. Although still relatively young, they are worn out in the endless struggle to maintain their daily drug intake. Tired and sick, they live at the threshold of death.

If their condition had been related to an honorable cause, there would be no limits to the efforts to rescue them. If it were a new type of cancer hitting computer workers, or a contagious disease spreading among professional athletes, money would not be an issue and hospitals would work overtime. This is not the case when it comes to these drug users.

We know that such simple measures can improve their survival ability: methadone, controlled doses of heroin, needle exchanges, and clean localities for using needles. And most of all, general social and medical services are needed. Unfortunately, these measures are taken only with rare exception. In most systems, including my country, Norway, doctors are not allowed to function as doctors when life-threatening conditions are believed to be "caused" by drugs. The drug user might be seen as "deserving to suffer." Worse, if the drug user receives treatment, his neighbor might be tempted to use drugs knowing that the danger to a drug user's life is not quite that significant. Within penal law, this type of thinking is classified as an example of deterrence or general prevention. But to think like this in medicine represents an anomaly. Most doctors think that Hippocrates had a point when claiming that the doctor's obligations are first and foremost to treat the individual patient, not to deter that patient's neighbor. A growing uneasiness among doctors regarding their function as warriors in a penal law directed against drugs might lead to one of the first major moves toward a greater medical autonomy in the drug arena.

Another cost has to do with money, but not the money of the warriors, the czars and their officers, the customs officers, police, judges, and prison guards; the war provides jobs for them. Many earn their living by fighting drugs, and the prison industry is great for many interests. But one type of cost that is particularly disturbing is the uncontrolled flood of money from the drug users to the drug dealers. The illegality of drugs has caused a trade system to develop that is even more uncontrolled than ordinary international trade. Taxation becomes impossible, giving some parties undue advantages. It is not easy for ordinary businesses to buy a factory when some bidders appear with unlimited resources. It is not surprising that the drug-control empires meet opposition from established businesses on the right wing of the political map; usually they are the most vigorous supporters of law, order, and pain for the outcast.

Some would add strained international relations to the list of costs in this war, but this matter is complicated, particularly if we look into state interests. Who gained and who lost when we examine the Panama invasion? In whose interest is it that the military systems of Latin America are modernized to increase efficiency in the war against drugs? And when it comes to Western military systems, who was not interested in alternative targets when the cold war ended? Enemies should not die, but should be brought to near-death defeat. United States' extension of its drug agenda to countries outside its own borders (cf. Kevin F. Ryan in this volume) might prove highly useful in preserving the country as the leading military world power.

The victories in the drug war are few, but the costs are considerable, as are the effects of the great length of time that has passed. Cannabis, heroin, cocaine, and crack have all been seen as the ultimate threats to civil society. More recently, the focus has been on the drug "ecstasy," so much so that the old threats have lost their central position in the competition for attention. And, as pointed out by Beckett and Sasson in this volume, the media need new angles. Two new sources appear: drug users and scientists. Drug users have had time to organize, and in this process have also given the enemy a human face. The scientific community has had time for more sober studies and reflections. Many of the first panics were nurtured by claims from rather simplified statements on the approaching "doomsday." But then followed the scrutiny of the first reports, and the doomsday was declared postponed. Inger Sagatun-Edwards' article in this volume on the supposed need for special measures against illegal drug use by pregnant women exemplifies this process. With more time, it has also been possible to place the various panics in an historical perspective. Schivelbusch (1981), on the history of stimulants, and Berridge and Edwards (1981) on "Opium for the People," are relevant early examples.

Which brings us back to Hans Magnus Enzenberger.

The empire builders could not build until the time was ripe, the wheel was invented, boats were constructed, population surplus was available, or the discrepancies between ideals and realities became embarrassingly visible. This is also true for the great de-builders; the time had to be right. Gorbachev's influence was essential, but he could not have made his historic contribution in the 1960s. The situation within the drug-control empire is of the same character. When is the time ripe? When will the dissonance for the doctors acting under command of penal law become so great that they break out of the ranks, disobey the commanders, show civil disobedience, and act as ordinary doctors again? And concerning the economy, when will the upsetting effects on the more ordinary business system be so strongly felt and expressed among powerful figures and in the media that right-wing opposition will crack the front?

As for the scientific community, an increasing amount of data and analysis provide fertile ground for critique. In Norway, the leader in the field of legal thinking on punishment and deterrence, Professor Johs Andenaes, calls the war against drugs the greatest criminal-political mistake of this century. At a recent meeting of the American Criminological Association, Alfred Blumstein expressed much of the same view in his presidential address. Additionally, there is the growing literature, including this book, that describes the construction of a problem and the intellectually untenable situation in which the empire builders have placed themselves. What goes on is a cultural elaboration preparing the ground for a shift in the meaning given to drugs in modern society. The time seems to be ripe for a de-builder.

Nils Christie
University of Oslo

Preface

This volume examines the various anti-drug campaigns—"drug wars"—that have taken place in the United States, and their effects and implications on the criminal justice system. Included are critical discussions about several drug wars, beginning with the anti-opiate campaign following the enactment of the Harrison Act in 1914, all from the social constructionist perspective. Constructionists believe that a combination of political opportunism, media profit maximation, and a desire among criminal justice professionals to increase their spheres of influence has led to many misguided drug policies. Not ignoring the fact that the use and abuse of drugs can lead to numerous forms of harm, the editors present several alternatives to the drug-war solutions that have been used throughout the world.

Acknowledgments

The writing and editing of a book involves the contributions of many people. Whereas authors and editors receive credit in the form of having their names on the covers of books, these other people, who often remain in the background, are almost as responsible for the books seeing the light of day as are the authors/editors. A first such individual is Joy Pollock, the ACJS/Anderson Monograph Series Editor. She not only supported and encouraged us for the better part of two years, but she also provided detailed suggestions and recommendations on each of the chapters.

Editing a book, we were warned, is a thankless job. You will be chasing contributors, be forced to hound them, and not be successful in obtaining their cooperation most of the time, we were told. It would be easier to write the book ourselves, the conventional wisdom indicated. Nothing could be further from the truth. Working with the authors of these chapters has been a genuine pleasure. Notwithstanding their heavy workloads, they have invariably found (and made) time to respond to our requests promptly.

Finally, two individuals at Sam Houston State University deserve credit for their contributions. Joann Davis and Kay Billingsley edited, copy-edited, and typed the entire manuscript. If it had not been for their assistance we would not have met any of the deadlines.

Contents

1

The Social Construction
of Drug Problems:
An Historical Overview

Eric L. Jensen
University of Idaho

Jurg Gerber
Sam Houston State University

The criminal justice system in the United States has undergone substantial changes in the past decade. Most of these changes are a result of the 1986 War on Drugs (Nadelmann, 1993; Gordon, 1994; Irwin & Austin, 1994; Jensen & Gerber, 1996). The scope of these alterations in the contemporary American criminal justice system is matched only by those of the due process revolution of the 1960s and 1970s. Several of these major changes include:

- the police have been pressured to increase arrests for drug violations,

- with the advent of the civil forfeiture of assets policy, law enforcement officials have been accused of "policing for profit,"

- several states that had decriminalized the possession of small amounts of cannabis products have recriminalized this behavior,

- court systems are overloaded with persons charged with drug offenses,

- stiff mandatory sentences have been enacted for drug offenses,

- sentences for crack-related offenses have become extremely punitive,

1

- attempts have been made to criminalize women's drug-related behaviors during pregnancy,

- the military has been used for drug-related law enforcement functions,

- prison populations have increased dramatically for drug offenses.

Furthermore, the new severe punishments for drug-related offenses fall disproportionately on members of racial and ethnic minority groups.

These direct outcomes of the War on Drugs on the justice system have also been accompanied by the expansion of the civil powers of the state and private employers into new areas of our daily lives in an effort to combat the drug problem. Examples of these combative efforts include the civil seizure and forfeiture of assets in drug cases and the use of child protection laws to remove children from the custody of mothers accused of drug use during pregnancy. In addition, drug testing, which has historically been restricted to convicted felons with drug problems, has become relatively common in the workplace and among student athletes.

These expansions of criminal justice system tools into the civil arena have greatly increased state control over citizens and private employers' control over their employees. However, because these controls are outside the jurisdiction of criminal courts, due process protections are often not required.

The influence of the United States drug policy is not limited to the American system of justice. The federal government has exported its orientation toward dealing with drug problems throughout the western hemisphere and to Europe, both by example and through explicit political pressures on policymakers in other nations. This most recent "discovery" of the drug problem, the related fundamental shifts in the nature and operation of the American system of criminal justice, and the influence of the 1986 War on Drugs in the United States and on Canadian drug policy are the subjects of this book.

PERSPECTIVES ON THE CREATION OF SOCIAL PROBLEMS: OBJECTIVE HARM AND SOCIAL CONSTRUCTIONISM

Two competing perspectives exist in the sociological literature on the creation of social problems: the objectivist perspective and the social constructionist theory. The objectivist perspective defines a social problem as a societal condition that causes harm to individuals or to society as a whole (e.g., Basis, Gelles & Levine, 1982). According to this perspective, harm to people or the social order is the observable (or objective) reality by which a social problem is gauged. For example, the drug problem would be thought of as worsening if more people were using illegal drugs, or if an increase in violence was found to be associated with the drug trade.

One criticism of the objectivist perspective is that "not all harmful conditions are considered social problems" (Best, 1989:xvi). The inequitable treatment of racial and ethnic minority groups in America, for example, has only periodically been perceived as a social problem by the dominant group (e.g., from the mid-1950s through the mid-1960s), even though structurally-based inequality has been a fact of life for subordinate group members for centuries.

In line with the objectivist perspective, the emergence of a social problem would lead to public policy that is a politically neutral response to the objective conditions. A growing body of research has indicated that this has not been the case with criminal justice policies (Reinarman & Levine, 1989; Gerber et al., 1990; Jensen, Gerber & Babcock, 1991; Gordon, 1994; Beckett, 1995a). Since illegal drug use has long been perceived of as one of the most destructive and "evil" forms of deviance in American society, and has been associated with "dangerous classes" of people by claimsmakers, we should expect the political and policy-making rhetoric surrounding this issue to be highly value laden (Lindesmith, 1940; Bonnie & Whitebread, 1974; Reinarman, 1994a).

In contrast to the objectivist perspective, the social constructionist theory proposes that a social condition becomes a social problem only when groups or collectivities bring attention to it and influence people to think of it as problematic. According to an influential proponent of the social constructionist theory, it

> attempts to describe and explain how new definitions of social problems emerge, how troublesome persons or social arrangements are identified, how institutions are created to deal with them . . . it is attempting to explain how society, *through an essentially political process, discovers* . . . its problems (Spector, 1983-1984:11-12, emphasis added).

Since the 1970s, numerous scholars have used the constructionist theory to study how social conditions come to be perceived as problematic. Some have treated social problems as unique phenomena (Spector & Kitsuse, 1977), while others have studied them using social movement theory and resource mobilization theory in particular (e.g., McCarthy & Zald, 1973, 1977). Another development in this theoretical work was to combine these two perspectives, as in the work of Mauss (1975, 1984, 1989) who argued that social problems were a type of social movement. There may be social movements without a social problem, but every social problem must be created by a social movement.

Mauss (1975) proposed that problems arise from the grassroots level of activism in a series of five stages: (1) a condition is seen by only a few people as problematic (incipiency), (2) organizations are formed that champion the issue as problematic (coalescence), (3) governmental agencies recognize the existence of a problem and respond to it (institutionalization), (4) the movement then begins to fall apart largely through its own success (fragmentation), and (5) may eventually disappear (demise). Crucial to this model is the notion that the movement begins with some popular concern (incipiency and coalescence), followed by official recognition. Furthermore, an assumption is made that these movements are what McCarthy & Zald (1973, 1977) called *classical social movements*. In such movements, social movement organizations are seen as comprising primarily "beneficiaries," that is, people who benefit directly from social movement organization success. Conversely, adherents and supporters of professional social movement organizations are often "conscience" supporters, people who do not directly benefit in the case of organizational success. They participate in and support the organization for other reasons.

Other studies have revealed that some social problems are created by government officials acting on their own behalf. They may champion a cause based on their personal or organizational interests, lay claim to a condition as falling under their purview, and *then* attempt to build public support for their claims (Chauncey, 1980; Randall & Short, 1983). In this instance, what Mauss called institutionalization *precedes* public awareness and concern. As will be discussed later in this chapter, in our analyses of the 1986 War on Drugs in the United States (Jensen et al., 1991) and in Canada (Jensen & Gerber, 1993) we found this to be the case. Politicians championed drugs as a social problem before the public expressed concern over them in opinion polls. Building on the work of Randall & Short (1983) we created a modified version of Mauss's five stages of social problem/social movement development. The first two stages, incipiency and coalescence are similar to the original model. There *may* be an initial awareness of a condition as potentially problematic (incipiency), which *may* be followed by the emergence of social movement organizations (coalescence). However, the two stages that follow are very different under these circumstances:

> 3. Creation and Policy Formation. The creation and policy formation stage is central to this model. In this stage, powerful interests such as politicians or governmental agency personnel claim the existence of an undesirable condition, argue for the legitimacy of their claims, and develop a solution for the politically constructed problem in an attempt to advance their own interests.

> 4. Legitimation. By publicizing their claims, politicians or other state officials attempt to create or strengthen public support for their position. In addition, these state problem

constructors must establish the legitimacy of their claims and remedies in order to support their political or organizational interests (Jensen et al., 1991; Jensen & Gerber, 1993).

Eventually the issue may become fully institutionalized in governmental policies and bureaucracies (e.g., the War on Drugs gave rise to the creation of a federal "drug czar"), or it may wither away (e.g., the War on Poverty).

An important aspect of the social construction of social problems is what Best (1989) referred to as typification. Claimsmakers not only bring attention to conditions that they consider problematic, they also "characterize a problem's nature" (Best, 1989:xx). That is, the people who construct problems usually define the cause of the problem and recommend solutions to it based on their interests and stake in the issue. For example, Reinarman and Levine (1989) pointed out that the New Right felt threatened by changes in society and set out to impose what they referred to as "traditional family values" into national policy during the 1980s. Part of their agenda was to reinforce the perception of social problems as simply the consequences of individual moral choices, without regard to the complex interplay of social, economic, and political factors (Reinarman & Levine, 1989).

Thus, social constructionism focuses on both the political processes and claims-making typification that define conditions as problems. Perceptions of the nature of problems are also created that often reflect the interests of the claimsmakers, rather than an objective description of the issue.

THE SOCIAL CONSTRUCTION OF UNITED STATES DRUG WARS PRIOR TO 1986

The United States has a long history of socially constructed drug panics and "wars." For various political, moral, and economic reasons discussed, a war on drugs is declared, claims are made, solutions proposed, counterclaims are made, and some form of compromise is reached. The war is subsequently either declared won, or public and political attention drifts away to a new issue. However, eventually drugs reemerge as a political and social issue.

We trace in this section the history of drug wars in the United States prior to the 1986 War on Drugs. Two main drug wars and several smaller ones occurred in the twentieth century. The campaign against opiates in the early years of the century focused on the use and medical prescription of opium, morphine, and heroin. In the 1930s, a nationwide campaign against marijuana resulted in federal legislation. Following World War II, in the 1950s amidst the

Red Scare, the harshest federal anti-drug laws to date were enacted. This, in turn, was followed by a counter movement in the 1960s and 1970s that focused on the decriminalization of marijuana. In the 1970s, President Nixon waged his war on drugs; by 1986, the country was ready for another major war.

The Anti-Opiate Campaign

The first drug law in the United States was a city ordinance in San Francisco enacted in 1875 that prohibited the smoking or possession of opium, the operation of opium dens, or the possession of opium pipes. Nevada then enacted a statute that outlawed the retail sale of opium in 1877. Twenty other states, many in the West where most of the Chinese lived, subsequently passed similar laws (Bonnie & Whitebread, 1974). Since smoking opium was mainly limited to the Chinese, these laws were clearly intended to facilitate the social control of this minority group through the use of the criminal justice system (Bonnie & Whitebread, 1974; see also Quinney, 1970). These laws were passed at a time when the Chinese were perceived as a threat to the jobs of the white working class. The Chinese had originally been drawn to the United States around 1850 by the California gold rush. When the gold rush tapered off, many Chinese went to work as laborers on the transcontinental railroad. With the completion of the railroad came a labor surplus in California and hostilities against the Chinese developed. Numerous violent attacks against the Chinese occurred in the gold camps and cities of the West during the 1870s and 1880s. Legal actions against the Chinese culminated in 1882 with the Chinese Exclusion Act which forbade Chinese from entering the United States.

Although smoking opium was criminalized in the late 1800s, opiates in other forms were as accessible during the nineteenth century as aspirin is today. Physicians dispensed morphine and heroin directly to patients and wrote prescriptions for these drugs, pharmacies sold opiates over the counter without prescriptions, even grocery stores and mail order houses sold opiates. An Iowa survey, for example, found 3,000 stores in the state where opiates were sold in the mid-1880s. Opiate drugs (i.e., opium and morphine) were most commonly consumed in the form of patent medicines. They were sold under such names as Ayer's Cherry Pectoral, Mrs. Winslow's Soothing Syrup, and Godfrey's Cordial—a mixture of opium, molasses for sweetening, and sassafras for flavoring. These patent medicines were recommended for a wide variety of ailments including pain, coughs, "women's troubles," diarrhea, and dysentery (Brecher, 1972:3-6).

While the nonmedical use of opiates was not considered respectable and was even thought of as immoral in some circles in the nineteenth century—a vice as reprehensible as dancing, smoking tobacco, and gambling—it was not as subject to a severe societal reaction as it is today. Employees were not fired for addiction, spouses did not divorce each other for being addicted, and children were not taken from their homes and placed in foster homes or institutions if their parents were addicts. In short, addicts were free to participate fully in the life of the community (Brecher, 1972:6). Prior to the criminalization of opiates and the stigmatization of addicts as outsiders, being an addict was not related to many of the problems associated with addiction today such as poor health, street crime, and being engulfed in a drug subculture.

Why did the opiate situation in the United States change so drastically? As might be expected, the answer lies in the anti-opiate movement. This movement emerged from a complex of commercial, religious, and nationalistic interests. Around the turn of the century, American missionaries overseas initiated a drive for the international control of opiates. This moral crusade was led by the Right Reverend Charles H. Brent, Episcopal Bishop of the Philippine Islands. Whereas the religious interests based their concerns on a Christian ideology that emphasized discipline and responsibility, economic conflicts between British, Chinese, and American business interests also contributed to the movement. For many years the British had been shipping opium grown in India to China, but some Chinese saw this as unfair competition. American missionaries saw it as the ruin of the Chinese people, and members of the American business community wanted to divert the Chinese trade in their direction (Brecher, 1972:48). At the request of the Right Reverend Brent, President Theodore Roosevelt called for an international conference on opium, which took place in Shanghai in 1908 and led to The Hague International Opium Conference of 1912. The Hague Conference passed a resolution calling for international controls over opiates.

Paralleling this international drive against opiates was a campaign in the United States against the patent medicine industry led by Dr. Harvey Wiley, Chief of the Bureau of Food and Drugs, and his following of crusading journalists known as "muckrakers." Their efforts were primarily responsible for passage of the Pure Food and Drug Act of 1906 which required that medicines containing opiates be labeled as such.

The institutionalization of the anti-opiate movement came with the passage of the Harrison Act of 1914. While the Act prohibited the importation of opium for smoking, it was primarily a licensing and taxing device that allowed pharmacists and physicians to continue prescribing narcotics. Manufacturers of patent medicines were exempted from the licensing and tax provisions of the Act if their products contained less than a specified amount of opiate. Brecher (1972:49) concluded, "Far from appearing to be a prohibition law, the Harrison Narcotic Act on its face was merely a law for the orderly marketing of opium, morphine, heroin, and other drugs . . . It is unlikely that a single legislator realized . . . that the law . . . would later be deemed a prohibition law."

Law enforcement officials, particularly the Narcotics Division of the Treasury Department which was created by the Harrison Act to enforce its provisions, interpreted the phrase "in the course of his professional practice, only" as prohibiting physicians from prescribing opiates to addicts. Even though the conceptualization of addiction as a disease and support for the medical treatment of addicts were prevalent among the public and physicians at the time, the Narcotics Division set out on a two-pronged campaign to criminalize opiates and change public attitudes about these drugs.

With this apparent justification in the Harrison Act, law enforcement officers in 1919 began to arrest physicians for writing prescriptions for opiates in the course of treating addicts. The courts were often in agreement with the law enforcement position, and in a series of decisions during the next three years (1919-1922), the Supreme Court effectively prohibited physicians from prescribing narcotics to addicts.

In conjunction with its efforts to increase its jurisdiction over drugs and eliminate the role of physicians in drug treatment, the Narcotics Division launched a campaign to "educate" the American public about the "evils" of opiates and the drug addict. The core of this public relations (or legitimation) effort has been called the "dope fiend mythology." This mythology contained the following elements: the drug addict is a violent criminal, the addict is a moral degenerate (i.e., a liar, thief, etc.), drug peddlers and addicts want to convert others into addicts, and the addict takes drugs because of an abnormal personality (Lindesmith, 1940). The Narcotics Division made extensive use of the media in its "educational" campaign about the dangers of "dope fiends." The propaganda disseminated by the division often contained false, sensational charges such as the widespread addiction among children and the physical effects of opiate addiction that included insanity; diseased lungs, hearts, and kidneys; rotting of the skin; and sterility (Dickson, 1968).

The Narcotics Division solidified its jurisdiction over opiates with the U.S. Supreme Court decision in *United States v. Behrman,* 258 U.S. 280 (1922) which held that physicians could not supply drugs to addicts even in an effort to cure them. The Narcotics Division had succeeded in its drive to eliminate the medical treatment of addicts, criminalize opiates, and change public attitudes toward the addict and addiction through a series of carefully selected test cases and its "educational" campaign. Commenting on the situation five decades ago, the eminent sociologist Alfred Lindesmith concluded that, "The treatment of addicts in the United States today is on no higher plane than the persecution of witches of other ages" (1940:208). With its bureaucratic control over the opiate problem established, the Division withdrew from active agitation and enjoyed its expanded enforcement role until the 1930s when the next anti-drug campaign was initiated (Mauss, 1975).

Thus, the shift in handling drug users and abusers from the health care system to the criminal justice system created the context for the types of illegal drug problems that the United States experiences today. Users are now heavily stigmatized; forced to obtain drugs at extremely high black-market prices from illegal sources; involved in drug subcultures in order to obtain drugs; ostracized from the mainstream society; often are required to resort to property crimes and prostitution in order to obtain money to pay for the drugs; suffer many negative health consequences of addiction that are largely related to their subcultural lifestyle; and learn the value system of the subculture that includes a set of justifications for their harmful lifestyles.

The Criminalization of Marijuana

A number of states passed anti-marijuana legislation before a federal statute was enacted. Between 1914 and 1931, 29 states, most of which were in the West, passed anti-cannabis statutes. The states leading this drive were those with large populations of immigrants from Mexico or the Caribbean such as Colorado, Texas, and Louisiana (Bonnie & Whitebread, 1974). As with the earlier anti-opiate laws, the specters of racism and scapegoating were major influences on the passage of these laws. Mexicans and blacks were portrayed as drug-crazed violent criminals who were destroying communities throughout the West and Southwest. An editorial in a San Antonio newspaper in 1917 stated, in part: "The men who smoke this herb become excited to such an extent that they go through periods of near frenzy, and worse, it is always aggressive as the crimes which have been committed in garrisons, armories, barracks, and the humble suburbs of Mexico [attest]" (as cited in Bonnie & Whitebread, 1974:36).

The racist rhetoric surrounding these anti-cannabis campaigns was fueled during the early stages of the Depression by the existence of a labor surplus pool. From 1900 to 1930, a large wave of Mexicans had immigrated to the United States to escape the chaotic conditions of revolutionary Mexico and in search of better economic conditions. Then in 1929-1934, the federal government established a program of repatriation that was responsible for deporting hundreds of thousands of Mexicans (and United States citizens of Mexican descent). Thus, the circumstances underlying the passage of these anti-marijuana statutes at the state level were remarkably similar to those surrounding the enactment of laws prohibiting smoking opium in the late 1800s.

When the Narcotics Division was reorganized as the Bureau of Narcotics in 1930 it seemed content with its role in the fight against drugs. As of 1932, the Bureau advocated state jurisdiction over marijuana and did not consider marijuana use to be a major problem. In 1934, Commissioner Harry J. Anslinger and the Bureau reversed this position, however, and began a legitimation drive to convince the public and lawmakers that a "marijuana menace" plagued the nation (Bonnie & Whitebread, 1974:97-117). These efforts resulted in the passage of the Marijuana Tax Act in August 1937. Becker (1963) claimed that this anti-marijuana drive was a personal campaign of Anslinger. The commissioner was a virulent moral entrepreneur who led a drive to gain public and congressional support for passage of federal anti-marijuana legislation. Dickson (1968) noted that public concern with marijuana was negligible prior to the passage of this statute, and similar to its actions with the Harrison Act, the Bureau mounted an anti-marijuana campaign only after the legislation was passed. The Bureau's annual budgetary appropriations declined beginning in 1933, and Dickson (1968:155) argued that it reacted as any threatened organization might by trying to appear to be more necessary and attempting to increase its scope of operations. The result of this response was the Marijuana Tax Act and the Bureau's subsequent "public education" or legitimation campaign. Thus, Dickson (1968) interpreted the Bureau's anti-marijuana drive as a crusade generated by an organizational fight to survive. Bonnie and Whitebread (1974) noted that another important reason behind Anslinger's championing of anti-cannabis legislation was to eventually establish a federal-level drug law. This was not a simple task in an era of states' rights politics and ideology. In order to achieve this end, Anslinger became the dominant claimsmaker in this legislative battle. He first used the strategy of declaring a "marijuana menace" in 1934 in support of the passage of uniform drug laws at the state level, and later to gain passage of the federal Marijuana Tax Act of 1937. For example, one 1935 Bureau statement read: "Police officials in cities of those states where it is most widely used estimate that fifty percent of the violent crimes committed in districts occupied by Mexicans, Spaniards, Latin-Americans, Greeks, or Negroes may be traced to this evil" (as quoted in Bonnie & Whitebread, 1974:100). A widely circulated pamphlet published by the Bureau in 1936 stated:

> Prolonged use of Marihuana frequently develops a delirious rage which sometimes leads to high crimes, such as assault and murder. Hence Marihuana has been called the "killer drug." The habitual use of this narcotic poison always causes a very marked mental deterioration and sometimes produces insanity. . . .
>
> While the Marihuana habit leads to physical wreckage and mental decay, its effects upon character and morality are even more devastating. The victim frequently undergoes such moral degeneracy that he will lie and steal without scruple. . . . (as quoted in Bonnie & Whitebread, 1974:109).

In addition, Anslinger ordered the Bureau's agents throughout the nation to support this legitimation process through direct lobbying and "educational" efforts (Bonnie & Whitebread, 1974:95).

Each of these three views has credibility; Anslinger was clearly a moral crusader who championed the anti-drug theme and the accompanying "dope fiend" mythology throughout his long and unrelenting tenure as dean of the federal narcotics enforcers. Dickson's analysis of the organizational response to external pressure threatening survival of the Bureau added a valuable dimension to our understanding of the creation of the marijuana "problem." The thorough historical analysis conducted by Bonnie and Whitebread (1974) revealed a complex of organizational and political reasons underlying the actions of Anslinger and the Bureau in expanding the criminalization of cannabis products.

Two major points emerging from these studies of the origins of the Marijuana Tax Act of 1937 are the racism involved in this process, particularly in the early stages of state-level activities, and the entrepreneurial efforts of Harry Anslinger and the Bureau of Narcotics in creating the "marijuana menace," manipulating public opinion on the issue and, thus, legitimating its position on the criminalization of cannabis products. Once again, state agents were powerful claimsmakers in the creation of a national drug "problem."

With American involvement in World War II increasing, the Bureau was unable to generate continuing interest in the problem. However, the drug problem was "rediscovered" in the early 1950s.

The Anti-Narcotics Revival

The Bureau revived its anti-drug drive after World War II with this effort coalescing around the Kefauver Committee on Organized Crime in 1951. The Bureau claimed that illegal drug use was exploding, particularly among teenagers. There may have been some truth to these claims since organized crime had mounted an effort to expand heroin marketing in the ghettos of America and admissions to treatment programs were rising. The emphasis on teenagers appears to have been less credible, however.

This was a period of fear and suspicion across the nation. The Red Scare was a dominant theme in America. It should not be surprising that the fear of communism was also linked to the newest drug scare. As Bonnie & Whitebread (1974:209) noted, "A spy was behind every tree and a narcotics peddler right behind him. . . . The two sinister characters behind the tree were perceived to be one and the same. . . . Political cartoons and commentaries quite often attributed increased drug traffic to the efforts of Chinese Communism to dominate and demoralize American youth."

The institutionalization of this revival movement was marked by the passage of the Boggs Act in 1951, which set stiff minimum prison terms for violations of federal drug laws and for the first time included marijuana in the same category of drugs as heroin and cocaine (Bonnie & Whitebread, 1974:204-210). The subsequent Narcotic Control Bill of 1956 mandated even harsher sanctions for federal drug violations. These statutes were a reaffirmation of the "get tough" methods championed by the Bureau.

The dominance of a punitive approach to the drug problem continued throughout the 1950s. Around the end of the decade, however, Alfred Lindesmith—a long-time critic of this approach—the American Medical Association, and the American Bar Association challenged the Bureau's point of view and spoke out for a medical alternative in the treatment of addicts (Mauss, 1975). This objection to the Bureau's authority in drug-related matters and its punitive approach to handling addicts was expedited with the retirement of its crusading director, Harry J. Anslinger, in 1962.

The Reform Movement

Within one month after the retirement of Anslinger, the first White House Conference on Narcotic and Drug Abuse was held. This event signaled official recognition of the incipiency of the reform movement. Scientists and other national leaders at the conference concluded that anti-drug efforts were inaccurate and hindered progress in ameliorating drug problems (see Mauss, 1975).

Later in the 1960s, members of the scientific community were joined in their attack on the punitive approach to drug use by user groups. Following the early lead of Timothy Leary and Richard Alpert who advocated the spiritual benefits of hallucinogens, user groups such as BLOSSOM (Basic Liberation of Smokers and Sympathizers of Marijuana) and NORML (National Organization for the Reform of Marijuana Laws) were organized with the goal of decriminalizing marijuana.

These user groups were reflective of a new type of illicit drug user. The "hippie" movement drew its drug-using members from the middle- and upper-middle classes. When widespread use of illicit drugs became common in the suburbs and on college campuses, the stereotype of drug "fiends" as violent, crazy perverts was no longer credible. The punitive approach also eventually came under fire from middle-class parents and legislators whose children were arrested and sometimes sentenced to prison for possession or sale of marijuana or hallucinogens. The drug problem could no longer be treated as a distant lower-class malady, for it had invaded mainstream America.

The reform movement entered the institutionalization stage during the late 1960s. At this time, methadone maintenance programs emerged as a medical treatment for heroin addicts. Methadone is a synthetic drug similar to heroin but it is administered orally in treatment instead of intravenously to minimize its euphoric effects and eliminate the ritual of using needles. Addicts on methadone maintenance are able to lead relatively normal lives and many are employed.

Other indicators of the institutionalization of the reform movement were the passage of the Comprehensive Drug Abuse Prevention and Control Act of 1970 and the National Commission on Marijuana and Drug Abuse report on marijuana in 1972. Among its several features, the Comprehensive Drug Abuse Prevention and Control Act reduced penalties for first-time possession of marijuana to probation for one year or less with the possibility that the record could be expunged (Musto, 1987). The extensive National Commission report recommended that marijuana be decriminalized. While this recommendation was emphatically rejected by the Nixon administration, as of 1982 several cities and 11 states containing about one-third of the United States population had decriminalized possession of marijuana. Another 17 states had significantly reduced penalties for possession of small amounts of marijuana to the level of a minor misdemeanor (Akers, 1985:128). The number of persons arrested for possession of marijuana dropped by almost 50 percent in California in 1976 as a result of decriminalization, with a savings of at least $25 million to the state (see Clinard & Meier, 1979). In addition, research indicates that marijuana use did not increase significantly in states that decriminalized possession (Single, 1989).

The Nixon Administration Drug War

The drug war promulgated by the Nixon administration was heavily influenced by political motives. In interviews with former high-ranking officials in the Nixon administration, Baum (1996) was told that the 1970s war on drugs was intended to gather political support for President Nixon from working-class and middle-class whites, many of whom had traditionally voted Democratic by associating cannabis and other illegal drugs with the student left, opponents of the war in Vietnam, and young African-Americans. Nixon and his strategists then extended the popular appeal of this argument by claiming that drugs and crime were strongly linked. Thus, the youth movements of the time, emerging minority self-empowerment movements, drugs, and crime became one-in-the-same in the minds of many Americans. This was a clear example of scapegoating the problems of society on various "dangerous classes" of people and intertwining the evils of drugs through these claims in order to gain political support. For example, Baum (1996:13) quotes an entry made by H.R. Haldeman, Nixon's White House Chief of Staff, in his personal diary: "[President Nixon] emphasized that you have to face the fact that the whole problem is really the blacks. The key is to devise a system that recognizes this while not appearing to." Variations on this strategy have been used successfully by the political right, not only during the Nixon years, but continuing through the 1980s and 1990s.

Components of the Nixon drug war included strengthening law enforcement efforts with infusions of federal monies; expanding drug abuse prevention through research, education, and treatment—including methadone maintenance programs; and reducing the flow of heroin into the United States from the major source at the time, Turkey. The latter component was apparently relatively successful. The most important legacy of the Nixon war on drugs, however, was the creation of a modern political rhetoric connecting youth, minorities, drugs, and crime—rhetoric that has persisted in the minds of Americans for two decades, largely due to the crusading efforts of the New Right.

Thus, the remainder of the 1970s was characterized by liberalized marijuana possession laws at the state and local levels, a continuation of methadone treatment programs for those addicted to opiates and synthetics, and policies of supply reduction (including then-President Carter's use of the herbicide paraquat on Mexican cannabis fields). In the early 1980s, the rhetoric crafted by the Nixon administration was again brought into the political arena by the New Right.

THE 1986 WAR ON DRUGS IN THE UNITED STATES

In one way, the 1986 War on Drugs in the United Statets can be seen as simply another reincarnation of the seemingly eternal struggle against illicit substances. Opiates were the focus at the turn of the twentieth century, marijuana in the 1930s, and narcotics again in the 1950s. Illicit drugs in general, and crack in particular, emerged as the focus of another war in the second half of the 1980s. However, even if this is assumed to be the case, the question of timing remains. Why was the war declared in 1986, and not in 1980 or 1987? To answer this question we need to examine "objective conditions" of drug use and abuse, public opinion, and the political economy.

Trends in Illicit Drug Use

Much of the rhetoric used in 1986 implied that there had been a sizable increase in illicit drug use leading up to declaration of the war. As demonstrated elsewhere (Jensen et al., 1991), quite the opposite is the case. According to self-reported drug use, rates peaked in the late 1970s for most drugs and most age groups. Throughout the early 1980s, rates decreased or remained stable for most drugs among most demographic categories. Support for this assertion can be found in a number of studies. The most comprehensive series of studies is conducted by the National Institute on Drug Abuse (NIDA) every two or three years. According to these surveys most drugs showed a peak in use between 1979 and 1982 and then stayed fairly stable or declined throughout the early 1980s. The one exception was cocaine which peaked between 1982 and 1985 (National Institute on Drug Abuse, 1986).

Unfortunately, NIDA does not conduct its survey every year and thus we lack important information. The best annual study is the Monitoring the Future Study, based on a representative sample of all seniors in public and private high schools in the coterminous United States. Self-report data have been available for year since 1975 (see Table 1.1). One problem with this study is that it collects information on high school *seniors* and therefore does not include all students or *dropouts*. Assuming that drug use rates are higher among those who drop out than among students, the figures provided by the Monitoring the Future Study probably underestimate the extent of drug use among high school-aged youth. At the same time, there is no reason to assume that *trends* in drug use reported here differ significantly from those of all teenagers; with the possible exception of those living in disorganized inner-city neighborhoods.

Table 1.1
Trends in Lifetime, Annual, and Monthly Use of Illicit Drugs by Graduating High School Seniors

Class of	1975	1976	1977	1978	1979	1980	1981	1982	1983	1984	1985	1986	1987	1988	1989	1990	1991	1992	1993	1994	1995
% Reporting Use in Lifetime																					
Marijuana	47.3	52.8	56.4	59.2	60.4	60.3	59.5	58.7	57.0	54.9	54.2	50.9	50.2	47.2	43.7	40.7	36.7	32.6	35.3	38.2	41.7
Cocaine	9.0	9.7	10.8	12.9	15.4	15.7	16.5	16.0	16.2	16.1	17.3	16.9	15.2	12.1	10.3	9.4	7.8	6.1	6.1	5.9	6.0
Crack	N.A.	N.A	N.A	N.A.	N.A.	N.A.	N.A.	N.A.	N.A.	N.A.	N.A.	N.A.	5.4	4.8	4.7	3.5	3.1	2.6	2.6	3.0	3.0
% Reporting Use in Last Twelve Months																					
Marijuana	40.0	44.5	47.6	50.2	50.8	48.8	46.1	44.3	42.3	40.0	40.6	38.8	36.3	33.1	29.6	27.0	23.9	21.9	26.0	30.7	34.7
Cocaine	5.6	6.0	7.2	9.0	12.0	12.3	12.4	11.5	11.4	11.6	13.1	12.7	10.3	7.9	6.5	5.3	3.5	3.1	3.1	3.6	4.0
Crack	N.A.	N.A.	N.A.	N.A.	N.A.	N.A.	N.A.	N.A.	N.A.	N.A.	N.A.	4.1	3.9	3.1	3.1	1.9	1.5	1.5	1.5	1.9	2.1
% Reporting Use in Last 30 Days																					
Marijuana	27.1	32.2	35.4	37.1	36.5	33.7	31.6	28.5	27.0	25.2	25.7	23.4	21.0	18.0	16.7	14.0	13.8	11.9	15.5	19.0	21.2
Cocaine	1.9	2.0	2.9	3.9	5.7	5.2	5.8	5.0	4.9	5.8	6.7	6.2	4.3	3.4	2.8	1.9	1.4	1.3	1.3	1.5	1.8
Crack	N.A.	N.A.	N.A.	N.A.	N.A.	N.A.	N.A.	N.A.	N.A.	N.A.	N.A.	N.A.	1.3	1.6	1.4	0.7	0.7	0.6	0.7	0.8	1.0

Sources:

L.D. Johnston, P. O'Malley & J.G. Bachman (1996). *National Survey Results on Drug Use from the Monitoring the Future Study, 1975-1995*. U.S. Department of Health and Human Services, National Institute on Drug Abuse. Washington, DC: USGPO.

K. Maguire & A.L. Pastore, eds. (1996). *Sourcebook of Criminal Justice Statistics, 1995*. U.S. Department of Justice, Bureau of Justice Statistics. Washington, DC: USGPO.

Included in Table 1.1 are three drugs: marijuana, the most commonly used illicit drug; cocaine, a major focus of the 1986 anti-drug campaign; and crack, a form of cocaine and the main focus of the 1986 drug war. Marijuana use peaked in 1978 and 1979 and steadily decreased until 1992 before increasing again. In 1986, at the declaration of the war, about one-half of the high school seniors had tried marijuana, about two of five in the previous 12 months, and about one in four during the previous month. Cocaine use rates peaked in 1985, close to the beginning of the war, but what is most remarkable is the consistency of use rates between 1979 and 1986: about one in six seniors had tried it, one in eight had used it during the previous year, and one in 16 had used it during the preceding month. Crack did not emerge on the streets until late 1985 and figures are only available since 1986 and 1987. Few high school seniors in any year had tried it.

The use rates depicted in Table 1.1 may be considered high by some and thus be a justification for a war on drugs. On the one hand, most people who use illegal substances only use them on an experimental or occasional basis. On the other hand, extensive use of drugs is undoubtedly problematic for some users, their families, and communities. Thus there is a need for some form of intervention in those cases. However, what is interesting to us is the timing of the war on drugs. While there were some increases in some drugs prior to 1986, these increases were minimal and certainly did not support the claim of a new crisis in illicit drug use. The most dramatic increases occurred in the late 1970s but the war was not declared until 1986. Apparently factors other than the use of illicit drugs are to account for this fact.

Public Opinion and the Drug Issue

According to the social constructionist theory, claimsmakers try to influence and manipulate public opinion in their attempt to create a social problem. Public opinion polls let us examine to what extent the public viewed drugs as a problem prior to and throughout 1986. Furthermore, by looking at the *timing* of public concern over drugs, we can determine whether public opinion drove politicians and the media to focus on drugs or whether the public became concerned *after* receiving a steady diet of political and media information.

Polls conducted by the Gallup organization showed that the public was relatively unconcerned about illicit drugs throughout the early 1980s. In the reports released for the years 1981 to 1984, Gallup did not list illicit drugs as a separate category to the question concerning "the most important problem facing this country" (*The Gallup Report*, 1984). In 1985 and early 1986, illicit drugs was listed as a separate category, but only about three percent of the population chose it as the most important problem. As late as the middle of July, drugs were only a distant fourth among all problems facing the nation (*The Gallup Report*, 1986). At the same time, there was some public concern over drugs in schools, with drugs being viewed as the most important problem facing public schools in early 1986 (Gallup, 1986).

Once then-President Ronald Reagan declared a war on drugs in early August 1986 and the media had began an orgy of drug coverage primarily aimed at crack, public opinion changed dramatically. By the week of August 18, drugs had become the most important problem facing the nation according to a *New York Times*/CBS poll (Clymer, 1986). Furthermore, in a *U.S. News*/CNN poll in late August, 86 percent of the respondents indicated that "fighting the drug problem" was "extremely important" (*U.S. News and World Report*, 1986). Given the timing of the increase in public concern over drugs, it is clear that politicians were not driven to the issue by a concerned citizenry, but rather, they were at the forefront of the drug war bandwagon (see also Beckett, 1994).

Politicians such as President Reagan do not construct issues out of thin air. The campaigns they choose tend to be related to general ideological principles they hold or to the prevailing political climate. The early 1980s were a time of political conservatism. Ronald Reagan was elected on a conservative platform and the Republican party gained control of the Senate for six years. Also, driving under the influence of alcohol was a hot political issue in the 1982 and 1984 elections, along with an effort to raise the drinking age in all states to 21. It was in this political context that the youth-minorities-drugs-crime image could once again emerge as a hot button issue in 1986 (cf. Trebach, 1987; Reinarman & Levine, 1989; Gerber et al., 1990).

The media were also a major influence in creating the drug scare, as they often are in shaping social issues (Schneider, 1985). An examination of the *Reader's Guide to Periodical Literature* indicated that this was the case for the drug war of 1986 as well (Jensen et al., 1991). In the decade preceding 1986, several drug-related events received extensive coverage in the popular press. A number of celebrities were either arrested on drug charges or suffered adverse health consequences as a result of drug use. Also, throughout the early 1980s drug use among athletes attracted considerable media attention with the most notable event being the death of Len Bias, a top draft choice of the Boston Celtics, in June 1986.

Reinarman and Levine (1989) noted that news coverage of drugs, especially crack, exploded beginning in the spring of 1986. "In July 1986 alone, the three major TV networks offered 74 evening news segments on drugs, half of these about crack" (Reinarman & Levine 1989:541). Also, in the months prior to the 1986 November elections, a few selected national newspapers and magazines alone ran approximately 1,000 stories that mentioned crack. Orcutt and Turner (1993) demonstrated that workers in the print media distorted the findings of research studies to create an image of "a coke plague." In the fall of 1986, the CBS program "48 Hours on Crack Street" obtained the highest Neilsen rating of any similar news show in the previous five years (Reinarman & Levine, 1989:541-542).

In addition to the above "objective" factors that would focus political attention, and thus public opinion, on illicit drugs, some were more arbitrary. Politicians in democracies need issues to champion during elections. Crime control often serves this function and crime is therefore "politicalized" during elections:

> Politicians seize an opportunity to exploit public predispositions in order to gain political office. Politicalization, in other words, has more to do with gaining and retaining political office than with policy making . . . (Scheingold, 1984:38).

Drugs provided politicians, conservatives and liberals alike, with an election high in 1986. Controlling drug use was an attractive election issue for conservatives because it drew attention to "individual deviance and immorality and away from questions of economic inequality and injustice" (Levine & Reinarman, 1987:388). Liberals could likewise support anti-drug efforts because they could espouse treatment programs that exceeded those proposed by conservatives, without having to oppose the popular incumbent president. Regardless of ideological bent, politicians in 1986 loved drugs.

A second contributing factor to the 1986 war was the anti-drug campaign of First Lady Nancy Reagan. Early in her husband's presidency, she had been portrayed by the media as a cold and insensitive person whose chief concern seemed to be her wardrobe. In an attempt to change this image, she sought an issue to champion. Apparently she considered other issues (Beck, 1981), but settled on illicit drugs. While her campaign may have been little more than public relations at first, it provided the President with a launching pad in 1986.

Events in 1986

Our earlier review of *The Reader's Guide* and *The New York Times* (Jensen et al., 1991), highlights several events in early 1986 that drew political attention to illicit drugs. In late 1985 and early 1986, crack hit the streets in major cities in the eastern United States. Around that time, various community and church groups held demonstrations and vigils in New York City. In June 1986, Len Bias died as a result of a drug overdose, which was followed by the death of a football player, Don Rogers, only eight days later.

Between July 9, and October 28, 1986, the drug issue swept the nation. Articles were published showing that President Reagan was considering the possibility of a campaign against drugs, that he initiated such a campaign, and that then-House Speaker O'Neill and other Democratic leaders wanted a bipartisan effort to combat drugs. The Democrats introduced a major bill on August 1, followed a few days later by President Reagan's. By now the public had jumped on the anti-drug bandwagon, and illicit drugs shot up in the polls as a major problem facing the nation. As a result, politicians jockeyed for the most advantageous position of this wholesome, safe issue. Bills were then passed by both the House and the Senate, a compromise was reached, and President Reagan signed the $1.7 billion "Drug-Free America Act" into law on October 28, 1986. In a matter of a few months, illicit drugs had been reconstructed as a social problem and been institutionalized with the enactment of a major piece of federal legislation.

Political Activities in 1988 and 1989

Again in 1988 the presidential election campaigns lacked a major "hot" issue so the drug scare was reborn. Candidates began attacking each other as being "soft on drugs." Just before the 1988 elections, Congress passed a new, even more punitive and more expensive anti-drug bill, as it had before the 1986 elections (Reinarman & Levine, 1989:564). Even some political actors acknowledged the political posturing over the drug issue. Marlin Fitzwater, President Reagan's spokesperson, told the White House press corps that "everybody wants to out-drug each other in terms of political rhetoric" (as cited in Reinarman & Levine, 1989:565).

After the elections, President Bush's Drug Czar William Bennett announced further measures to combat the drug plague: prison capacities would be doubled and users as well as dealers would be incarcerated (Reinarman & Levine, 1989:536). President Bush also announced a crackdown on marijuana users. The vision of increasingly punitive actions against users and dealers resulting in exploding prison populations has since become reality (Gordon, 1994; Irwin & Austin, 1994).

IMPORTING THE UNITED STATES DRUG WAR TO CANADA

Canada has long been influenced by policy developments in the United States, but seemingly no one was expecting the immediate response of Prime Minister Brian Mulroney to this most recent American drug war. Two days after President Ronald Reagan declared a war on drugs in 1986, Mulroney made an unexpected announcement, added at the last minute to a speech: "Drug abuse has become an epidemic that undermines our economic as well as social fabric" (as cited in Erickson, 1992:248). It appears that even high-ranking government officials were not aware of the Prime Minister's intention to declare a war on drugs. As one top-level official in Health and Welfare Canada remarked: "When he [the PM] made that statement, then *we* had to make it a *problem*" (Erickson, 1992:248).

From an objectivist perspective, we would expect an increase in drug use or illegal drug-related problems to characterize the "epidemic" to which Mulroney referred. A review of the relevant data, including self-report studies, police reports, and health statistics, revealed little evidence to suggest an upswing in drug use or health problems related to drug use in Canada during the mid-1980s (Jensen & Gerber, 1993).

Similar to the situation in the United States, the onset of the Canadian war on drugs appeared to be based on political considerations. Although Mulroney and his Progressive Conservative party swept the nation for the first time in 26 years with an overwhelming victory in September 1984, "[I]n less than two years, the Tories had lost nearly one-half of their post-election support and had slipped to a second place standing in the public approval ratings" (Jensen & Gerber, 1993:455). Thus, were the seeds of the 1986 Canadian drug war sown. Unlike the United States where the drug war raged like wildfire through the media, public, and on both sides of the aisle, this was not a popular idea in Canada.

In line with Canadian public opinion, Mulroney also attempted to legitimate the national drug strategy cloaking drug policy in the rhetoric of prevention and education. In reality, however, his policies were primarily punitive, and the bulk of resources were designated for law enforcement (Erickson, 1992; Fischer, 1994a). As one observer commented, "Canada's bite is worse than its bark" (Erickson, 1992:250 ff.)

CONCLUSIONS AND IMPLICATIONS FOR THE CRIMINAL JUSTICE SYSTEM

As we have seen, the United States has experienced a number of drug wars. On the national scale, the anti-opiate drive followed the enactment of the Harrison Act in 1914, the anti-marijuana campaign in the mid- and late-1930s, highly punitive federal legislation of the 1950s, the Nixon drug war of the 1970s, and the 1986 War on Drugs together with its spin-offs in the 1988 U.S. presidential election season and in Canada. In contrast, the lone drug policy reform movement of the 1960s and 1970s included the decriminalization of possession of marijuana for personal use in a number of states. As an offshoot of the 1986 War on Drugs, however, several of these laws were eventually eliminated.

As we review these anti-drug campaigns in the United States, several common themes can be observed. First, on the national level, all of these drug wars were initiated by state agents or politicians who constructed the problem and then legitimized it to the public. The drug wars were socially constructed by state agents and others with moral, organizational, or political stakes in the issue. The anti-opiate war of the 1920s, the marijuana war of the 1930s, and the drug war of the 1950s were all rooted in the interests of the Bureau of Narcotics and its director Harry J. Anslinger. Politicians were also very active in declaring and executing these wars. The Nixon and Reagan-Bush drug wars were primarily politically motivated. This component of the origins of American drug wars closely fits the revision of social constructionist theory elaborated by Jensen et al. (1991) reviewed in this chapter.

A second commonality running through these drug wars is the use of the media to pass legitimating messages on to the public, and in many cases serving to sensationalize and magnify "drug crisis" themes. As Reinarman (1994a:96) has noted, "the mass media has engaged in . . . rhetorically recrafting worst cases into typical cases and the episodic into the epidemic." The media were major communicators of these messages in the drug wars of the 1930s, 1970s, and late 1980s. They were also involved in constructing and legitimating the anti-drug campaign of the 1950s perhaps to a lesser extent than in the other campaigns. Given the "evil" and "immorality" associated with illicit drugs in American culture (i.e., the dope fiend mythology and Nixon's revision of it), the specter of drug crises is fertile fodder for media coverage. The Beckett and Sasson chapter that follows presents a discussion of the media's role in the 1986 War on Drugs and of sentence disparities for powder and crack cocaine. The chapters by Brownstein, Leiber, et al. also discuss the role of media in constructing problems associated with drugs.

A third theme underlying the American drug wars is institutional racism. With hindsight, detecting the racism in the early anti-opiate and anti-marijuana laws is easy. For some, however, institutional discrimination will be less apparent in the current sentencing debate over powder and crack cocaine. Understanding the dynamics of society in our own time is often more difficult than reviewing the past due to the legitimation efforts by seemingly authoritative claimsmakers such as presidents, congressional representatives, agents of the criminal justice system, and the mass media. The following chapters by Beckett and Sasson, Webb and Brown, Everett, and Fischer reverberate with the theme of racism.

A fourth theme involved in the American drug wars is scapegoating illegal drugs as the causes of other public problems (see Reinarman, 1994a). Claimsmakers often link drugs to other societal issues in an attempt to blame the substance use and abuse for these other problems. In the 1930s, the United States was involved in the Great Depression and the Western and Southwestern regions of the country were experiencing a pool of surplus labor that contained a large number of persons of Mexican descent. Marijuana, the drug associated with this ethnic group, was an easy scapegoat for many of the economic problems and associated intergroup hostilities in these regions at the time. During the 1950s, the fear of communism swept the nation and Commissioner Anslinger connected the rise in heroin use to the efforts of the Chinese communists to overtake the youth of America. In the late 1960s and early 1970s, the nation was rocking from urban civil disorders and the Vietnam War protests. Illegal drugs once again became a political scapegoat for much deeper problems in the nation. During the 1980s and continuing into the 1990s, the searing effects of major structural economic shifts that began in the mid-1970s reached a tainted fruition leaving behind millions of working families with little hope for the future and an explosion in the urban underclass (Wilson, 1987). Once again, drugs are a ready scapegoat for the loss of hope, increasing violence in low income neighborhoods, and a rising fear of crime.

What are the implications of anti-drug campaigns for the criminal justice system? The most obvious ramification is that a whole range of behaviors associated with distributing, obtaining, and using illicit substances has come under the purview of the criminal justice system. Since those defined as criminal by the laws are participating in these behaviors of their own free will, these consensual crimes are much more difficult for law enforcement to detect and investigate than are the usual offenses that have a victim to file a complaint. This aspect of drug offenses has long put pressure on law enforcement to extend the intrusiveness of their techniques for enforcing drug laws, thus often violating established due process protections.

In addition, the criminalization of substances creates a lucrative market for those willing to profit from the sale of illegal drugs. When the only source of supply is illegal, the prices charged for the drugs are exorbitant and profits are large. This serves to attract people and organizations into the sale of illegal drugs and provides incentive for them to expand their markets. Even with strenuous law enforcement efforts directed at illegal drugs and a rebirth of extremely punitive sanctions for drug offenses during the past decade, given the attractiveness of huge profits in drug sales—at least at the highest levels of the distribution system—and the desire of millions of people to use illegal drugs, the criminal justice system faces an impossible task as it seeks to eliminate the illegal drug trade. Indeed, critics are now attacking law enforcement for redirecting a substantial portion of its resources to apprehending drug offenders—most often marijuana users—thereby decreasing resources available to deal with violent crimes and serious property offenses.

Although each of the earlier drug wars has produced at least temporary effects on the criminal justice system—usually in the form of increased arrests and increased prison populations—the ramifications of 1986 War on Drugs for the criminal justice system and indeed expansions of social controls outside of the criminal justice system have far surpassed those of its predecessors (see the chapters by Sagatun-Edwards and Crowley), with the possible exception of the original federal criminalization efforts in the wake of the Harrison Act. These implications for criminal justice policy and the civil arena are discussed in the chapters that follow.

The 1986 War on Drugs has also been widely exported to other nations. The United States has become the moral and political leader in the fight against crime in general (Christie, 1994), and a worldwide campaigner against illegal drugs in particular. Important for the purposes of this book is that the United States' efforts have been influential in setting a punitive, prohibitionist tone rather than a rehabilitative or public health direction for global drug policy (see the Ryan, Fischer, and Erickson and Butters chapters).

Finally, given that the United States' war strategy has completely failed, voices advocating alternative solutions to problems associated with illegal drugs have become increasingly louder. On the forefront of positive change at this time is the harm-reduction movement. The goals of harm-reduction policies are to reduce the harm to the drug users/abusers and to the communities and societies in which they live, including the harm generated by the criminalization of the substances. The chapter by Erickson and Butters explains this perspective and discusses examples of harm reduction policies in effect around the world today.

2

The Media and the Construction of the Drug Crisis in America

Katherine Beckett
Indiana University

Theodore Sasson
Middlebury College

The media play a crucial role in shaping public perceptions of political and social issues. Research suggests, for example, that media consumers are more likely to identify issues that receive prominent attention in the national news as the nation's most important problems (Bennett, 1980; Iyengar & Kinder, 1987; Leff, Protess & Brooks, 1986; McCombs & Shaw, 1972). There is also evidence that the content and framing of media products shape public perceptions of social issues and influence the formation of political opinions about them (Beckett, 1995b; Gamson, 1992; Iyengar, 1991; Roberts & Doob, 1990; Sasson, 1995).

Researchers analyzing the impact of exposure to media stories about crime have also found a link between the content of these stories, assessments of the crime problem, and support for particular crime control policies (Roberts & Doob, 1990; Roberts & Edwards, 1989; Surette, 1992). For example, survey research indicates that heavy consumers of violent television crime shows are more likely to see the world as a violent and frightening place and to adopt a "retributive justice perspective" (Roberts, 1992; Surette, 1992). While these findings document a correlation rather than a causal relationship, experimental studies also indicate that those who are exposed to media depictions of violent crimes are subsequently more likely to perceive other crimes as more serious and to support punitive anti-crime measures (Roberts & Edwards, 1989). Similarly, those who read media accounts of sentencing decisions are more likely to see them as "too lenient" than are people who obtain their information from court documents (Roberts & Doob, 1990). While it is too simple to say that media discourse *causes* changes in public opinion, it does appear to be a crucial component of the context in which opinions about criminal justice matters are formed.

Media representations of crime-related matters may also affect criminal justice practitioners and politicians, independent of their effect on public opinion (Surette, 1992). In accounting for their legislative initiative on the crime and drug issues, for example, politicians in the 1980s often cited increased media coverage of the drug problem as evidence of the public concern to which they felt compelled to respond (Beckett, 1997b). Officials may also perceive a high degree of media interest in crime-related issues as an opportunity for political exposure or as a sign that public concern is likely to increase in the future (Surette, 1992).

In sum, both the extent and nature of media images have some influence on the opinion formation and policy-making processes. There is reason to suspect, therefore, that media coverage of the "drug crisis" in the 1980s played a role in justifying and perpetuating the war on drugs. As many analysts have pointed out, journalists drew a great deal of attention to the spread of "crack" cocaine in the inner city and depicted this problem mainly as the consequence of insufficient punishment and control (Beckett, 1995b, 1997b; Brownstein, 1991; Reeves & Campbell, 1994; Reinarman & Levine, 1989; Reinarman & Levine, 1995). Concern about the drug problem and support for punitive antidrug policies also reached record levels during the late 1980s, and these attitudinal shifts played an important role in legitimating the expansion of the criminal justice system.

In what follows, we describe the main themes that characterize the news media's representation of the drug problem at the height of the drug war. In the second section, however, we suggest that chinks have appeared in the edifice of this construction of the drug problem. The appearance of this alternative discourse was triggered by the 1995 congressional decision to uphold those provisions of the Anti-Drug Abuse Act that mandated five year minimum terms for even small-scale crack offenders. In the debate that ensued, more critical perspectives on the drug problem received a significant amount of exposure in the news media. Previously ignored aspects of the drug problem—including the social and economic conditions that shape the use and distribution of drugs, the racially biased consequences of current sentencing practices, and the over-representation of black youth in the criminal justice system—were identified in the mass media as important components of it. Indeed, some stories went so far as to suggest that many aspects of what is now considered the "drug problem" are actually drug *policy* problems (Reinarman, 1994b). This challenge to the hegemony of the "law and order" approach suggests that more critical perspectives on the drug issue may—under certain circumstances—appear in the news media; that history need not be read as prophesy. Finally, drawing on the insights of the literature reviewed in the first section, we offer a tentative explanation of this development and discuss its implications for efforts to influence popular discourse and policy on drugs.

IMAGES OF THE DRUG PROBLEM IN THE NEWS

The selection and representation of "newsworthy" events is a complex social process (Gans, 1980). From the infinite pool of events and occurrences, news workers must determine which of these constitute "news" and identify the appropriate "spin" for each story. This representational process is far from self-evident; the same facts and events may be understood and represented in a number of different ways, and their interpretation will depend on the social location, worldview, and interests of the interpreters (Edelman, 1988; Gamson, 1992; Gusfield, 1981). An increasing crime rate, for example, might be depicted as evidence of the breakdown of "law and order" or of increased socioeconomic inequality and the need for policies that reduce it.

News workers' selection and framing of media stories are influenced by the claims-making activities of public officials and public agencies (as well as the interest of news organizations in garnering audience share and meeting production demands) (Gans, 1980; Molotch & Lester, 1974; Sigal, 1973). Journalists' reliance upon "official" sources is quite well-documented (see Fishman, 1978; Gans, 1980; Morgan, 1986; Nimmo, 1964; Sigal, 1973; Whitney et al., 1989). For example, Sigal (1973) found that "numerically, the most important sources of information are the officials of the U.S. government," and concluded that

> while resistance to direct forms of control has hardened in
> the press, susceptibility to news management has spread. . .
> The routines and conventions of reporters' work incline
> them to accept the words of the officials without probing
> beneath them on their own (Sigal, 1973:123).

Similarly, Whitney et al. (1989:170) found that 72 percent of all sources for network television news were government officials or leaders of political groups or institutions.

A number of factors help to account for journalists' reliance upon public officials. Officials are often seen as objective and authoritative, and thus lend legitimacy to the often ambiguous journalistic enterprise (Becker, 1967; Gans, 1980; Hall et al., 1978; Herman & Chomsky, 1988; Schudson, 1978). Journalists' need for a regular and frequent supply of appropriately formatted information from geographically concentrated sources also contributes to this pattern (Epstein 1973; Gans, 1980; Tuchman, 1978: Whitney et al., 1989). Official sources thus provide the mantle of objectivity and a steady flow of information upon which journalists depend. While sources are not typically able to determine the content of media stories (Erickson, Baranek & Chan, 1991), there is evidence that sources are often able to influence news content (Beckett, 1995b; Molotch & Lester, 1974).

Crime news is particularly compatible with the ideological biases and organizational needs of the news media: the regular provision of information from law enforcement and other government officials means that crime stories can be produced quickly and regularly, and on the basis of information obtained from sources considered to be legitimate authorities (Fishman, 1978; Sherizen, 1978). This practice—combined with the media's tendency to look to other media outlets (especially the *New York Times*) for confirmation of its news judgment and its financial interest in sensationalistic and dramatic stories—often leads to the creation of what Fishman calls "crime waves" (Fishman, 1978). "Crime waves" occur when news workers—looking primarily to each other and a limited number of "authoritative" sources for a sense of "what's news"—focus on a particular type of crime and dramatize the nature of the threat posed by it. Many of those analyzing the news media's coverage of the "drug crisis" of the 1980s emphasize its complicity in the creation of a "drug-related crime wave." "Crime waves" are thus a particular type of "moral panic," that exist when "a condition, episode, person or group of persons emerges to become defined as a threat to societal values and interests; its nature is presented in a stylized and stereotypical fashion by the mass media . . ." (Cohen, 1972:9; see also Goode & Ben-Yehuda, 1994).

Constructing the Drug Panic

Studies analyzing the construction of the drug issue in the 1980s suggest that the media played a crucial role in generating public concern about drugs and support for punitive anti-drug policies. Three central claims support this assessment. First, relative to earlier and later periods, coverage of the drug issue during the late 1980s was extensive. Second, the framing of the drug issue emphasized the pharmacological properties of crack cocaine as a cause of drug-related violence and individual motivations for involvement with drugs, thus implying the need for criminal justice solutions to the drug problem. Third, the media frequently advanced factually erroneous claims about drugs. Each of these themes is explicated below and illustrated in the *Newsweek* cover story reprinted in Box 2.1.

Box 2.1

"It is cheap, plentiful and intensely addictive . . . the crack craze is spreading nationwide. . . . Crack has captured the ghetto and is inching its way into the suburbs. . . . Wherever it appears, it spawns vicious violence among dealers and dopers. . . ."

Rock and crack represent a quantum leap in the addictive properties of cocaine and a marketing breakthrough for the pusher. Sold in tiny chips that give the user a 5-20 minute high, crack is often purer than sniffable cocaine. . . . The cycle of ups and downs reinforces the craving and . . . can produce a powerful chemical dependency within two weeks. . . . .

There are ominous signs that crack and rock dealers are expanding well beyond the inner city . . . "In the past six months every city, county and almost every little town has been hit by the crack epidemic," says John J. Barbara of the Florida Department of Law Enforcement.

. . . Crack and rock are spreading because cocaine is so widely available in the United States and because the justice system has been unable to thwart the cocaine trade at any level. Police in every city where crack is now a major problem argue that the courts are too lenient with drug offenders, and they may be right. . . . "We are not thinning out the ranks and making any impact. We are not *deterring*," Cusack says. "As a matter of fact, the opposite is happening. What's the risk? So few are getting caught and the risk of prosecution is so remote that we are encouraging people to traffic." (Selections from "Crack and Crime," *Newsweek*, June 16, 1986, by Tom Morganthau.)

Highlighting the Drug Issue

Media coverage of the drug issue increased somewhat after President Ronald Reagan laid the framework for the war on drugs in October 1982, but drug coverage increased most dramatically after 1985 (Merriam, 1989). Several factors help to explain this. First, in April of 1986, the National Institute of Drug Abuse (NIDA) launched its campaign titled "Cocaine: The Big Lie." During the spring and summer of 1986, 13 public service announcements affiliated with this campaign aired between 1,500 and 2,500 times per month on 75 local television networks. (By contrast, the "Just Say No" announcements aired 1,100 times per month at their peak in 1982-1983 [Forman & Lachter, 1989].) The cocaine-related death of Boston Celtics' star recruit Len Bias in June 1986, and President Reagan's increased interest in the subject, also catalyzed journalistic attention to the drug issue.

By July 1986—the month that football celebrity Don Rogers also died from a cocaine overdose—the quantity of "drug stories" was truly staggering: the three major TV networks aired 74 evening news stories about drugs during that month alone (Reeves & Campbell, 1994). By the November elections, NBC news had aired more than 400 stories about drugs (consuming an "unprecedented" 15 hours of air time) and a handful of major newspapers and magazines had produced roughly 1,000 stories about crack (Reinarman & Levine, 1995). *Time* and *Newsweek* each ran five cover stories on drugs in 1986. Attention to the drug issue diminished a bit during 1987 but intensified once again in 1988. For example, between October 1988 and October 1989, *The Washington Post* ran 565 stories about the drug crisis (Reinarman & Levine, 1995). In sum, media coverage of the drug issue increased slowly after 1982, grew more dramatically in 1985-1986, and remained relatively high until the outbreak of the Persian Gulf War in early 1991.

Framing the Drug Problem

The framing the drug problem during this time is also striking. Using a modified version of Gamson's "frame analysis" techniques, Beckett (1995b, 1997b) distinguished four "packages" used to frame news coverage of the drug issue in the 1980s. One of these packages—*Get The Traffickers*—identified "preventing narco-traffickers and drug pushers from terrorizing our nation's citizens" and persuading children to "just say no" to drug use as the primary solution to the drug problem (1995b:169). A second package—*Zero Tolerance*—emphasized the need to "get-tough" with "casual users" (as well as dealers). The main "alternative" to these "get-tough" packages was *Need More Resources*, which suggested that politicians were using the drug issue for political gain and that the government was not devoting sufficient funds to the anti-drug effort. Finally, *War Fails* suggested that harm reduction should serve as the goal of drug policy and that drug prohibition increased rather than decreased the harm associated with drug use.

To measure the relative prominence of each of these packages in the mass media, Beckett (1995b, 1997b) examined a large sample of television news stories that focused on the drug problem. This analysis revealed that the two "law and order" packages—*Get The Traffickers* and *Zero Tolerance*—were depicted most frequently (and were strongly associated with the presence of state officials as news "sources"). In fact, more than one-half of all package displays in the television news sample signified the *Get The Traffickers* frame, and an additional one-quarter depicted *Zero Tolerance*. By contrast, *Need More Resources* and *War Fails* were depicted in just 12 and 10 percent (respectively) of all package displays. In sum, television news coverage of the drug problem overwhelmingly represented it in ways that implied the need for "tougher" anti-drug policies.

Reeves and Campbell (1994) also document the ascendance of "get tough" themes in nightly news coverage of cocaine during the 1980s. Earlier in the decade, they suggest, the typical cocaine-related story focused on white recreational users who snorted the drug in its powder form. These stories frequently relied on news sources associated with the drug treatment industry and emphasized the possibility of recovery. By late 1985, however, this frame was supplanted by a new "siege paradigm" in which transgressors were depicted as poor and nonwhite users and dealers of crack cocaine. At the same time, law enforcement officials emphasizing the need for law and order responses to the drug problem took the place of the medical and treatment experts previously identified as drug authorities. And as the 1980s progressed, journalists increasingly used an overtly "campaigning" voice to demonstrate their clear disapproval of the drug scene and those who populate it. Camera crews also began using handheld cameras to cover crack house raids from the vantage point of the police (Reeves & Campbell, 1994).

The changing identity of drug authorities and the increasingly moralistic and dramatic tone of drug-related stories were clearly related to the initiative of "moral entrepreneurs" (Becker, 1963) in drawing journalists' attention to the crack problem. For example, Robert Stutman, director of the Drug Enforcement Agency's New York office, made a concerted effort to alert the New York media to the presence and dangers of crack cocaine:

> It was time to make this information public. Through my spokesman . . . I released the contents of the intelligence division report [on the spread of crack cocaine] to the newspapers. The reporters dug into the data and found a gold mine of stories in the accounts of the effects of crack. Armed with the reports' data, they visited crack houses and followed agents on raids to crack mills. And the reports they prepared intensified the pressure for federal action . . . (Stutman, 1992:218).

As a result of this initiative, coverage of cocaine increased dramatically in *The New York Times* and, later, in other media outlets that followed the *Times'* cue (Danielman & Reese, 1989).

In sum, analyses of news coverage of the drug crisis suggest that particularly after 1986, the "law and order" perspective on the drug issue predominated. This construction of the drug problem was associated with the initiative of law enforcement and politicians and with the depiction of minorities as the main transgressors in the war on drugs.

Erroneous and Misleading Claims

At the height of the drug war, the media promulgated misleading and often inaccurate information about the drug problem. For example, media accounts during this period claimed that drug use was "pandemic"—sometimes "epidemic"—and thus analogous to a "medieval plague" (Reinarman & Levine, 1995). In fact, the available evidence suggests that most categories of drug use were declining in the 1980s; National Institute of Drug Abuse data indicate a downward trend in the use of all illicit substances other than cocaine. Even with respect to cocaine use, the data are somewhat ambiguous. Although the proportion of high school seniors and young adults reporting cocaine use in the past year or past month did increase slightly prior to 1986 (Jensen, Gerber & Babcock, 1991), lifetime use of cocaine by youth and young adults peaked in 1982 and had consistently declined since that year (Jensen, Gerber & Babcock, 1991; Reinarman & Levine, 1995). In all other age groups, NIDA's Household Survey indicates that cocaine use was decreasing. In sum, "these data reveal a picture of overall decline in the use of illicit drugs since the late 1970s and early 1980s. . . . the increases in [two measures of] one illegal drug among two age groups in the population do not support the claim of a new 'crisis' in illicit drug use" (Jensen, Gerber & Babcock 1991:655). As Orcutt and Turner (1993) show, statistical artifacts and graphic images were nonetheless used to dramatize and demonstrate the veracity of the claim that cocaine use among the young was a crisis of "epidemic" proportions.

The nature of the drug problem was also presented in misleading ways. News stories about crack often claimed that addiction to the drug is "instantaneous" and depicted the violence associated with crack as a consequence of its pharmacological properties (Brownstein, 1991; Reinarman & Levine, 1995). Claims about the addictiveness of crack were clearly exaggerated; in fact, many crack users are not instantly or inevitably "addicted" (Reinarman & Levine, 1995; Reinarman, Murphy & Waldorf, 1994; Waldorf, Murphy & Reinarman, 1991). This over-emphasis on the pharmacological origins of addiction ignores a body of research demonstrating that the distribution and intensity of drug abuse is related to social, psychological, and economic conditions (Currie, 1993; Peele, 1985; Reinarman, Murphy & Waldorf, 1994; Waldorf, Murphy & Reinarman, 1991).

The media's emphasis on the chemical properties of crack also obscured a more accurate and nuanced understanding of the relationship between crack and violence. Research suggests that much of this association is a product of the illegal nature of the drug trade and the socioeconomic context in which battles over market share are fought (Brownstein, Ryan & Goldstein, 1992; Goldstein et al., 1989). The media's tendency to over-emphasize the chemical causes of crack-related violence led it to exaggerate the "random" nature of drug-related violence, the threat it posed to "innocent bystanders," and the extent to which this violence was "spilling over" into white and middle-class neighborhoods (Brownstein, 1991).

Finally, the media paid a great deal of attention to (African-American) women who consumed crack cocaine while pregnant and advanced ominous predictions about an "epidemic of crack babies" who would grow up to be "tomorrow's delinquents" (Reinarman & Levine 1995:214). Images of small, undernourished "crack babies" dramatized the severity of this new social problem and helped to generate support for efforts to prosecute women who used drugs or alcohol during their pregnancy (Beckett, 1997a). The impact of these images was intensified by widespread claims that the damage caused by prenatal exposure to drugs was inevitable, extreme, and permanent.

In fact, there is considerable uncertainty about the causal relationship between drug use and adverse birth outcomes (Coles, 1992; Lutiger et al., 1991; Mathias, 1992; Mayes, 1992; Strandjord & Hodson, 1992; Woodhouse, 1994; Zuckerman & Frank, 1992). Many early studies did not control for the compounding effects of poor medical care, improper nutrition, and the use of alcohol and/or tobacco (Coles, 1992; Lutiger et al., 1991; Woodhouse, 1994). More recent studies that control for these factors indicate that early claims regarding the nature and permanence of the damage caused by prenatal exposure to cocaine were exaggerated (Drucker, 1990; Lutiger et al., 1991; Mathias, 1992; Mayes, 1992; Strandjord & Hodson, 1992; Woodhouse, 1994; Zuckerman & Frank, 1992). These studies also suggest that more than two-thirds of crack-exposed infants suffer no adverse consequences at birth and that both prenatal and postnatal interventions may prevent or ameliorate developmental problems for those infants who are affected by their prenatal exposure to drugs (Chasnoff et al., 1992; Humphries, 1993; Mathias, 1992). While some of the media's exaggeration of the consequences of prenatal drug use reflects the medical field's "rush to judgment" on this issue,[1] it is noteworthy that the newer (and more optimistic) studies have not received nearly the media exposure that the earlier and more alarming reports did.

Explaining the Drug Panic

The saturation coverage of the drug issue—largely depicted as a problem of immoral and nonwhite users and dealers laying siege to middle-class white America—was thus predicated on false and misleading claims, most of which reinforced the notion that the best way to deal with the drug problem is through the enforcement of criminal law and the expansion of the criminal justice system. How can we explain the complicity of the media in the Reagan and Bush administrations' war on drugs? The 1980s was, of course, a period in which crack cocaine became more available in many American inner cities and in which several celebrities died under circumstances that implicated cocaine. Furthermore, there is reason to suspect that the harm associated with drug abuse (particularly among the poor) increased with the spread of crack—hospital data indicate that the number of drug-related emergency room visits increased throughout the late 1980s and early 1990s (Goode, 1989; Johnston, 1989). Finally, it is true that the crack trade spawned a great deal of violence in the inner city (Brownstein, Ryan & Goldstein, 1992; Goldstein et al., 1989).

Still, there was nothing inevitable about the sudden journalistic attention to the issue or the media's promotion of the "law and order" perspective on the issue. As was mentioned earlier, NIDA survey data indicate that most categories of drug use were declining throughout this period, and the data on prevalence hardly support the claim that cocaine use was "epidemic." More importantly, the media's promotion of the "law and order" approach to the drug problem cannot be seen simply as a response to the harm associated with the spread of crack (there are clearly other ways of responding to this harm), and may have done more to exacerbate it than alleviate it. Finally, as harmful as crack and the crack trade may be, far more destructive social practices (including the lack of prenatal care for poor children, underemployment, low wages, the absence of universal health care, and the public health consequences of alcohol and tobacco consumption) were not the subject of media hype in the way that crack cocaine was (Reeves & Campbell, 1994; Reinarman & Levine, 1995).

Thus, while the spread of crack has had tragic consequences for some inner city communities, the complicity of the media in the war on drugs cannot be explained in these terms. Instead, the active participation of journalists in the creation of a moral panic over drugs largely reflects a convergence of political, bureaucratic, and journalistic interests. In what follows, we consider the roles of conservative politicians, bureaucrats in federal law enforcement and treatment agencies, and news organizations in the creation of the drug crisis of the 1980s.

Conservative Politicians

The drug control initiatives launched by politicians in the 1980s were a component and extension of the federal government's "war on crime," an effort that dates back more than 30 years. Despite the allocation of most crime-fighting responsibilities to state and local governments, the "crime issue" became highly politicized during Goldwater's 1964 presidential bid. In the years that followed, crime-related issues were often depicted in ways that suggested that urban social ills stem not from deindustrialization, social inequality, or racial discrimination, but from the immoral actions of the minority poor (see Beckett, 1997b; Gans, 1995; Katz, 1989; Reeves & Campbell, 1994; Reinarman & Levine, 1995). This ideological campaign has been politically useful in a number of ways. First, conservatives have used the issues of crime and drugs to deflect attention from the way in which government and corporate policies have exacerbated urban social problems and suggested that these problems are best understood as a consequence of "bad people." These images and associations have done much to legitimatize the replacement of social welfare with social control as the principle of state policy (Beckett, 1997b). Second, the "wars" on drugs and crime—and the images of the dangerous and undeserving underclass upon which they rest—have enabled conservatives to drive a wedge through the Democratic Party's interracial coalition and realign the electorate along racial lines (Edsall & Edsall, 1991).

The groundwork for the most recent anti-drug campaign was initiated by the Reagan administration in the early 1980s. Initially, the administration focused on the problem of street crime, but drugs were prioritized when it became clear that federal jurisdiction over conventional street crimes is severely circumscribed (Beckett, 1997b; see also Zimring & Hawkins, 1992). In 1982, Reagan established the general ideological framework of the anti-drug effort.[2] In the bureaucratic scramble that ensued over anti-drug funds, both federal law enforcement and treatment agencies released a great deal of anti-drug "information," which in turn stimulated media interest in drugs.

Drug Enforcement and Treatment Agencies

Motivated by the increased availability of anti-drug funds and the possibility of enhancing their turf and authority, federal drug enforcement and treatment agencies worked doggedly to promote journalistic attention to drugs. Coverage of the drug issue increased gradually after 1982, and as was noted above, grew significantly after 1985 (Merriam, 1989). In April, 1986, NIDA began its most ambitious outreach program, "Cocaine, the Big Lie." During the rest of the spring and summer, the DEA and other government officials also issued hundreds of press releases and gave innumerable interviews. As was mentioned earlier, law enforcement agencies invited journalists to ride along and film drug "busts." These entrepreneurial efforts paid off; if not in reduced drug use, then at least in terms of bureaucratic budgets. Between 1981 and 1993, federal spending on drug enforcement increased from less than $2 billion to more than $12 billion (Reinarman & Levine, 1995). Law enforcement was a much bigger winner than drug treatment/prevention agencies, which actually saw declining revenues during this period (Beckett, 1997b).

Journalists

News stories are, in the final analysis, written and reported by journalists working for media organizations. Why did news workers fall into lockstep with the Reagan administration and the various drug control agencies? To a significant extent, journalists' collusion in the war on drugs reflects the fact that covering the "drug crisis" from the point of view of law enforcement agencies (and especially film footage of drug "raids") satisfied the media's interest in dramatic and sensationalistic news. The ride-along footage of drug busts, the touring of enemy territory, the grave assessment of casualties—all of these made for exciting television. And the excitement registered in ratings. The CBS special "48 Hours on Crack Street," for example, was the highest rated of any similar program in five years (Reinarman & Levine, 1995). News agen-

cies' interest in the dramatic and sensational also helps to explain why journalists were loathe to drop their dubious claims concerning the "epidemic"
nature of crack use, the "random" violence it spawned, and the inevitable harm
caused to "crack babies."

The prevalence of enforcement personnel and public officials as sources in
drug-related stories also helps to account for journalists' adherence to the
administration's line on drugs. For example, Beckett (1995b, 1997b) found that
85 percent of the sources appearing in a large sample of 1980s national network TV news coverage of drugs were associated with the federal government.
(Of these, the vast majority were either associated with the Executive Branch
or federal law enforcement agencies.) To assess the impact of reporters'
reliance on these sources, Beckett compared the frames advanced by these federal officials with the frames advanced by other sources. The findings of this
analysis confirm the key role of official sources in shaping the news: 88 percent of the statements made by official sources signified one of the two law
and order frames (*Get Tough* or *Zero Tolerance*), while non-state actors mobi-
lized these frames only 44 percent of the time.

By 1987-1988, however, some stories on the drug crisis were more reflective and nuanced. A few reporters began to point out, for example, that the
violence associated with the distribution of crack was concentrated in a handful
of neighborhoods (Reeves & Campbell, 1994). Some also began calling attention to the opportunistic uses of the "cocaine crisis" by politicians and the
mass media (Reeves & Campbell, 1994). While many reporters who engaged
in such "second thoughts" demonstrated no penchant for irony—they uniformly failed to recognize their own complicity in promoting drug hysteria—they
did introduce the notion that crack is as much a "political" issue as a public
health or criminal justice problem.

In sum, as a result of the media's interest in the dramatic and its reliance
upon politicians and law enforcement authorities, media coverage of the drug
issue in the late 1980s was characterized by exaggeration and distortion. By
1988, more nuanced and self-reflective reports on the drug issue began to
appear but these did not significantly undermine the dominant construction of
the "drug crisis."

Consequences

News coverage of the drug issue in the 1980s heightened public concern
about drugs and encouraged people to identify law enforcement as the appropriate solution to this complex social problem. During the peak of the drug war
(1989), 64 percent of Americans named drugs as the number one problem facing the nation. Public support for punitive measures also increased in the
1980s (Beckett, 1997b). While it is possible that receptivity to the "tough"
rhetoric of the wars on crime and drugs is more superficial than is commonly

supposed, the public's apparent acceptance of the drug warriors' rhetoric nonetheless legitimated the "get-tough" policies of the war on drugs—policies that have in turn made the single largest contribution to the growing rate of incarceration among minorities (Tonry, 1995).

The news media's cultivation of law and order attitudes on the issue of drugs also had the effect of reinforcing a more general shift to the right: "During a period when people believed that the greatest risk to their well-being came from random violence perpetrated by drug users and traffickers—a notion constructed by the media—attention and resources were diverted from the more intractable social and structural problems" such as homelessness, AIDS, unemployment, and racism (Brownstein, 1995b:58). During the same period, welfare programs to provide support to the poor were represented as causes of drug addiction and crime rather than their solutions (Beckett, 1997b; Sasson, 1995). Indeed, the construction of the crime and drug crises as "underclass" problems resulting from insufficient social control laid the ideological foundation for the Republican-led assault on welfare and affirmative action. Finally, Sanders and Lyon identify a more direct consequence of the media's complicity in the war on drugs. By treating the drugs (and the deviant individuals who use and sell them) as the main cause of urban crime and violence, the news media encouraged criminal justice personnel to prioritize disciplining drug offenders above all else (1995:35-36).

CHALLENGING THE DRUG WAR IDEOLOGY

In 1995, a new, more critical discourse on drugs commanded attention. The precipitating cause of this shift was the 1995 congressional decision to retain the controversial federal sentencing laws that entail far more serious penalties for crack offenders than for any other class of drug law violators. Below, we give some background on this decision, describe the media coverage of the ensuing controversy,[3] and offer a tentative explanation of the changing nature of drug news.

The Sentencing Laws

In 1984, after more than 10 years of deliberations, Congress enacted the most sweeping and dramatic reform of federal sentencing procedures aimed at correcting what was considered to be a pattern of undue leniency—the Sentencing Reform Act (U.S. Sentencing Commission, 1991). The Act also called for the establishment of an independent agency (the U.S. Sentencing Commission) to develop guidelines that would structure judicial discretion and decisionmaking with respect to sentencing. Around this time, Congress began to adopt a series of "mandatory minimum" sentencing statutes. In 1986, the Anti-

Drug Abuse Act tied mandatory minimum penalties for drug trafficking directly to the amount of drugs involved, thereby limiting the range of factors that judges may consider in determining the appropriate punishment. Most significantly, this legislation required a mandatory minimum sentence of five (and up to 20) years for the simple possession of five or more grams of crack cocaine and 20 years for any offender who engaged in a "continuing drug enterprise" (U.S. Sentencing Commission, 1991). By way of comparison, the five year mandatory minimum sentence for simple possession applies to powder cocaine only when the quantity reaches 500 grams—*100 times the threshold for crack*.

In May 1995, however, the Federal Sentencing Commission recommended that Congress abandon those provisions of the Anti-Drug Abuse Act that penalize crack offenders more severely than any other type of drug law violator. The Commission further suggested that those found with small amounts of crack (or powder) cocaine should be placed on probation as long as they did not also engage in violence or possess an illegal firearm. In October—shortly after the Million Man March in Washington, DC in which the Reverend Jesse Jackson and others denounced the crack laws as "unfair," "racist," and "ungodly"—Congress voted to ignore the Sentencing Commission's recommendations and uphold existing sentencing statutes. President Clinton subsequently approved Congress' decision, arguing that punishing crack offenders more harshly is appropriate because crack is more likely to be associated with violence and therefore takes a greater toll on the communities in which it is used and distributed.

The Breakdown of Hegemony

That Congress and the President ultimately decided to uphold the sentencing laws that have contributed so much to the growth of the federal prison population is not, at this point, surprising. What was unusual was the intensity and nature of the debate triggered by the Sentencing Commission's recommendations and Congress' decision to ignore them. Suddenly, public discussions of the drug issue expanded to include several critical themes. Moreover, while most of the figures participating in these discussions were high-ranking legal and political authorities, some spokespersons from non-profit organizations (e.g., The Sentencing Project, a group that advocates alternatives to incarceration) and grass roots community groups (e.g., the Atlanta-based prisoner advocacy group Seekers of Justice, Equality and Truth) also contributed to the discussion.

The first of the new, more critical themes attributes the distinctively punitive crack sentencing laws and their selective enforcement to racial bias. While most news stories and editorials treated the racially disparate impact of the new drug laws as unforeseen and unintentional, many pointed directly to the possibility that the refusal to modify them was racist. "If these were young white men going to jail," *The New York Times* quoted a defense attorney as saying, "[the sentencing disparity] would not exist. So the war on drugs is essentially being borne by the black community." The same article quotes the Washington, DC director of the American Civil Liberties Union:

> How can you go to an inner city family and tell them their son is given 20 years [for using crack], while someone in the suburbs who's using powdered cocaine in greater quantities can get off with 90 day's probation? When people understand the truth about the way these laws are imposed, the fact they've had no deterrent [sic], and the race-based nature of these prosecutions, then I think a sleeping giant is going to roar *(New York Times,* October 28, 1995).

News stories also reported the Sentencing Commission's finding that while NIDA survey data indicate that most users of crack are white, over 90 percent of all crack defendants charged in federal courts—and thus subject to harsh federal penalties—are black. In a lengthy article, *The Los Angeles Times* reported the results of its own investigation into federal crack prosecutions in Los Angeles County. In 1993-1994, the newspaper found there were no federal prosecutions in Los Angeles County of white defendants on charges related to crack cocaine. During the same period, however, 183 whites were prosecuted in L.A. County courts—where penalties are less severe—for crack-related offenses. The article drives home its point with a quote from a federal district judge: "More blacks are being punished with these crack laws than whites. A red flag has gone up. Now we must work toward a system that is more fair" (*Los Angeles Times,* May 21, 1995).

News stories and editorials during this period also emphasized that racially biased drug laws and their enforcement—rather than an increase in criminal behavior—are largely responsible for the increasing rate of incarceration among African-Americans. News stories expressing this theme often quoted Marc Mauer, assistant director of The Sentencing Project, or a report issued by the same organization, to suggest that the growing rate of incarceration among African-Americans "primarily reflected changes in enforcement policies that have resulted in a greater number of defendants receiving prison sentences, especially for drug offenses, rather than an increase in the number of crimes committed by black men" (*Washington Post,* October 5, 1995).

A third new theme, appearing less frequently than those mentioned above, suggested that drug use is a social problem related to long-term poverty and unemployment. An example of this theme, as well as additional examples of the others, appears in the *Boston Globe* column extracted in Box 2.2. In sum, discussions of the drug issue were—following the Congressional decision to sustain current sentencing laws—less monolithic, more democratic, and more likely to include critical perspectives on the drug issue.

Box 2.2

"The forces that keep many of his brothers in prison are obvious to Ijalil, one of the young black inmates who make up more than half the population of the Suffolk County House of Correction. . . ."

"I don't care what society says, black men do want to take care of their families. . . But if the doors to higher-paying jobs aren't opened for you, hey, the first order of the day is survival. So you sell a little reefer. And if you get caught, you're in the system from there on out". . . .

. . . the Sentencing Project, a Washington group . . . reported that one in three black men between the ages of 20 and 29 is either in prison, on probation or on parole. . . . Criminal justice professionals agree that the nation's "war on drugs" has focused primarily on low-level drug dealers, a majority of whom are black. . . .

The implications of the high incarceration rate remain deeply troubling for the black community. There are fewer young men for women to marry and start stable families. Doing time has become a fact of life in many city neighborhoods. . . .

Sociologists say there is still another troubling and self-perpetuating trend: the high imprisonment rate leads to the stigmatizing of all blacks, especially young men, who are viewed by many police and whites as being associated with crime. . . .

Imprisonment also fuels underemployment and joblessness. . . . "In lots of communities. . ., a 15-year-old can't get a job at the 7-11, but he can get a highly responsible job as a crack dealer." (Selections from "Inside Views on Black Incarceration Issue," *Boston Globe*, October 20, 1995, by Anthony Flint.)

Explaining the Change

Why the sudden change? How can we explain the inclusion of these more critical perspectives on the drug problem? Three main factors help to account for this shift. First, the controversy over the racial dimensions of the crack/powder cocaine sentencing disparity occurred during the same period as the O.J. Simpson murder trial. Extensive news coverage of this case frequently highlighted racial differences in assessments of Simpson's guilt and the fairness of the justice system. For example, the media reported that 66 percent of African-Americans believe the justice system is racist, compared with only 37 percent of whites *(USA Today,* March 21, 1995). The discovery of the "Furman tapes" drew further attention to the problem of racial bias in the criminal justice system (as had the video-taped beating of motorist Rodney King by several Los Angeles police officers several years earlier). Thus, in the background of the controversy over the crack/powder sentencing disparity was increased media attention to the problem of racism in the legal system, as well as African-Americans' distrust of that system. It appears that these developments sensitized journalists to these issues and convinced them of their suitability for more detailed news coverage.

More significantly, the Federal Sentencing Commission's report on penalties for offenses involving crack cocaine represented a partial breakdown of elite consensus behind the drug war. This breakdown meant that high ranking officials in the government and judiciary—i.e., individuals who satisfy conventional journalistic standards as "authoritative" and "objective"—were now criticizing components of the United States drug control policy. As argued above, the virtual absence of such "establishment critics" during the drug panic of the 1980s contributed to the one-sided nature of the news coverage during that period. The significance of the Sentencing Commission report in creating space for dissident voices on the drug issue is demonstrated by its widespread use in the framing of drug-related stories during this period.[4]

Finally, the claims-making activities of progressive advocacy organizations also help to account for the changing nature of news stories on drugs. The partial breakdown of elite consensus behind the drug war created the opening for non-elite claimsmakers, and critics seized the opportunity with alacrity. The Sentencing Project was especially successful in this regard. The organization's 1995 report on blacks in the criminal justice system (in which it was found that one in three young black men is under some sort of criminal justice supervision on any given day) was cited in numerous news stories and editorials. While elite dissensus created space for progressive perspectives, the fact that the new space was exploited was a product of the independent and skillful initiative of non-elite critics of the drug war.

CONCLUSION

This chapter has argued that news coverage of the drug issue during the 1980s helped to fuel support of the war on drugs by sensationalizing and exaggerating the "epidemic" nature of drug use, misrepresenting key aspects of the drug problem, and by framing the issue almost exclusively as a matter of law and order. The chief architects of the drug crisis were Presidents Reagan and Bush and their lieutenants in the various drug control agencies. Journalists, however, were also complicit in the creation of a moral panic over drugs. Seduced by the dramatic possibilities for drug coverage and reluctant to look beyond public officials for information and perspective, news workers traded independence and professional skepticism for the chance to ride along with police on "crack-house" raids. The news coverage that resulted, we have argued, helped to legitimatize the increasing incarceration of minority youth and a range of conservative social and economic policies.

More recently, however, news coverage of the drug issue has expanded to include a number of critical themes and dissident voices. This democratization of public discourse was triggered by the Federal Sentencing Commission's 1995 report recommending that harsh federal mandatory sentences for possession of crack cocaine be reduced. The Commission's report signaled a crucial fracture in elite consensus on drug policy and therefore provided journalists with an establishment news source critical of current drug control policy. The opening created by the Sentencing Commissions' report was then exploited by progressive advocacy organizations, especially The Sentencing Project, as an opportunity to call attention to the overextension of the criminal justice system and its implications for the African-American community.

The recent publication of a series of essays criticizing the drug war in the conservative newsmagazine *The National Review* suggests that elite consensus in support of the drug war has fragmented even further. The contributors—including the magazine's editor William F. Buckley and Baltimore Mayor Kurt Schmoke—declared the drug war a failure, identified drug prohibition (as opposed to drug use) as an important cause of urban crime and violence, warned against the "creeping attrition of civil liberties," and called for one form or another of drug legalization (*The National Review*, February 12, 1996 and July 1, 1996; see also *The Economist*, June 8, 1996). Financial support from elite philanthropists also appears to have been crucial to the adoption of legislation legalizing the medical use of marijuana in California and Arizona. The drug warriors persist, but they can no longer do so without prominent opposition from within the circles of power. The time is ripe for the mobilization of more critical perspectives to counter those that have dominated discussions on the issue of drugs thus far.

NOTES

¹   It appears that medical researchers "expected" cocaine and other drugs to have an adverse effect on the fetus (Koren et al., 1989). This study of papers examining the effects of cocaine on fetal health found that, controlling for rigor in methods and measurement, studies that showed that ingestion of cocaine had adverse effects on the fetus were five times more likely to be published than those that found no effects (Koren et al., 1989). This realization has led some to condemn the medical field's "rush to judgment" on the issue (Mayes, 1992; Woodhouse, 1994).

²   For example, upon ascension to office in 1980, the Reagan administration compiled a list of all of the studies funded by NIDA that used the word "social" and used this list to determine which studies would no longer receive government funding (cited in Reinarman, 1994b: 225).

3   This argument is based on an analysis of all stories related to illegal drugs appearing in three news weeklies (*U.S. News & World Report, Time, Newsweek*) and five
metropolitan newspapers *(Boston Globe, New York Times, Chicago Tribute, L.A.
Times, Atlanta Journal/Constitution)* during two sampling periods. These included
April-May, 1995—immediately following release of the U.S. Sentencing Commission's report—and September-November, 1995—the period during which Congress
debated and rejected the Sentencing Commission's recommendations.

4   This argument is informed by research that suggests that the extent to which
political elites are united has important implications for media coverage, and that
elite dissensus was an important precondition for the emergence of more critical
perspectives on the Vietnam War in the news (see Hallin, 1989; Herman &
Chomsky, 1988).

3

United States Drug Laws and Institutionalized Discrimination

Gary L. Webb
Michael P. Brown
Ball State University

INTRODUCTION

Although anti-drug legislation is oftentimes thought of as a contemporary social phenomenon, the federal government has attempted to regulate drugs throughout most of the history of the United States. Anti-drug legislation is said to be for the good of society—to rid society of the immorality associated with drug use; to reduce drug-related health problems; and/or to maintain or establish social order. Generally, however, such laws tend to be concerned less with the drugs they purportedly target than with those who are perceived to be the primary users of the drugs (Morgan, 1990). Many drug statutes have been roundly criticized for treating one group differently than another (i.e., being racist). Used in this way, anti-drug laws are institutionalized mechanisms by which the socially powerful pursue their own political and economic interests (Morgan, 1990).

This chapter will first provide historical evidence of how anti-drug laws have unfairly targeted minority groups. Laws regulating opium and marijuana are cited as examples. Then, the current laws that differentiate between crack and powder cocaine are examined. It will be shown that they are likewise discriminatory, especially toward African-Americans.

ANTI-DRUG LAWS OF THE PAST

Opium Use and the Chinese Immigrant

In 1875, the United States embarked on an anti-drug campaign aimed at controlling the consumption of opium (Helmer, 1975). It is a notable year in United States history because, according to Helmer (1975:20), it marks "the first attempts to legislate against drug use." It is also important to mention that this legislation was not initiated after evidence was gathered that showed that opium was somehow harmful to individual users or to society in general, but rather as a result of misguided concerns over a failing labor market.

Anti-Chinese sentiments were probably expressed from the first time Chinese immigrants set foot in the United States. These sentiments, however, grew within certain segments of the white culture, namely among those who competed with the Chinese for jobs in the gold mining and railroad construction industries. The economy was on the decline—with the completion of the railroads, resulting in substandard wages and a scarcity of jobs—and Chinese laborers became the target of their white counterpart's anger (Helmer, 1975). The following describes the basis for anti-Chinese sentiments as they pertain to the gold mining industry.

> They [whites] were ready to attack the Chinese in the mining fields, not because the Chinese were responsible for reducing the economic condition of the whites but because the Chinese were prepared to accept the terms of wage labor dictated by the companies to an extent that the white forty-niners were not. This in turn, meant that the companies could afford to drop the wages of the white laborers, as long as there was a ready supply of Chinese who, if not happy, were at least willing to accept it. To stablize [sic] the labor market in the mining fields and hold the line on the level of wages, the whites turned their attack from the source of economic power [i.e., the companies that owned the mining fields] to the source of labor competition, and attacked the Chinese to drive them off the fields (Helmer, 1975:20).

Similar sentiments were expressed by whites toward Chinese laborers in the railroad construction industry (Helmer, 1975). Chinese laborers represented unwanted competition in an industry with few job opportunities, and extreme steps were taken to remove them from the labor market.

To accomplish this end, white laborers—reacting to the large capitalists' desire to keep the Chinese as a low-wage labor source—launched a propaganda campaign against the use of opium, a component of the Chinese culture

(Helmer, 1975). Despite the lack of documented evidence of widespread opium use among the Chinese (or other groups for that matter) prior to the mid-1870s, social demonstrations against opium were held and attempts were made to halt immigration from China (Helmer, 1975). Rumors spread about the morally degenerative effects of opium smoking, and with them came increased public fear (Blum, 1969). Articles were written for public consumption, supposedly based upon eyewitness accounts of how individual citizens were at risk of being attacked by opium-crazed Chinese offenders. Society, too, was said to be at risk as prominent citizens were supposedly being lured into a subculture of sin.

To be sure, the rhetoric portrayed opium smoking as having spread beyond Chinese immigrants to other ethnic and socioeconomic groups. Its social and moral consequences were described as being so deleterious and foreboding of further discord that in 1875, San Francisco, California, passed an ordinance forbidding the smoking of opium (Kane, 1882). The conditions under which the ordinance was passed were perceived by a nineteenth-century writer in the following manner:

> The practice [of smoking opium] spread rapidly and quietly among . . . gamblers and prostitutes until the latter part of 1875, at which time the authorities became cognizant of the fact . . . that many women and young girls, and also young men of respectable family, were being induced to visit the [opium] dens, where they were ruined morally and other-wise, a city ordinance was passed forbidding the practice under penalty of a heavy fine or imprisonment, or both (Kane, 1882:1).

The San Francisco ordinance was the first of many of its kind as the rhetoric pertaining to opium smoking spread throughout the west coast. Then, in 1914, with the passage of the Harrison Act, the federal government forbade the Chinese living in America to import or manufacture opium that could be smoked in the United States (Latimer & Goldberg, 1981). Only Americans could import or manufacture smoking opium.

As can be seen, early anti-opium laws were initiated in an attempt to func-tionally exclude the Chinese living in the United States from fully participating in the labor market. Although these laws were initially held out as a panacea to the problems associated with opium addiction, they provided an institutional means by which the Chinese could be discriminated against. The prejudicial attitudes that were held by many United States citizens are captured in a state-ment contained within a 1877 report issued by the California Senate: "whites cannot stand their [Chinese] dirt and the fumes of opium, and are compelled to leave their vicinity" (Committee on Education and Labor, 1877:19).

Marijuana Use and Mexican-Americans

Sentiments against the use of marijuana, much like those that brought about anti-opium ordinances, were grounded in racism (Sandor, 1995). However, with regard to marijuana, it was Mexican immigrants (and other marginalized groups such as Caribbeans and blacks) who were the targets of claimsmakers. Seen as a threat to American culture and the American way of life, Mexican immigrants were negatively portrayed as drug-crazed criminals—made immoral and violent by their use of marijuana—who were responsible for the moral collapse of many communities throughout the West and Southwest (Bonnie & Whitebread, 1974). By 1931, Americans were so biased toward Mexicans and their use of marijuana that 29 states, most of which had large Mexican and Caribbean populations, had passed anti-cannabis statutes (Bonnie & Whitebread, 1974).

Mexican immigrants continued to be the scapegoat when the Depression brought about a surplus labor pool. Frustrated, bitter, and insecure about their economic future, many Americans pointed to Mexicans as a primary cause of their economic strife (Inciardi, 1990). They were said to be taking low-paying jobs away from unemployed American laborers (Inciardi,1990).

Until the mid-1930s, efforts to establish anti-cannabis legislation were found at the state level. But in 1934, the first of many steps was taken to control the use marijuana through federal legislation. In that year, Harry Anslinger, Commissioner of the Bureau of Narcotics, embarked upon a campaign to convince the public and law makers that America was experiencing a "marijuana menace" (Bonnie & Whitebread, 1974). To that end, although there was no scientific research to support his position, Anslinger held steadfast to his claims that marijuana was capable of turning sane, law-abiding citizens into heinous criminals (Inciardi, 1990).

Lured by the sensational nature of Anslinger's moral crusade, the mass media unwittingly assisted in bringing about federal anti-cannabis legislation by likewise alleging that a relationship existed between marijuana use and criminal behavior (Helmer, 1975). Marijuana was reported to bring people to commit almost any type of violent act, including sex crimes and murder (Freedman, 1987). It was also considered to be the cause of criminal insanity and delinquency (Musto, 1973).

In 1936, Anslinger took the final steps necessary to establish federal legislation to control marijuana use. He declared the marijuana controversy to be one of the most pressing problems facing the United States (Inciardi, 1990). Anslinger also stated that marijuana was comparable in strength to heroin (*Scientific American,* 1938) and more socially deleterious than opium (Himmelstein, 1983).

By the time the Marijuana Tax Act was introduced to Congress in 1937, there was little opposition. Nearly everyone supported Anslinger's version of the truth about marijuana. It was "killer weed"; the "assassin of youth." In August 1937, President Roosevelt signed the Marijuana Tax Act into law.

Anslinger accomplished what he had set out to do. The public was both hostile toward and fearful of Mexican immigrants and marijuana (Musto, 1973). Federal anti-cannabis legislation was considered necessary in order to save our nation from the ravages of marijuana and its primary users—Mexican immigrants.

Historical evidence suggests that the anti-Mexican rhetoric in general and laws regulating the use of marijuana in particular were parts of an overall strategy to remove Mexican immigrants from the labor market (Helmer, 1975). The Depression had created a surplus labor force that the market was unable to absorb (Helmer, 1975). As Helmer (1975:56) describes it: "Public concern about marijuana grew because Americans wanted to drive the Mexicans back over the border, for reasons which had nothing to do with the nature of the drug or its psychological effects." Therefore, the social forces that brought about anti-cannabis statutes were similar to those that prohibited smoking opium in the late 1800s.

A CONTEMPORARY CASE STUDY: POWDER VERSUS CRACK COCAINE

The war on drugs in the mid-1980s, say claimsmakers, was declared to stop the spread of crack cocaine and the increase in violent crime that it left in its wake. The advocated response by the media and the legislation enacted by Congress to address the ravages of drugs, that is the popular mechanisms by which American society was thought to be salvaged, involved a combination of more laws, strict and widespread enforcement of laws, and punitive laws taking the form of mandatory prison sentences. Initially, mandatory prison sentences were enacted for drug traffickers; later, mandatory penalties were extended to possession cases.

The consequences of harsher penalties for drug law violators and aggressive law enforcement practices are staggering. From 1981 to 1992, the most recent available data, the number of offenders imprisoned for drug-related crimes increased by 231 percent (Administrative Office of the United States Courts, 1981; U.S. Department of Justice, 1996). The majority of this increase can be attributed to the mandatory sentences enacted by Congress (U.S. Bureau of Prisons, 1987). Moreover, while 72 percent of convicted drug offenders received an incarceration sentence in 1981, as many as 90 percent received an incarceration sentence in 1992 (Administrative Office of the United States Courts, 1981; U.S. Department of Justice, 1996).

Mandatory sentencing laws enacted at the state level have had a similar effect on state prison populations. From 1980 to 1990, the percentage of state prison admissions for drug offenses increased from seven percent to 32 percent (Gillard, 1993). In other words, while 9,000 offenders were incarcerated for drug crimes in 1980, about 104,000 were incarcerated in 1990 (Gillard, 1993). In 1992, 61 percent (or 170,941) of state prison admissions were for drug offenses (U.S. Department of Justice, 1996).

Drugs were the nation's primary concern at the time the war on drugs began (Andreas et al., 1991-1992), and billions of dollars have been spent over the last decade on efforts directed at the eradication of drugs in the United States. Yet, in spite of its priority and the resources allocated to fight the war on drugs, the problem is said to persist. In 1988, the height of the crack era, *The New York Times* (1988) reported that while 1,872 kilograms of cocaine were smuggled into the United States in 1981, the amount had increased to as much as 35,970 kilograms by 1987.

In that same year (1987), Trebach, discouraged by the drug war, asserted:

> After seven years of a multi-billion dollar drug war, our prisons are filled to record levels, violent drug traffickers pollute our cities, and drug abuse is rampant. Despite the most aggressive drug war campaign in history, so much cocaine has been imported since 1981 that the price has dropped to one-third its former level. While some of our children now find it more difficult to buy marijuana, many find it much easier to buy crack and cocaine (Trebach, 1988:2).

It seems that each day the mass media report on how drugs—especially crack cocaine—are slowly eating away at the moral fibers of American culture, culminating in societal decay and, ultimately, its destruction. As it did at the beginning of the war on drugs, crack cocaine continues to incite fear today; it is portrayed by the popular media to be associated with crime in general, and random violence and gangs in particular (Hamid, 1990; Inciardi, Lockwood & Pottieger, 1993; Lockwood, Pottieger & Inciardi, 1996) In addition to trying to explain where they went wrong, that is why the war on drugs has been described as an abysmal failure, Congress is faced with perhaps an equally important dilemma: they are being accused with having passed a law that discriminates against African-Americans.

The Controversy

Under federal law, there is a five-year mandatory prison sentence for offenders convicted for possession of five or more grams of crack cocaine. For offenders convicted on powder cocaine charges to receive the same sentence, they would need to have 500 grams in their possession. That is a 100:1 ratio—known today as the "hundred-to-one rule," a substantial disparity in sentence punitiveness (Moore, 1995).

Congress contends that when the law was passed, little was known about crack cocaine (Moore, 1995). It was believed that crack cocaine was so much more dangerous than powder cocaine that the disparity was warranted: that crack cocaine users were more crime-prone and more violent than powder cocaine users (Gest, 1995). It has been also posited that crack cocaine was so new that data were not readily available to assess the racial implications of mandatory prison sentences (Gest, 1995).

Notwithstanding, the evidence is in now. Research indicates that while crack cocaine users tend to be more crime-involved than powder cocaine users (Lockwood, Pottieger & Inciardi, 1996), crack cocaine users do not appear to be more violent than powder cocaine users (Lockwood, Pottieger & Inciardi, 1996). According to Lockwood, Poittieger, and Inciardi (1996), it is not the type but rather the amount of cocaine that is used that predicts violent criminal conduct.

Furthermore, the National Institute on Drug Abuse (NIDA) reports that from 1988 to 1991 crack cocaine use had remained relatively steady and in some instances showed a downward trend in use (NIDA, 1988, 1991). These surveys reveal that the prevalence rates for crack cocaine were, with the exception of heroin, lower than any other drug. The 1988 NIDA survey estimated that approximately 2.5 million people (age 12 and older) had at one time in their lives tried crack cocaine, about 1.3 percent of the population; in the past year, about one million (.5% of the population) had tried crack for the first time; and during the month prior to the administration of the survey, 484,000 used the drug (.2% of the population). By 1991, the NIDA estimated that 3.9 million people had used crack (about 2% of the population), one million (.5% of the population) had used crack during the previous year, and 479,000 (.2% of the population) had used the drug during the month preceding the survey.

The NIDA (1991) also estimates that of those who use crack cocaine, nearly 50 percent are white, 36 percent African-American, and 14 percent Hispanic. Conversely, about 93 percent of those convicted on crack cocaine charges are African-American, five percent are white, and three percent are Hispanic (Moore, 1995). As a consequence of mandatory sentences for crack cocaine offenders, African-Americans serve terms that are approximately 41 percent longer than their white counterparts (Moore, 1995). The U.S. Department of Justice (1993) reports that African-Americans served an average of 98 months for federal drug offense convictions; whites served 74 months. Furthermore, the war on drugs has been blamed for placing approximately 25 percent of African-Americans between the ages of 20 and 29 under correctional control—they are in jail or prison or serving probation or parole sentences (Mauer, 1990).

Moreover, the war on drugs has been shown to have increased the level of racial disparity among the imprisoned population. Blumstein (1982, 1993), in two separate studies, found race to be an important predictor in whether drug offenders were imprisoned. For example, approximately 20 percent of the racial disparity in incarceration rates is unexplained by the disproportionate representation of African-Americans at the arrest stage of the justice system process. Unexplained racial disparity in incarceration rates varied substantially by crime type: approximately three percent for homicide, five percent for aggravated assault, 16 percent for robbery, 33 percent for burglary, 46 percent for larceny-theft and motor vehicle theft, and 49 percent for drug offenses. Langan (1985) likewise found minorities were overrepresented among the imprisoned population. He did not examine drug offenders specifically, but rather chose to concentrate on robbery, burglary, larceny, simple assault, and aggravated assualt. Nevertheless, Langan's (1985) findings support Blumstein's research (1982, 1993): approximately 20 percent of the overrepresentation of imprisoned racial minorities was left unexplained.

Responding to the Disparity in Sentences

In 1993, the Chief Judge of the United States District Court in Nebraska sentenced four African-American offenders for dealing crack cocaine to sub-stantially shorter periods of incarceration than what the federal statute required. He cited racism as the reason for diverging from federal guidelines. The judge wrote: "Members of the African American race are being treated unfairly in receiving substantially longer sentences than Caucasian males who traditionally deal in powder cocaine" (*Omaha World Herald,* 1993:1). A year later, the Eighth Circuit Court of Appeals overturned the sentence, indicating ". . . that even if the guidelines are unfair to African-Americans, that is not enough to justify a more lenient sentence than called for under the [federal] guidelines" (Walker, Spohn & Delone, 1996:159). Several federal judges have felt so strongly that mandatory sentences are unfair, especially for young, first-time drug offenders, that they have refused to hear drug cases; some federal judges have resigned their positions (Kerr, 1993).

The hundred-to-one rule has been contested in other appeals, but to no avail. Consistently, federal appellate courts have ruled that the disparity in fed-eral sentencing guidelines does not violate the equal protection clause of the Fourteenth Amendment to the Constitution (Walker, Spohn & Delone, 1996) [see, for example, *United States v. Thomas,* 900 F.2d 37 (4th Cir. 1990); *United States v. Frazier,* 981 F.2d 92 (3d Cir. 1992); *United States v. Lattimore,* 974 F.2d 971 (8th Cir. 1992)]. Moreover, the Second Circuit Court of Appeals posited—despite evidence to the contrary— that compared to powder cocaine, ". . . crack's social impact may warrant the tougher penalties" (Moore, 1995:388).

Meanwhile, in 1994, the U.S. Sentencing Commission recommended that Congress re-examine the disparity in sentences for crack and powder cocaine. Congress agreed by, in turn, asking the U.S. Sentencing Commission to offer procedures by which the punishments for crack and powder cocaine might be equalized (Moore, 1995). But after considering the Commission's proposals, Congress voted to maintain the disparity (Gest, 1995). As the final blow to any possibility that the laws would be changed, President Clinton signed the bill to retain the disparity.

Explanations for the Disparity in Sentences

Explanations have been offered to explain sentence disparity for crack and powder cocaine offenders. These explanations are important because within them one is able to ascertain whether contemporary crack cocaine laws are discriminatory. The following outlines two of the more popular explanations.

Powder Cocaine is Hollywood, Crack Cocaine is Harlem

According to Moore (1995), it is no accident that laws pertaining to crack cocaine are more severe than those for powder cocaine. While the mandatory sentences were being formulated there

> . . . was the unspoken assumption that crack was a far more dangerous drug than powder cocaine. Crack was perceived as the drug of choice for the dangerous black underclass. High on ruinous potion, these criminals prowled the inner-city streets . . . Powder cocaine is also bad. But its users are perceived as crazed hedonists, amoral but not dangerous. In popular mythology, cocaine is Hollywood, crack is Harlem (Moore, 1995:388).

Thus, according to Moore (1995), two forces influenced the passage of mandatory prison sentences for crack cocaine users in the mid-1980s. First, Congress was under the mistaken assumption that crack cocaine was more dangerous than powder cocaine; and second, affected by racial prejudice, the use of crack cocaine by African-Americans, considered by lawmakers to be a crime-prone race, was perceived to be a dangerous combination.

Belenko (1993) offers yet another explanation for the punitive crack cocaine laws. He contends that like other anti-drug campaigns, crack cocaine was primarily built upon

> unsubstantiated fears that (1) the particular drug made its users lose control and become violent; (2) the drug was highly and quickly addictive, and drug "pushers would make this drug available in every nook and cranny of the nation, where it would soon virtually enslave the populace"; and (3) those addicted would turn to crime to sustain their craving for the drug. (Belenko, 1993:10)

The concern of crack cocaine gained in saliency when it spread to the urban areas populated primarily by the poor and minorities (Reinarman & Levine, 1989). As Belenko (1993:9) asserts, ". . . the use of crack by the urban poor provided political leaders with a convenient scapegoat for both diverting attention from pressing social and economic problems and blaming a specific powerless group for social disaster."

On the other hand, the war on crack is unlike other anti-drug initiatives. Belenko (1993) states:

> What makes the crack phenomenon unique among drug scares is that the drug emerged into the drug subculture at a time when momentum was indeed building toward strict punishment of drug users and dealers, with a presidential administration [i.e., Reagan] that had a strong ideological bent toward individual accountability and an aversion for sociological or economic explanations for social problems. And, with crack arriving in the midst of a national election year campaign, politicians would find it difficult to avoid speaking out strongly against this latest drug "menace." In the political climate of 1986, silence about the issue would too readily be interpreted as being "soft" on drugs. In this way, the political debate over crack quickly deteriorated into demonstrations of "toughness" against drug abuse (Belenko, 1993:9).

Hence, when the disparity in sentences between crack and powder cocaine was reconsidered in 1994, Congress was aware that scientific research had demonstrated that crack was no more addictive or dangerous than powder cocaine (Moore, 1995; Lockwood, Pottieger & Inciardi, 1996). Yet lawmakers voted to maintain the disparity for their own personal gain. Although it is conceivable that the perceived relationship between crack cocaine and crime had originally influenced the making of laws that resulted in the sentence disparity between crack and powder cocaine offenders, scientific research had disproven that crack was more likely to lead to criminal behavior than powder cocaine (Lockwood, Poittieger & Inciardi, 1996) when the laws were reconsidered in 1994. Therefore, it appears that stiffer penalties for crack cocaine offenders are tainted by politics and racial prejudice.

Congress is not the only culprit. There is a tendency in American society, especially among whites, to associate African-Americans with criminal behavior (Wilbanks, 1987). To ascertain the extent to which prejudicial attitudes impact upon the sentences imposed upon offenders, however, has proven to be a formidable task for criminal justice researchers. In part, this is due to the complex ways in which prejudice may influence justice system processing. MacLean and Milovanovic (1990), for example, indicate that:

While biases sometimes operate directly within the criminal justice system, at times they are "extra-legal" in that they operate within a broader society to make minorities more vulnerable to criminal justice scrutiny. Sometimes these biases are the direct result of a specific characteristic, and sometimes they are indirect in that they result from a combination of characteristics. Thus we may see direct discriminatory effects of race on outcomes in criminal justice processing or we may find the indirect effect of race in combination with class and/or gender in these outcomes (MacLean & Milovanovic, 1990:1).

Police Practices and the War on Drugs

There appears to be no fiscal constraints on expanding the criminal justice system. Expenditures in other areas may decrease, such as those for education, but there appears to be a bottomless pit of financial resources available for supporting the expansion of the criminal justice system. Increasing the number of police officers on the street is a priority in this endeavor. And the police have been given their marching orders: take drugs off the streets. For the decade of the 1980s, as crack cocaine plagued inner-city streets, arrests for drug-related crimes increased by 126 percent (Maguire & Flanagan, 1990). And from 1985 to 1989, arrest rates rose from 200 to 400 per 100,000 people (Blumstein, 1996). This increase can be explained by a concerted effort mounted by the police on inner cities to impact upon the growing crack trade.

"Although laws are in theory applied to all violators, they are in fact applied in a discriminatory fashion against minorities" (Chambliss, 1996:250). Common everyday law enforcement strategies have resulted in a racial disparity in arrests (Walker, Spohn & Delone, 1996). The police can actively "seek out" drug law violators, but they tend to be restricted to responding to complaints of personal and property crimes (Kraska, 1992). Available evidence suggests that police tend to target minority group neighborhoods in the pursuit of drug law violators, while leaving middle-class white neighborhoods virtually untouched (Walker, Spohn & Delone, 1996). Such a law enforcement strategy is discriminatory, and has resulted in a disproportionate number of minority arrests leading to incarceration sentences. According to the U.S. Department of Justice (1995), from 1980 to 1994 the number of African-American males confined to jails and prisons throughout the country increased by 225 percent. The incarceration rate for African-Americans for that same period (1980-1994) was seven times that for whites (Bureau of Justice Statistics, 1981, 1995).

Sometimes discrimination in arrest practices are overt. Take, for example, "Operation Pressure Point" in New York City. The New York City police department "cracked down" on drug dealers, who happened to be racial minorities, while at the same time scaring off the buyers who had driven into the city from their white suburban middle-class neighborhoods (Zimmer, 1991). Or consider "Operation Hammer" by the Los Angeles police department. This police operation was intended to target suspected gang members and drug dealers. All of the arrestees were either African-American or Hispanic, most of whom had to be released for lack of evidence (Hoffman, 1993). "Operation Hammer" neither reduced gang membership nor did it reduce drug crime (Hoffman, 1993).

CONCLUSIONS

The history of anti-drug laws in the United States is wrought with institutionalized prejudice toward minority groups. This chapter showed how the Chinese and Mexicans were targeted for exclusion from the labor market under thin veils of legislation aimed at making opium and marijuana illicit drugs. To achieve this end, propaganda campaigns were launched depicting the Chinese and Mexicans and the drugs they used as dangerous and immoral.

The war on drugs, from its conception—when Congress passed mandatory prison sentences for crack cocaine offenders—to its present day implementation—when the police target inner-city streets primarily occupied by young African-Americans, is likewise racist. Furthermore, similar to previous anti-drug legislation, the present war on drugs emphasizes punishment, the incitement of fear, and the creation of a crisis that suggests if crack is not immediately addressed it will destroy society (Reinarman & Levine, 1989). The war on drugs is also similar to previous anti-drug legislation in that it identified a minority group that was easily used as a scapegoat (Reinarman & Levine, 1989).

To be sure, the war on drugs has had far reaching consequences. Millions of drug offenders, primarily African-Americans, have been placed under the control of the justice system, for longer periods of time and serving harsher penalties. "Increased police surveillance, mandatory prison sentences, and more severe penalties have never effectively reduced crime" (Chambliss, 1996:255). What it has done effectively, however, is turn the African-American community into a community of convicts (Chambliss, 1996).

> Men hardened by the experience of jail and prison; women with husbands, lovers, their children's father, brothers, uncles, and nephews with criminal records; men stigmatized and unable to break the stigma; men used to the brutality by police, prosecutors, jailers, and other inmates. Men return with experiences of being raped, threatened, and assaulted by police and inmates. Some return to the community with AIDS and other diseases contracted while in jail or prison (Chambliss, 1996:253).

The reasons for this paralyzing war are complex. Unlike previous campaigns against drug use, there was no explicit attempt to exclude a particular racial group (namely African-Americans) from the labor market. Instead, as Belenko (1993) explains:

> The strong reaction to crack was probably grounded in the simultaneous occurance [sic] of several social, economic, and political trends: concerns about the intractability of a growing underclass, a shaky economy and the ongoing decline of the United States as a world economic power, a continuing trend away from rehabilitation and toward punishment of criminals, and a philosophy of zero tolerance for drug use and user accountability fostered by the Reagan Administration (Belenko, 1993:155).

Nevertheless, it is apparent that this war on drugs is rooted in the professional aspirations of political leaders whose personal gains are their primary concern. By inciting fear about crack and the purported danger crack users posed to society, politicians were able to sidestep the truly difficult questions pertaining to American society and the state of the economy.

With decriminalization unlikely in the foreseeable future, alternative policies that are considered superior to the current strategy of imprisonment have been proposed. One such proposal is based upon research that suggests that court-ordered drug treatment programs would be more cost effective, decrease drug consumption, and reduce the social costs of drug use more than the conservative measures associated with the current drug war (Justice Research, 1994). A report issued by Justice Research (1994:1) indicates that "the costs of crime and lost productivity due to cocaine use are reduced by $7.46 for every dollar spent on treatment of heavy [drug] users, compared with a savings of 52 cents per dollar for domestic enforcement." The report also notes that in order to reduce cocaine consumption by one percent it would take an additional $1 billion spent on domestic enforcement, interdiction, and source-country control. Conversely, "drug treatment would [only] require an additional $34 million to achieve a one percent reduction in cocaine consumption" (Justice Research, 1994:2).

Others suggest that the extensive use of fines would be better than the current policy that relies so heavily upon imprisonment. However, as Belenko (1993) points out, such a strategy would disproportionately affect poor, minority defendants. Unable to pay the fine, poor defendants may face more severe sanctions.

Neither court-ordered treatment nor fines address the potentially damaging effects of the stigma associated with a criminal conviction. Civil commitment, when used as a diversion from criminal prosecution, holds much promise.

When used in this way, treatment for drug addiction can be initiated outside of the justice system. Previous experience with these programs, however, suggests that terms of commitment need to be regulated so as not to exceed the amount of time served had the drug user been processed formally by the justice system (Belenko, 1993).

History clearly indicates that the potential for racism exists whenever attempts are made to regulate drug use. If drugs are to be regulated, a rational, humane approach needs to be adopted. Such a strategy may leave fewer opportunities for differential treatment (i.e., racism) than past or present drug control policies.

4

The Drugs-Violence Connection: Constructing Policy from Research Findings

Henry H. Brownstein
University of Baltimore

Policy-making is a form of reality construction. That is, public policy is a social artifact constructed by individuals with power and authority in the face of competing claims about what problems need to be solved and what solutions are most appropriate. This chapter demonstrates how research is used in the process of policy construction by showing how the same findings from a study of the relationship between drugs and violence were interpreted and used to support two different claims about what should be the federal drug policy in the United States.

THE CONSTRUCTION OF PUBLIC POLICY

Ultimately, policymakers do their job by setting priorities and allocating resources (Brownstein, 1991). They consider the level of available resources, the competing demands for those resources, and their own values and beliefs and make decisions about (1) what problems are worthy of a public response, and (2) what level of resources should be allocated to address those problems in a meaningful way. This process of making policy moves from problem identification and definition; through program and policy design, development, and implementation; to the evaluation of outcomes; and finally to decisions about resource allocation (cf. Brownstein & Goldstein, 1990; Bullock et al., 1983; Mayer & Greenwood, 1980; Portney, 1986).

59

To set priorities and make decisions about resource allocation, policymakers need information and advice (Brownstein, 1991). Information has an objective quality in that it is offered independent of any personal or social value orientation. Advice is value-laden; it is offered as a recommendation in favor of or opposed to a particular decision or action and is meant to persuade (see Lee, 1978; Merton, 1949). Any number of interested parties may offer advice to those who are engaged in the process of making policy, including not only individuals working within a policy-making establishment, but also individuals and groups such as lobbying organizations, recognized professional specialists, and official agencies and agents (Brownstein, 1995a). Their advice inevitably is presented in the form of a claim about what is known and what should be done (on claims making, see Best, 1989, 1990; Spector & Kitsuse, 1974, 1987).

Claims and the people who make them operate in social realms inhabited by others making claims about the same social issue or phenomenon (Spector & Kitsuse, 1987:72). In this marketplace of claims (cf. Best, 1990:15), claimsmakers compete and collaborate for acceptance of their claims by those with the power and authority to make policy. Public policy is the product of that competition and collaboration.

THE SETTING

From 1982 to 1995, I was employed by the New York State Division of Criminal Justice Services, an Executive Branch agency. Over my 13-year tenure with the government, my title changed from program research specialist, to principal research specialist, to special assistant to the executive deputy commissioner, and finally to chief of the Bureau of Statistical Services. During this same time, the name of the office changed first from the Office of Program Development and Research (OPDR) to the Office of Policy Analysis, Research, and Statistical Services (OPARSS), and then to the Office of Justice Systems Analysis (OJSA). As OPDR became OPARSS, and then OJSA, our agency commissioner became the governor's director of criminal justice and our executive deputy commissioner his assistant director. Their job was to set the criminal justice agenda for the governor and our job, as staff, was, in theory, to advise them.

Our office was designed to contribute to making criminal justice policy under the assumption that policy was made through a rational and orderly process. To this end, it had three bureaus: Statistical Services, Research and Evaluation, and Policy and Program Development. The idea was for the Statistical Services Bureau to collect data and maintain data systems for the production of official statistics, such as the Uniform Crime Reports. The Research Bureau was intended to use these data and statistics to do research on criminal justice issues and concerns. The statistics and research findings would be used by the policy analysts in the Policy Bureau to advise the director of criminal justice, who in turn would advise the governor.

THE DRUG CRISIS AND THE ROLE OF RESEARCH

If policy-making were truly a rational and orderly process, research would play an important role in that process. The general purpose of research is to "[develop] new knowledge by drawing upon past knowledge" (Merton & Moss, 1985:680). Through basic research, new knowledge "is of a kind that adds to general understanding of uniformities that go beyond any particular class of applications; it adds to the intellectual capital that comprises scientific knowledge" (Merton & Moss, 1985:680). In policy-making settings, where research is intended to be applied to problem solving, researchers are supposed to "[draw] upon that capital to arrive at new methods of achieving practical objectives that are themselves outside the sphere of basic knowledge" (Merton & Moss, 1985:680). Armed with this capital, an empirically-based body of knowledge, researchers could and should be an important source of information and advice for those who are making policy (cf. Barak, 1988; Brownstein, 1991; Brownstein & Goldstein, 1990; Merton, 1945).

Unfortunately for researchers who want to contribute to public policy, policy-making is neither rational nor orderly. Policy is driven instead by the dynamics of the competition and collaboration of claimsmakers as they strive to advise and influence policymakers. In this highly competitive marketplace of claims, researchers are at a disadvantage. Professional lobbyists, political constituents, and anyone else with a vested interest argues in this arena for their own favored position. In these forums, researchers historically have taken shelter behind the ideal of scientific objectivity. From that stance, they are able to play the limited role of provider of information, but hesitate as researchers to offer advice favoring even those positions supported by their research findings (Brownstein, 1991).

Researchers are further limited in their ability to contribute to policy by their relegation to particular stages of the policy-making process (cf. Merton, 1945). Typically, researchers are perceived by policymakers as potential contributors only to the evaluation of programs and policies. However, it is at the earliest stage of the process, when decisions are being made about the priority level of problems and the significance of competing claims, that the greatest contributions can be made. At that stage, researchers should be able to "focus attention on certain alternative lines of action by ascribing greater weight to certain types of evidence" (Merton, 1945:410).

Crack cocaine presented itself to policymakers in New York State in the summer of 1986. The news media sensationalized the story (Brownstein, 1995b) and the public demanded action. The response of the media, the public, and the politicians was so powerful that crack cocaine was identified as a problem before anyone could determine how or why it was a problem (cf. Reinarman & Levine, 1989). For the governor's office, this created a demand to respond to a crisis the parameters and dimensions of which had yet to be defined. Researchers and policy analysts in my office were called upon to provide the missing information.

A number of questions were asked. For example: How does crack cocaine compare to powder cocaine? How are drug offenders currently being processed by the criminal justice system? What might be the impact on criminal justice resources of harsher penalties for drug offenders? Office staff responded with volumes of memoranda and briefing materials. Largely, they addressed the systemic questions, almost exclusively playing their customary role as a source of information rather than advice.

Another set of questions involved the nature of the problem of crack cocaine. How was it a problem? What other problems were associated with it? In terms of criminal justice policy, the problem was quickly defined in terms of the relationship between crack and violent crime. Coincidentally, at that time I was co-investigator on a federally-funded study of the relationship between drugs and homicide in New York.

THE DRUGS AND HOMICIDE STUDIES

With funding from the National Institute of Justice, in 1986 the state agency for which I worked and Narcotic and Drug Research, Inc. (later to be called National Development and Research Institutes, Inc., NDRI in either case) were jointly engaged in a study of the drug-relatedness of the more than 1,700 homicides reported to the police in New York State in 1984. The study involved an examination of all police records of reported homicides for that year to determine the extent and nature of drug involvement in homicide. In the summer of 1986, the study was just under way and no data file was ready for analysis. Nonetheless, preliminary findings were reported in the memoranda and briefings were delivered that summer to the governor's office.

The crack cocaine crisis did not fade quickly away. From 1986 to 1990, the news media in New York constructed a compelling and sensational story about crack cocaine and its relationship to violence (Brownstein, 1995b). For example, in 1986 an article in *The New York Times*, "Opium Dens for the Crack Era," described a crack house in Queens and told the story of a young girl who had sex with the owners of the house in exchange for the drug (May 5). A 1988 *New York Daily News* article, "Crack Whips Killing Toll," linked crack cocaine to the record number of homicides in the city that year (December 30). In a September 1990 article in the *New York Magazine*, "All About Crime," the author wrote, "Drugs are probably an even greater factor in the crime wave than commonly imagined" (Greenberg, 1990:22).

The claims of the media about drugs and violence contributed to growing public fear. Naturally, the government responded. In 1987, just after his election to a second term, New York Governor Cuomo said in his annual address to the state legislature:

> This year, we must intensify our efforts as never before in the face of the emergence of crack—the extraordinarily potent, highly addictive and relatively inexpensive cocaine derivative. The lightening speed with which this lethal drug has spread through society is evident in substantial increases in drug-related deaths and demands for treatment by drug users. Crack has also been accompanied by rising incidents of violent crime, including robberies and murders. We must attack this new menace by enacting stiffer penalties for its sale and possession (Cuomo, 1987:39).

Three years later, in 1990, the governor found and gave the mayor of New York City the financial resources to support 5,000 additional police officers to wage the war against crack-related violent crime (Associated Press, 1990:B10).

Our studies of drugs and homicide were conducted in this environment of fear. As the news stories and governor's speech made clear, the media and the government had quickly decided on a course of action: getting tough with drug users and dealers (cf. Gordon, 1990). However, the need for information was great and the situation was still uncertain enough that claimsmakers could contribute to the formulation of particular strategies and tactics that would be used to "get tough." So federal funding became available for Drug Relationships in Murder 2 (DRCA-H2), a follow-up to the original study, with the focus now on crack cocaine and New York City.

For this latter study, during active police investigations data were collected on homicides that took place between March 1, 1988, and October 31, 1988, in four geographical patrol zones of the city. Following a request from the office of the state director of criminal justice (also the commissioner of the state agency where I worked), both the commissioner of the New York City Police Department (NYPD) and the chief of detectives directed homicide squad commanders from these zones to have their detectives complete a form requesting case-specific information, particularly in terms of drug relatedness, for each homicide they investigated during the eight months of the study. The data collection forms were included as part of the routine paperwork of each case investigation. In addition, the project director of the study team was a retired NYPD detective, and he interviewed each squad commander or representative about each case. The data were kept in the detective's case folder for each case, until a case was closed or the data collection period ended (December, 1988).

Seventeen of the 75 police precincts in the city (at that time) were included in the study. During the study period, there were 414 homicides in the four areas combined, accounting for about one-fourth of the 1,896 homicide victims in the city in 1988. The 414 homicides involved 441 victims and at least 496 perpetrators.

The analysis of these drugs and homicide study data was grounded in a conceptual framework that considered three different ways that drugs could be related to violence (Goldstein, 1989). *Psychopharmacological relationships* involve violence due to long- or short-term drug ingestion; *economic compulsive relationships* involve violence due to the compelling need for drugs during an economically oriented crime; and *systemic relationships* involve violence due to the traditionally aggressive patterns of interaction in the system of drug trade and use.

Findings of the research were reported to the social scientific and criminal justice research communities as well as to policymakers in the state and federal governments. The most prominent publication was a 1989 article in the journal *Contemporary Drug Problems* (Goldstein et al., 1989). Findings reported from the research included the following:

- Almost 53 percent of the 414 homicides were identified as drug-related.

- Of the drug-related homicides, 74 percent were systemic; most of these involved disputes between drug dealers over territory (36%), the robbery of a drug dealer (20%), or an assault to collect a drug-related debt (14%).

- Of the drug-related homicides, most involved trafficking in crack (60%); 84 percent involved trafficking any form of cocaine, including crack.

- Of the systemic drug-related cases, most (62%) involved primarily crack.

- Of the psychopharmacological drug-related cases, most involved primarily alcohol; all alcohol-related cases were psychopharmacological.

- Of all the homicide events, only three involved primarily heroin.

- Among the homicide victims in drug-related cases, only 29 (13%) were strangers to their killer, and only four (2%) were innocent bystanders.

The researchers/authors remained objective, issuing findings as information rather than advice. For example, the conclusion of the 1989 article noted, "The foregoing data should clearly focus attention on the crack distribution 'system' as the primary source of crack-related homicidal violence" (Goldstein et al., 1989:684). This left others to use the findings to give advice to policy-makers who would define the problem and determine how and where to allo-cate resources to deal with the consequences of crack cocaine.

USING RESEARCH TO MAKE POLICY

Perhaps the most important and certainly the most prominent finding of the second drugs and homicide study was that crack-related violence was most often systemic and rarely was psychopharmacological (Goldstein et al., 1989:682). This finding made sense then, and does now, in the context of other research that had established the peculiar characteristics of crack cocaine as a product, and of the early forms of crack distribution as a market (see Belenko, 1990; Falco, 1989; Inciardi, 1987; Johnson, Hamid & Sanabria, 1992; Reuter, MacCoun & Murphy, 1990; Vera Institute of Justice, 1992). It also made and makes sense in the context of research that concluded that early crack markets were particularly violent when compared to other drug markets (see Belenko, 1990; Mieczkowski, 1990; Office of the Attorney General, 1989).

The findings of this research had clear policy implications. They did sug-gest that violence was, in fact, a problem associated with crack cocaine, but more precisely that crack-related violence was a problem of the markets rather than users. They also showed that the victims of crack-related violence were predominantly the people who lived in the poor, minority communities where crack was being sold, and even there they mostly were people directly involved with markets. Thus the findings were supportive of policies that shift-ed criminal justice resources toward the control of crack markets and crack dealers. Policymakers in New York did not heed the message of these findings. They followed the lead of the media and pursued a policy that got tough on everyone involved with crack cocaine, including the users, who were actually the victims of the drug.

While state policymakers in New York paid little heed to the research findings, others on the federal level were interested. Given the policy relevance of these findings, they were widely known even before the first DRCA-H2 article was published in 1989. However, since the researchers who had con-ducted the study had taken an objective stance, it was left to those who used the findings to interpret them as they pleased and to use them to make claims and offer advice based on their own interpretations. The following are two cases that demonstrate how the pre-publication findings were interpreted and then used by others to make claims to policymakers making policy about crack and violent crime. (This section is derived from an article originally written for the *Sociological Practice Review* in 1991.)

The first case involves use of the findings by a national organization advocating reform of national drug policy. Staff of the Drug Policy Foundation in Washington, DC had obtained a pre-publication draft of the article that would later appear in *Contemporary Drug Problems*, which they adapted for publication in their newsletter.

Under the names of the authors of the yet-to-be-published article, a brief item with the title "Most Drug-Related Murders Result from Crack Trade, Not Use" (Goldstein et al., 1990) appeared in *The Drug Policy Letter*. The newsletter piece highlighted the main findings of the research, emphasizing the extent to which crack-related homicides were linked to the crack market rather than to crack use. The newsletter adaptation concluded, "The foregoing data should clearly focus attention on the black-market crack distribution 'system' as the primary source of crack-related homicide violence" (Goldstein, 1990:9).

The conclusion in the newsletter adaptation was taken almost verbatim from the article that was not yet published in a professional journal. The most notable difference was that in the journal article the statement about the systemic nature of crack-related homicidal violence was included as a small part of a section titled "Discussion" (Goldstein et al., 1989:684). In the newsletter adaptation it was highlighted. Another more subtle difference was that the researchers in the journal article innocuously suggested that perhaps attention to crack cocaine should be focused on the crack market. The newsletter article emphatically advised policymakers to direct criminal justice resources allocated for dealing with the problem of crack cocaine away from drug users.

The second use of the drugs and homicide research findings in support of a policy position involved a pre-publication draft of the article made available to staff of the office of the United States attorney for the Southern District of New York. An assistant United States attorney was preparing a brief for a case being presented to the United States Court of Appeals for the Second Circuit. The focus of the brief was an incident involving police officers who had forced entry into an apartment from which they knew drugs were being sold. At issue was the question of whether it was proper to withhold particular evidence against the defendants. Specifically, the appeal questioned whether a warrantless entry had been justified.

As it was eventually written, the brief describes the incident as follows: A confidential informant told police that drugs were being sold out of a particular apartment. Police then observed the apartment and saw several people arrive, stay briefly, and leave. They followed and stopped one person they saw leaving, learning thereby that "armed men were selling cocaine and marijuana" from the apartment. After about three hours of surveillance, an undercover police officer entered the apartment to make a purchase. Once inside he purchased five dollars worth of marijuana. He also observed several armed men, quantities of marijuana and cocaine, and additional weapons. He reported this to his colleagues and they returned to the apartment where they knocked on the door and identified themselves as police officers. As they waited, they heard noise and received information by radio that people were leaving the apartment through a window. At that point, they forced entry, arrested five people, and confiscated quantities of weapons, drugs, and money, all of which had been in "plain view" (*United States v. Errol MacDonald,* 1990).

One defendant in the case had his lawyer move prior to trial that evidence recovered from the apartment be suppressed due to warrantless entry. The motion was denied. The defendant was found guilty of possession with intent to distribute cocaine and marijuana, and of using or carrying a firearm. Later, the appeals court ruled that the evidence should have been suppressed since "the agents lacked exigent circumstances for their warrantless entry into the apartment" (*United States v. Errol MacDonald,* 1990). The case was remanded to district court to determine whether the defendant "had standing to contest the search of the apartment" (*United States v. Errol MacDonald,* 1990). The district court upheld the conviction, but the government "petitioned for rehearing of the portion of the panel opinion addressing [the defendant's] suppression claim" (*United States v. Errol MacDonald,* 1990).

The concern of the government in this case was the acceptance of drug and weapons involvement as exigent circumstances in a case for warrantless entry. As was stated in the brief prepared for the appeal, "It has long been recognized by this Court that the existence of serious ongoing crimes, such as the narcotics and weapons offenses involved in this case, is a highly relevant factor in the exigent circumstances analysis" (*United States v. Errol MacDonald,* 1990). In the brief, this argument was supported by the statement: "The courts' often-expressed concern about the extreme dangers posed by armed narcotics traffickers finds graphic support in statistics indicating that extraordinarily high numbers of violent crimes are drug-related, particularly in urban areas like New York City" (*United States v. Errol MacDonald,* 1990). This statement culminates in a footnote that refers to a half-page discussion of the 1989 drugs and homicide article.

The finding used in the brief that drug trafficking and violence are connected, support the position that police should have the right to enter a private residence without a warrant when they know that drugs are being sold from that residence. Effectively, the brief advises judges to establish a policy that permits warrantless entry in cases involving drug trafficking.

CONCLUSION

In its idealized form, policy-making is a rational and orderly process through which informed decisions are made regarding problem definition and resource allocation in pursuit of reasonable and realistic goals and objectives. In fact, policy-making is a nonrational, interpersonal, and political process through which demands for limited resources compete in a marketplace of claims that are grounded primarily in the interests and values of those who are making them.

Researchers are traditionally trained and socialized to treat their own work as science, their research findings as objective. From that position, any involvement in policy-making must assume that policy is made in a rational and orderly way. If it is not, then there is no need for objective findings to inform those who make the policy decisions. In the value-oriented marketplace of claims, there is an important place for claimsmakers and advice givers, but little need for those who provide only information.

In that policy-making is about problem definition and resource allocation, the findings of the drugs and homicide study had clear policy implications. The research showed that crack-related homicide is largely concentrated in communities and neighborhoods that are in or near drug markets. It showed that during the time when crack was being introduced to United States cities, an extraordinarily high proportion of homicides were drug-related. It showed that crack-related homicides involved mostly known drug settings, or people known to be associated directly and indirectly with drug use or drug trafficking or both. By conservative estimation, most of the homicides studied were found to have been related to drugs in one way or another. Most of those were related in a systemic way through the drug business, particularly in the case of crack-related cases; most psychopharmacological drug-related homicide cases were related to alcohol.

These findings were in the public domain through their inclusion not only in journal articles, but also memoranda and briefings to state and federal policymakers, newspaper articles about drugs and violence, articles in the newsletters of an advocacy organization, and even a legal brief presented in federal court. In each case, they were presented by the researchers as information. They were, however, interpreted and used by others to make claims and hence to advise policymakers.

The Drug Policy Foundation used the findings to support its position that drug users are not a source of criminal violence, so policymakers should not seek to criminalize those who use drugs. The office of the United States attorney for the Southern District of New York used the findings to support its position that since drugs are related to violence, when drugs are involved in other crimes, public safety officers may need to violate certain protections otherwise granted to citizens under law. The former is a liberal position, ultimately favoring the decriminalization of drug use. The latter is a reactionary position, favoring limitations on civil liberties.

The people who do research are most familiar with the subject of their research and therefore best able to interpret their findings. Allowing others who are less informed about the subject to advise policymakers, while researchers simply inform, diminishes the role of researchers in the policy-making process. Though neither the Drug Policy Foundation's newsletter article nor the United States attorney's brief had much of an impact on overall drugs and violence policies, other claimsmaking did.

The news media, for example, had espoused the position that drug-related homicidal violence had spread so that all citizens were at equal and greater risk of victimization. By defining the drug-related violence problem in terms of its randomness, the media generated widespread fear among the public. This, in turn, encouraged enhanced enforcement of drug laws in order to protect innocent citizens who believed they were potential targets of violence at the hands of drug users and traffickers.

The drugs and homicide study findings did not support the media position. In fact, claims based on those findings would have contradicted the claims being made by the media. From the research, the claim could have been made that the growing level of homicidal violence was largely a product of uncontrolled and volatile drug markets. In that sense, the problem of drug-related violence would have been defined in terms of its focus on particular communities. This would have encouraged the allocation of more resources to those communities faced with drug problems. It would have favored programs that empower and support communities in trouble, such as drug treatment programs, programs to care for people with drug-related health problems, education and training programs, housing programs, and so on.

Drug policy in the United States in the late 1980s and early 1990s—the years when crack cocaine markets emerged and expanded—favored law enforcement over treatment and prevention. (Beginning in 1989, the Office of National Drug Control Policy, of the office of the U.S. President, annually released a report on drug policy called the *National Drug Control Strategy*. According to that report for the years 1989 to 1995, approximately 60 percent of all funds allocated for drug programs in the United States in any given year are directed to criminal justice or interdiction programs.) More resources are spent on criminal justice and interdiction programs, and fewer resources are devoted to drug treatment, health care, and social services for people living in or near communities and neighborhoods with drug problems.

Researchers do need to adhere to the standards of their profession for doing research. They need to continue to provide information to those people whose job it is to make policy. However, their responsibility should not end there. Given the knowledge and understanding of particular subject areas they acquire from their research, they need to contribute to policy-making by participating in the marketplace of claims by sending recommendations to policymakers, writing editorial articles for popular journals and magazines, writing op-ed pieces for newspapers, and generally summarizing their research findings and conclusions in the form of policy recommendations.

5

A Constructionist Analysis of Newspaper Reporting of Gang Problems in a Midwestern State

Michael J. Leiber
Kent L. Sandstrom
Tina Engstrom
University of Northern Iowa

Marlana Puls
Sam Houston State University

During the past decade, gangs have become defined as a major social problem in America (Curry et al., 1993; Maguire & Pastore, 1995; Pryor & McGarrell, 1993). Widespread concern about gangs and gang activity has been fostered by many interrelated factors; including growing intolerance of crime, greater anxiety about youth violence and drug use, increased emphasis on "family" values and ties, and heightened racial and urban tensions. Concern about gangs has also been reinforced by the mass media, particularly by media accounts emphasizing the violent and often tragic consequences of gang activity for youth, families, and communities. Some analysts (Beckett, 1994; Hagedorn, 1994a; Zatz, 1987) contend that the media even generate public alarm about gangs by linking them with threatening imagery, such as drug abuse, drug dealing, and violent street crime. By framing gangs in this manner, the media allegedly encourage community members to perceive and respond to gangs (or groups of youth construed as gangs) as a kind of "social dynamite"

(Hagedorn, 1994b; Zatz, 1987). In so doing, the media play a key role in shaping public definitions of gangs as a serious community problem.

In this chapter, we examine the nature of the relationship between media coverage and rising public concern about gangs. We consider the interested parties (or claimsmakers) and guiding political agendas—such as the war on crime and war on drugs—that influence media reporting of gangs as a social problem. We investigate two key questions: How are media reports on gangs and gang activities influenced by the interests and agendas of various claimsmakers? Moreover, what images do these claimsmakers mobilize in defining gangs and how does this imagery become salient in media coverage of gangs and gang-related themes? In addressing these questions, we draw on a social constructionist perspective that presumes that (1) claimsmakers play a significant role in defining gangs as a social problem, and (2) claimsmakers' attempts to associate gangs with threatening imagery such as drug offenses will be a central theme in the definitional process. We examine and illustrate the validity of these presumptions based on a content analysis of newspaper reporting on gangs and gang-related themes in a Midwestern state between 1981 and 1994.

THE CONSTRUCTION OF GANGS
AS A SOCIAL PROBLEM

For objectivist theorists, evidence of an increase in gang formation and participation in illegal activity (e.g., drug use and dealing) is critical for explaining why this topic has become a focus of media and public concern. For social constructionists, on the other hand, an increase in gangs and gang-related illegalities is not as important as the role played by claimsmakers and the media and their agendas in defining these phenomena as problematic (Blumer, 1971: Jensen & Gerber, this volume; Spector & Kitsue, 1977). Put simply, social problems are more a matter of claims-making activities than objective conditions. As Best (1989) has argued, it is irrelevant whether certain conditions exist, such as the growth of gangs or gang involvement in drug-related activities. What matters is that people make claims about these conditions and seek to define them as problematic. Thus, the key factor involved in the construction of a topic as a social problem is what claimsmakers effectively say and do about the issue (Farrell & Swigert, 1982; Leiber, Jamieson & Krohn, 1993; Lynch, Nalla & Miller, 1989; Marx, 1981; Wright, Cullen & Blankenship, 1995).

At the present time, social scientists lack precise figures regarding the number of extant gangs and the prevalence of gang involvement in illegal activities. The general consensus is that gangs have increased and that gang members engage in more crime, delinquency, and/or illicit drug activity than nongang members (Esbensen & Huizinga, 1993; Horowitz, 1987; Howell, 1995;

Thornberry et al., 1993). Recent research indicates that the general public and law enforcement agencies view gang activity as rising and assume that gang members engage in more criminal and drug-related behavior than nongang members (Curry et al. 1993; Pryor & McGarrell 1993; Takata & Zevitz, 1990).

These official and public perceptions seem to be borne out by social scientific research on gangs and gang activity. For example, Miller's (1982) extensive study of youth groups in the United States suggested that gang activity was on the rise. Gang problems were reported in 18 of the 36 metropolitan areas he analyzed. Miller also noted that there were indications of an increasing probability of gangs in smaller cities and more rural environments (see also Hagedorn, 1988; Mays, Winfree & Jackson,1993).

In recent years, researchers have focused not only on the question of whether gangs are spreading but also on the question of whether gang members are more likely to engage in illegal behavior. Some analysts have discovered that gang members engage in higher rates of criminality and drug use than nongang members. For instance, in their longitudinal study of high risk youth in Denver, Esbensen and Huizinga (1993) found that gang members reported higher levels of delinquent behavior of all types compared to nongang members, including drug sales. Furthermore, although gang members did not specialize in any one type of delinquent activity, they did account for 57 percent of the street offenses of the entire sample.

Based on the above research, objectivist theorists might contend that the "gang problem" is clearly real and, thus, increased media reporting on gangs and gang activity is appropriate. However, despite the possibility that objective features of the gang problem exist, a number of factors lend support for a social constructionist perspective concerning the "reality" of the youth gang problem. First, it is difficult to derive an accurate estimate of the gang problem because of the complex issues involved in defining a gang (Thompson & Jason, 1988). For example, if a youth is with two to three other youth and he or she commits a crime in their presence, does this act constitute gang involvement in illegal behavior? Researchers and law enforcement agencies have responded to this question in different ways by using varying definitions of what constitutes a gang and gang activity (Esbensen & Huizinga, 1993; Klein & Maxson, 1989; Spergel, 1990). Different definitional criteria and subjective assessments of gang behavior raise questions of validity and generalizability.

Second, research methodologies often fail to capture the dynamics and intricacies involved in gang participation; such as how gangs get started, why youth join these groups, and what gang activity actually entails. This, in turn, can lead analysts to overreact to and misidentify gangs (Hagedorn, 1988; Huff, 1990; Mays, Winfree & Jackson, 1993; Winfree et al., 1992).

Third, perceptions of and reactions to gangs are also distorted by prevailing (and often "official") assumptions about how and why gangs form, particularly in small cities and rural settings. Many officials accept the notion that gang formation is fueled in these contexts by the migration of members from metropolitan areas who establish "satellite" gangs named after their former metropolitan gang (Hagedorn, 1988). However, Hagedorn's studies of gang formation and activities in Milwaukee, Wisconsin, challenge this conventional wisdom. His research highlights the role of the economy in creating and sustaining powerful strains to become a gang member and, in turn, to become involved in crime and drugs (1988, 1991, 1994a).

Finally, the presumption that gang members clearly exceed nongang members in crime and drug participation lacks clear-cut empirical support. While Esbensen and Huizinga (1993) found a correlation between gang membership and increased participation in delinquency and drug use, they also discovered that youth who joined gangs had high rates of involvement in these behaviors prior to becoming gang members. Moreover, Esbensen and Huizinga did not find evidence to support the notions that gang membership leads to drug dealing or that drug dealing is an organized gang activity that involves all members. Other researchers, such as Hagedorn (1994a, 1994b), have arrived at similar findings regarding gangs and drug-related activity. In fact, Hagedorn's analyses reveal that gang members vary greatly in terms of their involvement in drug activity and some members rarely or only briefly participate in such activity.

Overall, perceptions of gangs seem less shaped by "objective" factors, such as rates of gang participation in crime and drug use, than by images promoted by politicians, police officials, and the media, especially among mainstream adults (Tonry, 1995; Zatz, 1987). For example, in studying gang problems in Racine, Wisconsin, a city positioned between the metropolitan centers of Milwaukee and Chicago, Takata and Zevitz (1990) found that public perceptions of local gangs did not directly reflect the objective features of gang activity. By most local accounts, delinquent gangs were a social problem. Yet, adult and youth perceptions differed significantly with respect to local gang activity. Adults were almost twice as likely to view gangs as a serious problem than youths; also, they were less likely to have a full understanding of gangs (Takata & Zevitz, 1990:287, 302). Adult perceptions were shaped by images contained in police and media reports while the perceptions of youth were based on first-hand experience (Takata & Zevitz, 1990:302).

The findings of Pryor and McGarrell's (1993) survey on public perceptions of youth gangs in Indianapolis paralleled those obtained from Racine. The perceptions of Indianapolis respondents, however, were conditioned by their own neighborhood and other areas of the city (Pryor & McGarrell, 1993). Exposure to television news reports on youth gang crime fostered perceptions of gangs as a serious problem in the nonlocal context, but not within the immediate neighborhood. By contrast, in the local neighborhood, where perceptions of danger are generally lower, actual gang crime experiences with youth gangs and embeddedness in a neighborhood enhanced judgments of the severity of the problem. As in Racine, youths relied primarily on personal experience and, to a lesser extent, on others' opinions in formulating perceptions of their neighborhood. Conversely, adult respondents listed the media as their common source of information concerning youth gangs.

In both Takata and Zevitz's (1990) and Pryor and McGarrell's (1993) studies, adults relied on "official" assessments of the gang issue. Official assessments of such an issue typically reflect and arise out of a complex interrelationship between the media and influential claimsmakers. While researchers have not revealed the precise nature of this interrelationship, they have offered insight into how media reporting on social issues is influenced by political agendas championed by legislators, law enforcement officials, and other interested parties (e.g., Goode, 1989; Reinarman & Levine, 1989).

In related research on the media and the creation of "moral panics," Zatz (1987) focused on media coverage of gangs and gang issues in Phoenix, Arizona. Using a variety of data sources, she demonstrated how the interests of the media and another powerful claimsmaker, the police, coincided to promote the construction of Chicano youth gangs as a community problem. Most importantly, Zatz revealed how a "moral panic" emerged in response to the prevalence and activity of Chicano youth gangs when both the Phoenix police and media linked these groups to threatening social imagery (e.g., street crime and violence)—imagery that was incongruent with their actual behavior patterns (see also Davis, 1973; Fishman, 1978; Hagedorn, 1988; Roshier, 1975; Young, 1971). Zatz concluded that a combination of forces, including the media's desire for newspaper sales, the drive for external funding by the police, and racial tensions and bias, interacted to create and amplify the "problem" of Chicano youth gangs in the Phoenix area.

Given the concerns and debates that exist in the literature about the prevalence of gangs, their involvement in crime and drugs, and the role of the media in defining them as problematic, we examine the nature and context of media reporting on youth gangs in a Midwestern state. To date, no study has been conducted in this state to determine the extent of gang membership and gang activity in illegal behavior.

In our analyses, we seek to assess the relationship between reported gang incidents and media commentary on those incidents. We also seek to highlight the social forces and claimsmakers that affect media reporting on gangs as a social problem. Based on a social constructionist perspective and previous research, we anticipate that the political agendas and interests associated with the "War on Drugs" and the "War on Crime" will significantly influence media coverage of gang-related themes.

THE PRESENT RESEARCH

Content analysis of two newspapers was used to assess media reporting and the gang-related themes that emerged from 1980 to 1994. The newspapers come from two of the largest cities in this state. The first newspaper represents coverage for a county that has a total population of 123,798, with persons age 17 and younger comprising 31,402. Minority youth comprise 13 percent of those age 17 and younger, with African-Americans making up 77 percent of that figure. The largest city in the county has an African-American youth population of 19 percent. The other newspaper reflects a larger community with a population of 327,140 with persons age 17 and younger comprising 81,971. Minority youth make up 10.25 percent of those age 17 and younger, with African-Americans making up 47 percent of the nonmajority population. The newspaper in this community has a national reputation and is seen as the state's newspaper; thereby resulting in a larger readership. The two newspapers were selected on the basis of the size and diversity of the counties they served relative to others in this Midwestern state. The newspapers are designated as "Newspaper A" and "Newspaper B."

We collected information on the incidence of gang activity and commentary as reported in these two newspapers between 1980 and 1994. We identified an article as an "incident" when (1) an official report of an arrest, investigation, or a report was alleged or confirmed, and (2) follow-up information on an incident included reports on subsequent official and/or informal action, such as criminal justice and juvenile justice-related responses.

Commentary articles reflected reporting that was unrelated to a specific incident but may have focused on a specific incident in the form of editorials, letters to the editor, etc. To further delineate the role of interested parties in stimulating and sustaining gang membership and gang activity as a social problem, we further differentiated commentary by the source. The distinctions in the sources behind or at the focus of the commentary are: police, school, media, community, professional expert, legislature, and a category that encompasses the combination of two or more of the six sources.

In addition to distinguishing the type of reporting, the size of the article was measured to examine the prominence of the coverage and patterns of reporting over time. Column space was measured in one-quarter inches (Evans & Lundman, 1983; Leiber, Jamieson & Krohn, 1993).

Overall, we focused on the similarities and differences in the reporting of gang incidents and commentary on gangs as an issue for a 15-year-period for the two newspapers. Consequently, we positioned ourselves to examine trends and identify themes and the sources of those themes that may overlap or be unique to each community in the creation and maintenance of gangs as a social issue.

Utilizing a social constructionist approach and findings from previous research, we expected that commentary would be disproportionate to reported gang incidents in terms of the frequency and the total amount of space devoted to the topic. Additionally, we anticipated that the political agendas reflected in the war on crime and the war on drugs would play a significant role in producing the issue of gangs as a social problem. No specific expectations, however, guided the research regarding the precise role each claimsmaker had in this process. Therefore, our analysis is somewhat exploratory and meant to serve as a method for contextualizing the observed patterns in incident and commentary coverage by the two newspapers.

RESULTS

Before examining the role of interested parties and political agendas in the creation of gangs as a social problem, we assess the gang-related reporting patterns of the two newspapers to determine the extent of the "problem." Thus, the first stage of the analysis is descriptive in nature and involves an examination of the number and the amount of coverage given to gang-related incidents and commentary. Next, we identify the claimsmakers who fueled commentary focusing on gangs as a social issue. The final stage of the analysis involves a content analysis of newspaper articles to discover the context of the media coverage on gangs and gang activity and what themes are highlighted by the claimsmakers in the construction process.

Newspaper Reporting Trends

The number of incident and commentary articles covering the topic of gangs over the 15-year period is presented in Figure 5.1. The amount of column space devoted to gangs by each newspaper is provided in Figure 5.2.

For both newspapers, the topic of gangs did not become prominent as an issue until 1989 (Figure 5.1). In fact, reporting on gangs was sporadic prior to this time for Newspaper A; commentary articles appeared in 1981 (N=1), 1983 (N=1), and again in 1986 (N=6) and 1987 (N=3). During the years 1980 through 1988, Newspaper B reported no incident or commentary articles on the topic of gangs. This pattern of reporting for both newspapers is in line with Fishman's (1978) analysis and findings of media coverage of elderly crime in New York, and Leiber, Jamieson, and Krohn's (1993) study of reported drug involvement among professional athletes, and reflects that period prior to the establishment of the issue as a social problem.

Figure 5.1
Number of Articles Reporting Gangs by Newspaper, Type of Article, and Year

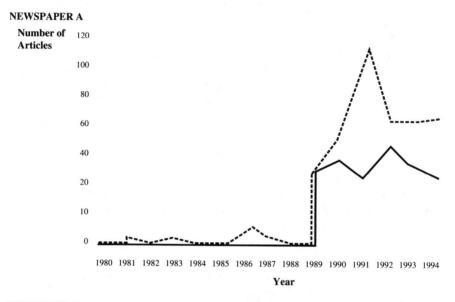

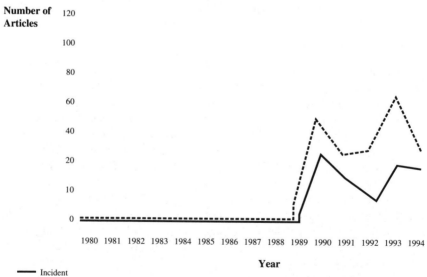

——— Incident

- - - - Commentary

The rise of newspaper coverage on gangs beginning in 1989 is similar to the increased attention paid to the topic nationwide (e.g., Hagedorn, 1988; Howell, 1995). After 1989, coverage increases steadily and, in turn, promotes solidification of the theme of gangs as a social problem. Although there are some differences between the two newspapers in terms of reporting trends, a decline in the total number of articles is evident for both media forums in 1994. Similar to previous research, however, the amount of coverage is still heavier than that period prior to the definition of the issue as a problem (e.g., Fishman, 1978).

Initially, we anticipated a greater proportion of incident articles would appear than commentary articles. As the topic of gangs became more attractive as an issue, we then expected an increase in the number of general commentary articles compared to incident articles and in the amount of coverage as measured by column space. The number of commentary articles and the space devoted to gangs are central factors in the creation of a topic as a social problem (e.g., Leiber, Jamieson & Krohn, 1993). Articles appearing in both newspapers, for the most part, conform to these expectations.

The increase in the reporting of commentary is strongest for Newspaper A where a rise in the ratio of reporting gang incidents relative to commentary begins in 1990 and peaks in 1992. For example, in 1992 the ratio is one gang incident article to every 5.5 commentary articles. A gang incident article was not among the first 11 articles appearing in Newspaper A. For Newspaper B, the ratio of gang incident articles to commentary increases in 1992 and then begins to decrease in 1994.

Distinguishing the amount of coverage by the column space devoted to the gang issue reveals similar patterns for the number and type of article reported (Figure 5.2), and supports previous research on the construction of social problems (e.g., Wright, Cullen & Blankenship, 1995). However, there are some notable exceptions that do not conform to expected patterns. For instance, for Newspaper A the amount of space devoted to gang-related incident articles is more than that given to commentary in 1993. Similarly for Newspaper B, proportionately more space is given to incident articles than commentary in 1990.

This part of the analysis has shown that gangs did not become a prominent issue until 1989. As expected, it also illustrated that commentary articles on gangs increased more dramatically than incident articles and played a significant role in shaping the topic of gangs as a social problem. Next, we assessed what role claimsmakers had in stimulating commentary on the issue.

Figure 5.2
Column Space of Articles Reporting Gangs by Newspaper,
Type of Article, and Year

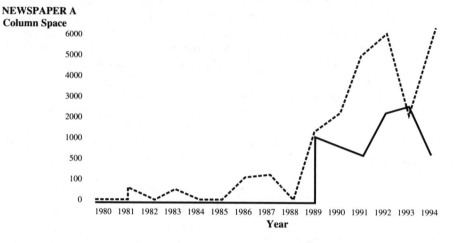

NEWSPAPER A
Column Space

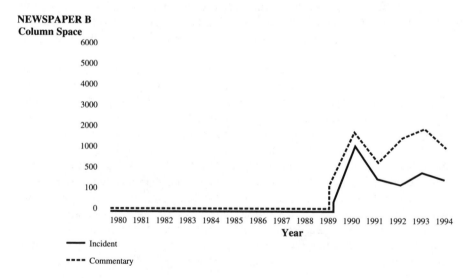

NEWSPAPER B
Column Space

——— Incident

---- Commentary

The Identification of Claimsmakers

Tables 5.1 and 5.2 provide the distributions of commentary articles differentiated by source and column space.

As illustrated in Table 5.1, the media itself was responsible for initiating a large share of the commentary articles in Newspaper A, followed by commentary that was driven by community concerns. The heaviest year of reporting was in 1991 (Figure 5.1) and it was at this time that both the media and concerns of the community dominated reporting on the issue of gangs. The media served as the source of 24 articles appearing in 1991 while community concerns prompted 28 articles during this year, the most for the 15-year timeframe observed. Commentary articles that focus on the community begin to decline in 1993. All other sources of the commentary appearing in Newspaper A represent a relatively small number of the articles, as well as devoted space, when compared to the role of the media and the community in generating attention to the gang issue. It seems important to note, however, that commentary driven by the legislature has almost tripled in frequency and devoted space when patterns in reporting are examined for the years 1989 through 1994.

The reporting of commentary articles by the source for Newspaper B reveals again that the dominant source fostering commentary is the media, particularly for the years 1992 through 1994 (Table 5.2). The year 1992 produced an extremely large amount of media commentary coverage (N=1,666). Unlike the trends seen in Newspaper A, commentary that focuses on community concerns plays a small role in directing attention toward gangs. In fact, this may be said of all other sources of commentary relative to the influence of the media. However, the number of articles and the amount of space given to police, school, community, and professional experts seem to be relatively more frequent and more evenly distributed compared to the media in the years 1989 through 1991. A noticeable increase is evident in reporting of police commentary articles in 1993 (N=15).

Gangs Within the Context of the
War on Crime and the War on Drugs

In the previous sections, we first provided a descriptive account of the frequency of articles and amount of column space devoted to gang issues. We also identified commentary by each source that was responsible for generating newspaper coverage. In the following discussion, we provide a content analysis of the reported articles to identify the themes that emerged from the newspaper reporting of gangs as a social problem. We focus special attention on what salient claimsmakers had to say about gangs, drugs, and crime. From this point, Newspaper A and Newspaper B will be referred to as "Community A" and "Community B."

Table 5.1
Reporting of Gangs in Newspaper A by Type of Commentary, Number, and Column Space, 1980-1994

Year	Police		School		Media		Community		Expert		Legislature		Combination	
	N	Column Space	N	Column Space	N	Column Space	N	Column Space	N	Column Space	N	Column Space	N	Column Space
1980	0	0	0	0	0	0	0	0	0	0	0	0	0	0
1981	1	78	0	0	0	0	0	0	0	0	0	0	0	0
1982	0	0	0	0	0	0	0	0	0	0	0	0	0	0
1983	0	0	0	0	0	0	0	0	0	0	0	0	1	70
1984	0	0	0	0	0	0	0	0	0	0	0	0	0	0
1985	0	0	0	0	0	0	0	0	0	0	0	0	0	0
1986	2	52	0	0	0	0	2	56	1	24	0	0	1	24
1987	1	6	0	0	0	0	0	0	0	0	0	0	2	162
1988	0	0	0	0	0	0	0	0	0	0	0	0	0	0
1989	3	128	0	0	10	350	4	126	2	56	3	286	7	358
1990	6	277	3	134	12	375	10	589	3	162	6	196	15	762
1991	10	365	4	108	24	1,003	28	1,328	4	150	9	698	27	1,481
1992	4	476	4	158	19	1,078	16	1,962	1	40	6	108	13	1,856
1993	5	584	2	108	30	1,636	2	756	0	0	8	338	14	1,834
1994	5	595	1	320	22	955	6	1,006	5	798	14	1,013	9	1,181

Table 5.2
Reporting of Gangs in Newspaper B by Type of Commentary, Number, and Column Space, 1980-1994

Year	Police		School		Media		Community		Expert		Legislature		Combination	
	N	Column Space	N	Column Space	N	Column Space	N	Column Space	N	Column Space	N	Column Space	N	Column Space
1980	0	0	0	0	0	0	0	0	0	0	0	0	0	0
1981	1	78	0	0	0	0	0	0	0	0	0	0	0	0
1982	0	0	0	0	0	0	0	0	0	0	0	0	0	0
1983	0	0	0	0	0	0	0	0	0	0	0	0	0	0
1984	0	0	0	0	0	0	0	0	0	0	0	0	0	0
1985	0	0	0	0	0	0	0	0	0	0	0	0	0	0
1986	2	52	0	0	0	0	2	56	1	24	0	0	0	0
1987	1	6	0	0	0	0	0	0	0	0	0	0	0	0
1988	0	0	0	0	0	0	0	0	0	0	0	0	0	0
1989	1	36	1	28	1	56	0	0	2	63	0	0	0	36
1990	4	156	5	202	8	234	11	146	3	110	4	100	18	1,880
1991	2	58	0	0	8	225	4	112	0	0	1	18	9	312
1992	3	165	0	0	19	1,666	0	0	2	93	0	0	2	170
1993	15	383	1	10	15	500	4	86	2	40	5	97	21	826
1994	1	28	0	0	15	536	3	151	1	30	1	50	7	218

The sporadic and infrequent coverage of gangs in the period from 1980 to 1988 may have been due either to the lack of gang activity or society's unwillingness to believe that a significant amount of crime was gang-related. With the exception of a few isolated commentary articles appearing in Community A during the early 1980s, the initial shift in concern about and coverage of gangs was triggered by gang-related killings that occurred in both Community A (1989, 1992) and Community B (1990, 1993) (Ewoldt, 1992; Wiley, 1993). The killing incidents in Community B, as well as a number of drive-by shootings in both communities, were linked not only to gangs but also to drugs and guns (Alex, 1992:1; Hovelson, 1993:19). Thus, actual reported gang-related activity was evident in both Community A and Community B. The topic of gang-related activity was also heightened by the Rodney King incident, the Los Angeles riots, and shootings at a state university (Alex, 1992; Community B, 1992a). In both communities, reports of gang-related activity in Los Angeles predominated media reporting, especially in 1992 (Farnhaen, 1993:A1; Community A, 1992).

These local and national incidents provoked a wave of community fear, particularly in Community A, and significant media attention in both communities. The media and politicians responded to the reported gang-related incidents and concomitant community fears by incorporating the gang topic within the larger war on crime and war on drugs. The gang-related incidents account for the disproportionate coverage in the number of articles and amount of space devoted to community and media commentary. Politicians' reactions and solutions to the perceived gang problem account for the increase in these commentary articles (Tables 5.1 and 5.2).

Three dominant themes emerged regarding the "gang problem" in both communities during the 15-year study. These interrelated themes were: (1) gangs are a serious problem; (2) gang members commit crime because of their involvement with drugs and access to guns; and (3) the gang problem can be solved by declaring and implementing a war on crime and war on drugs. The media, police, and politicians played key roles in fostering and feeding off these beliefs and in solidifying gangs as a social problem. Underlying the motives of the police and politicians were agendas that were often tied to budgetary resources, campaign elections, and gun control.

Estimates of the extent of gang membership in the state as a whole is 2,400 (Smith, 1993). In Community B, the figure cited is 400 persons who belong to one of four gangs (Hovelson, 1992). Media reports in conjunction with the police chief of Community B go so far as to state that gang activity "ebbs and flows and, like flood waters, gang violence is high now" (Clark, 1993). Again, keep in mind that these figures are purely speculative and are not based on the surveying of youths and adults to determine gang affiliation. Even if one accepted these unscientific estimates of gang membership as valid, questions arise regarding the extent to which gang members participate in illegal activity given the relatively low number of reported gang killings and incidents in both communities (Figure 5.1). Yet, these questions were largely ignored. In fact, some "experts" stressed the urgency of the gang problem despite the lack of incidents. For example, a local university professor stated, "If we don't move now, in the next year we'll have the most serious problem the state has ever seen" (Culpepper, 1990:A4).

Newspaper reports in both communities describe gangs in a manner similar to that described by Hagedorn (1988), who studied the media and law enforcement characterizations of gangs in Milwaukee and elsewhere. Gangs are perceived as organized groups who migrate from other cities, engage in illicit drug activity, and use guns to commit violent crimes. For example, one article stated, "Progression of gangs . . . has been fueled by hate, drugs, and an organized effort by gangsters in the country's largest cities to capture new markets" (Suk, 1993). Another example reflecting this sentiment, "Drug-dealing gangs from large cities are moving into Midwestern states, including . . . . They bring with them the drug-related violence of gangland style killings" (Newspaper B, 1990:A4). In another article, ". . . with these youth come connections to youth gangs and to the crack cocaine drug trade . . ." (Woolson, 1991).

These views are further echoed in the following headline and excerpts, "Crack, crime, and violence follow as gangs gain a foothold in the state" (Suk, 1993). ". . . officials . . . have seen an upsurge of gang interest in the state, mainly gauged by drug trafficking and violent crime" (Wiley, 1992:1). "Gang element cause for alarm, area leaders tell states panel" (Woolson, 1991). In this last article, not only is concern of gangs raised but the issue is tied to race and the belief that gangs are organized groups. For example, it was stated that "crack cocaine, racism, and economic despair have caused an outbreak of 'wanna-be' gangs" in Community B. "Crack cocaine is believed to be primarily associated with black gangs" and gang-related incidents are attempts to divert attention from drug trafficking activities (Woolson, 1991). In Community A, gangs were described as follows: ". . . street gangs can be broken down into three types—crack cocaine gangs composed almost exclusively of young blacks, white gangs with racist tendencies, and extortionist Asian gangs. All are dangerous and prone to violence . . ." (Suk, 1993:A1). In Community B, gangs were portrayed as waging drug wars in the streets (Hovelson, 1993:19).

The reason gang members commit crimes, residents believed, was because of their involvement with drugs and access to firearms. In Community B, one article stated, "Guns have become an increasing problem. . . . Juvenile court officials say the influx of crack cocaine has brought a new breed of young dealers, many packing pistols" (Powell, 1991b:A10). The police chief in Community B added to this portrayal by stating, "[our] county is the hub of drug activity. . . . More guns, drug sales and violence are escalating gang activities" (Powell, 1991a:A2). An affidavit for a search warrant in the county district court also stated, "These weapons are recognized to be tools of the trade and are used to protect drug traffickers and their inventory of cash on hand" (Powell, 1991a:A2). Even the high murder rate of the nation was blamed on gangs, drug addiction and the "ready availability of deadly high-powered weapons on many American streets" including those of this Midwestern state (Newspaper A, 1992b). Finally, the following quotes in commentary articles paint this bleak picture, "Today, drive-by-shootings or other types of gang generated gunfire seem to occur at least weekly, if not almost daily . . ." (Suk, 1993:A1); "increased numbers, older gang kids, more violence, more guns, more terrified people. The pattern is going to continue and expand" (Smith, 1993).

Residents in both communities, but especially in Community A between the years 1990 and 1992 (Table 5.1), became so terrified of gangs that they feared walking in their own neighborhoods. One resident stated, "You're driving through your own neighborhood, and you don't know if you're going to get shot. I thought it was a safe place. Now you can't go out for a walk" (Ballard, 1991:A4). Residents became so fearful that firecracker explosions were reported as gunshots (Ballard, 1991:A4). Shootings, particularly drive-by shootings, were perceived as gang-related despite the lack of evidence supporting such claims (Hartman, 1992).

In the wake of a perceived gang problem and growing community fear, politicians responded by couching the issue within the larger war on crime and war on drugs and the ideology and solutions associated with these efforts. Similar to other contexts, (e.g., Hagedorn, 1988), the ideology and the solutions were punitive in nature and reactionary. For instance, a lawmaker in Community B attempted to increase penalties for criminal gang activity by: (1) adding five years to the prison sentence of a criminal street gang member convicted of a felony, (2) sentencing a gang member convicted of any other public offense to an additional 180 days to one year in jail, and (3) refusing to allow early parole or deferred sentences, thereby forcing a convicted gang member to serve his or her entire jail term (Woolson, 1991).

The attorney general for this Midwestern state also contributed to the wave of conservative ideology by stating, "Our message to gang members and leaders is this: When we throw the federal book at you, it will be a knockout blow. There will be no bail, no probation, no parole, and you will be a long time in a federal penitentiary" (Newspaper A, 1992c:3b). The call for harsher laws and stiffer penalties underlay the bulk of the legislator commentary articles and, to a lesser degree, the community commentary articles. The latter articles also focused on residents' fear of violence and drugs (Tables 5.1 and 5.2).

The talk of a crime and drug control ideology paved the way for an array of law enforcement approaches that ranged from the hiring of more police to organizing special gang/drug task units, to establishing anti-drug trafficking laws, and imposing youth ordinances. For example, there was discussion of a dozen law enforcement agents joining forces to rid drug trafficking (Powell, 1991:A7). "By drawing off each other's individual expertise, funds, equipment, and manpower, they are collectively trying to combat the problem. Drug dealers will no longer be able to get rid of cops by 'crossing the border'" (Powell, 1991b:A7).

The anti-drug trafficking laws aimed to both increase the penalties for possessing drugs and make it illegal to recruit children younger than 18 to deliver or manufacture drugs (Roos, 1992:A4). One politician stated the anti-drug trafficking legislation was needed since "Gangs are recruiting people to come to . . . in the area of drugs knowing they'll get a hand-slap if they're caught" (Roos, 1992:A4). The youth ordinance targeted 16-year-olds and required them to be off the street by 11 p.m. unless accompanied by a parent or guardian (Ballard, 1991). The anti-drug laws and, in particular the youth ordinances, were criticized by some local community leaders as vague and potentially arbitrary in implementation. As one community leader stated, "If we could know what is in the mind[s] of the people, maybe I could buy an approach such as this. But I'm very concerned, because if you look at the language of the ordinance, what they've really done is create the crime of looking suspicious" (Powell, 1991b:A1).

Political agendas, fostering and mobilizing public fear, helped to cement the gang/drug issue as a social problem. Included in these political agendas were the law enforcement agencies' desire for more revenue and the politicians' desire for support for their election campaigns and their efforts to curb access to guns. As noted earlier, there was a significant increase in police commentary articles in Community B during 1993 (Table 5.2). The police chief in Community B used the issue of gangs and the wars on crime and drugs to convince the public that the police department needed more revenue to address this problem. One article heading stated, "[Community B] fears gang wars loom" (Hovelson, 1992). In the article, the police chief contended that the summer could become a "battleground" for big-city gangs trying to monopolize a lucrative drug market (Hovelson, 1992). In this same article, the chief had to defend this claim and his estimate of 400 gang members in light of criticisms that the comments were intended as a "political ploy" to combat a city council's request that the police department's budget for next year (1993) be cut by more than $400,000 (Hovelson, 1992:3).

In 1993, the chief admitted to using the gang issue as a means to obtain and protect resources but only after a reported shooting incident where someone was injured and another where shots were exchanged between passengers in two cars (Clark, 1993:A4). Both incidents were described by the chief as possibly gang-related (Langel, 1993:A4). The heading of the article containing the chief's admission read as follows: "[Police chief] on gang activity: I told you so" (Clark, 1993:A4). The chief stated that "the community's cold shoulder toward the problem can be partially blamed for the turf wars. . . ." "The failure of the community to address the problem allows them [(gangs)] to flourish and grow" (Clark, 1993:A4). At the same time, the chief also attributed a quiet summer in the previous year to weather conditions and successful police strategies for dealing with gang activity, such as narcotic arrests (Wiley, 1992:1). Furthermore, he believed his department's tough stance toward gangs and drugs resulted in the flight of gang members from the community and the "slow down of out-of-towners" (Wiley, 1992:1). Thus, the police chief used the gang issue not only as a means to protect and secure resources but also as a mechanism to provide evidence of good police work and the need for police protection, despite the lack of empirical proof that a significant gang problem existed. This finding supports Zatz's (1987) contention that the police are a central claimsmaker in the creation of "moral panics."

Politicians and others also used the fear of gangs and their involvement in drugs and crime for their own self-interest. Declaring war on gangs became a popular method of informing the public that one was tough on crime. Fighting crime and indirectly, gangs and drugs, became the focus of political campaigns. Former United States Representative Fred Grandy, for example, in his campaign for governor of Iowa, called for an end to parole, the building of more prisons, a death penalty, drug education programs, and the use of criminal statutes to combat mobsters to fight gang leaders (Yepsen, 1994:A1).

The gang/drug issue was also linked with campaigns by the media, the community, and especially politicians for controlling gun availability. As previously discussed, guns were portrayed as tools of the drug trade. Here are a few selected themes taken from newspaper headlines and stories to illustrate once again this linkage: "Youth death toll from guns still rising," "Guns for sale," "Reality is gangs with Rambo-styled assault weapons; everyday someone innocent becomes a statistic, caught in the crossfire of a drive-by shooting" (Newspaper B, 1991:10; Powell, 1991b:A1; Schram, 1994). This linkage, coupled with community fear, provided the avenue for legislators to push for gun control legislation and gun searches in public housing and school lockers (Newspaper A, 1994a; Newspaper A, 1994b; Newspaper B, 1991c).

CONCLUSIONS

The results of this study support past social constructionists' assessments of how the gang problem and other social problems, such as drug scares and crime waves, are conceptualized and amplified (Becker, 1963; Beckett, 1994; Fishman, 1978; Hagedorn, 1988; Leiber, Jamieson & Krohn, 1993; Musto, 1973; Zatz, 1987). Our findings offer the strongest support for a social constructionist approach or more specifically, a "cultural constructionist" rendering of the gang problem (Beckett, 1994). According to cultural constructionists, public perceptions of the nature of the gang problem are shaped by their popular representations. In turn, a strong association exists between media coverage, claims-making activities, and levels of public concern (Beckett, 1994).

Unlike objectivist theorists, cultural constructionists stress that public concern about gangs does not directly correspond to the actual incidence of gang-related involvement in crime or drug use. Instead, the politicization of "gangs" as an issue is largely a result of larger social, economic, and political forces that cause public insecurity (Beckett, 1994). Guided by prevailing political agendas, the media and claimsmakers feed upon this insecurity and propose perspectives and solutions that serve their own political or economic interests. Thus, increased media coverage and escalated claimsmaker emphasis on the "gang problem" are less a matter of "objective reality" than politics and economics.

Nevertheless, although cultural constructionists challenge objectivist assumptions about the correlation between public concern and the incidence of gang activities, they agree with objectivists in one respect. They accept the objectivist premise that shifts in public and media concern about gangs precede shifts in state (or elite) initiatives to define and address this problem. Our findings provide some support for this position. We detected that the emergence of public and media concern about gang activities seemed to precede state (and elite) initiatives to "frame" and handle it. Public concern and media coverage thus seemed to provoke claims making efforts which, in turn, influenced and reshaped public perceptions and media commentary on the gang issue. Unfortunately, claimsmakers' and media conceptualizations of this issue drew upon and perpetuated a distorted view of gangs—a view proposing that gangs participated exclusively in drug activities and gun shootings. This view intensified preexisting community fears and concerns regarding crime, drugs, and gang members. At the same time, it fostered unrealistic law enforcement strategies that benefited claimsmakers in some ways but failed to address a number of crucial questions, such as how and why gangs emerge, how and why they persist in various contexts, and when and why gang members participate in violence or drugs instead of more legitimate activities.

In concluding, we believe that the present study usefully extends previous research, especially through offering insight into the "symbolic politics" that surround claimsmakers' constructions of issues such as the gang problem. As several analysts have emphasized (Altheide & Snow, 1991; Edelman, 1988; Gamson, 1988; Gamson & Stuart, 1992; Manning, 1996; Robinson & Powell, 1996), we live in an era of "mass mediated political realities" where the skillful orchestration of symbolic messages by claimsmakers and "image managers" is formative in shaping political outcomes (Robinson & Powell, 1996:280). Hence, to understand how and why gangs become constructed as a problem, we need to examine how various claimsmakers interact with and influence the media, manage political symbols and, in so doing, shape public perceptions of gang members and their activities. This chapter has offered an important, beginning example of such an analysis of the gang issue.

6

The Evolution of the Federal Sentencing Guidelines for Crack Cocaine: Social Construction and Social Control

Ronald S. Everett
University of Idaho

DIFFERENTIAL PUNISHMENT

In the early 1980s, the media thrust crack, the reduced form of powder cocaine, into the public consciousness. The "pop, crackle, and glow" of crack, as portrayed in the media, generated widespread social concern in a relatively short period of time. Fear of urban violence and social disorder reportedly produced or exacerbated by crack use reinforced the dominant "get tough on crime" approach to political discourse and policy. Quickly, crack became a highly publicized and politicized campaign in the larger "war on drugs," a campaign characterized by extreme punitiveness. Thus, although penalties for the distribution of other drugs, including powder cocaine, led to harsh, mandatory minimum sentences, only crack cocaine carried a mandatory minimum for mere possession (U.S. Sentencing Commission, 1995).

The nexus of drugs and crimes has long been identified as a social problem in American society. However, the immediacy of this problem—and the public's response to it—has waxed and waned during the past 50 years. The purpose of this chapter is to investigate and review the creation of federal sentencing guidelines for crack cocaine. A social constructionist theoretical framework is used to interpret that process.

THE SOCIAL CONSTRUCTION OF
FEDERAL SENTENCING GUIDELINES

Competing Theoretical Models

The model concerned with objective conditions holds that public and political concern with the problem of drugs and crime merely reflects an accurate perception of empirical reality. Public opinion represents the objective evaluation of information or experience. The media present and reflect that public concern. Politicians and policymakers formulate public policy to address (change, ameliorate, eliminate) social problems. All problems from this progressive era perspective are solvable through scientific knowledge and correct social practice.

The constructionist perspective, rooted in the symbolic interactionist tradition, rejects the taken-for-granted assumptions of the objectionist's view of social problems. Instead, it focuses on the socially constructed nature of reality. It questions how a social issue becomes a "problem"—that is, how it becomes seen as something that is serious, public (rather than private), and correctable. It rejects the simple, linear objectivist model, replacing its focus on an obvious, empirical reality with the subjective meaning created through social activity. Constructionists concern themselves with how social problems are selected, interpreted, presented, and ultimately addressed through social policies.

The public arenas model shares the basic assumptions of the interactionist social construction model of social problems. However, the social construction model stresses the natural history of a particular problem. "Our model stresses the 'arenas' where social problems definitions evolve, examining the effect of those arenas on both the evolution of social problems and the actors who make claims about them" (Hilgartner & Bosk, 1988:55). The public arenas model stresses competition for public attention and the complexity of the process of collective definition.

MEDIA HYSTERIA AND THE DISCOVERY OF CRACK

The history of media coverage of crack cocaine varies in intensity and focus. One historical outline, extending from 1984 to 1992, progresses from the initial reports, to a media blitz, followed by a quiet time, then on to a new hysteria and finally to a steady-state of more balanced coverage (Belenko, 1993:24-28). Another model suggests that media coverage of cocaine, and specifically crack, proceeded in three phases: the initial phase (January 1981 to November 1985), is a "trickle-down" period ". . . in which what was once a decadent 'glamour' drug became increasingly available and abused by middle-class Americans" (Belenko, 1993:18); the crisis phase (December 1985 to November 1986), includes the discovery of crack as a specific element of the drugs and crime problem; and phase three, the aftermath of the crack crisis (November 1986 to December 1988), during which the war on drugs is solidified as a major political issue. Drugs and crime, supercharged by the overwhelming media attention to crack, politicized and moved these issues to the top of the social policy agenda.

Central to understanding the creation of the sentencing guidelines for crack is the role of the media. The specific problem of crack was discovered by the popular media beginning in the early 1980s (Reinarman & Levine, 1989). The social reality of crack was shaped and presented to the general public in a frenzy of media attention (Berger & Luckmann, 1966). In a very brief time frame, the problem of crack was made familiar and frightening, even to those segments of society far removed from the almost exclusive area of use—urban inner-city areas.

In constructing and presenting the problem of crack, the media focused on three general themes: (1) the claim that crack was in some manner more addictive than powder cocaine and caused greater individual and social damage (i.e., stories of crack babies and the exchange of sex for drugs because the desire was so strong); (2) there was a strong link to the violent crime of individual users with the suggested outcome that this would spill over into other neighborhoods and also to that of drug gangs as they vied for control of lucrative distribution areas; and (3) that the cost was low and the supply plentiful, making it easily obtainable even in the poorest neighborhoods.

The most widely recognized interpretation of the extreme public reaction was that crack animated a public fear of random and spreading violence that threatened to engulf previously safe communities (Brownstein, 1991). Less recognized responses to crack were that it represented either the ultimate temptation to the vulnerable or an effective pacification of the alienated. These more subtle themes were left mostly unexamined in the popular media. Recognizing any or all interpretations, crack seemed to represent a significant threat to urban communities already segregated from mainstream society and an unknown menace to the others (Massey & Denton, 1993). Subsequent research investigating these three assumptions has provided limited and often inadequate empirical support.

The notion that crack was more addictive, producing much greater social and psychological damage to individuals, families, and communities was a prominent theme in early media reports (Reinarman & Levine, 1989). Even in the mid-1980s, clear supporting evidence of this relationship was limited. It seems now upon examination that public perceptions and political response were driven by anecdotal and journalistic accounts (Belenko, 1993).

Congressional Action

Built on weak, and in many cases anecdotal evidence, arguments to increase the penalties for crack cocaine were developed in the Crime Control Acts of 1986 and 1988. The initial arguments were based on two primary concerns articulated in the media during the hysteria or crisis phase. First, the level of violence surrounding the distribution of crack was substantially greater than with other drugs, and second, the low cost and easy availability of crack was encouraging expansion of the user group and destroying the social fabric of many urban communities. Beginning at this time, crack was singled out for special public policy attention. Others have noted that the scope of media attention and public response have differed for crack, compared to early drug crisis eras (Reinarman & Levine, 1989; Brownstein, 1991).

1986 Crime Control Act

The Anti-Drug Abuse Act of 1986, contained within the Comprehensive Crime Control Act, established the basic structure of mandatory minimum sentences based on drug type and weight. Two levels of mandatory sentences, five and 10 years, were established. The general rationale for creating mandatory minimum penalties was to clearly delineate punishments that differentiated users from dealers. The five- and 10-year mandatory minimums were established to separate serious dealers from major dealers, respectively. A statement at the time by Senator Byrd clearly articulates the desire of Congress:

> For the kingpins—the masterminds who are really running these operations—and they can be identified by the amount of drugs with which they are involved—we require a jail term upon conviction. If it is their first conviction, the minimum term is 10 years (U.S. Sentencing Commission, 1995:119).

The increased penalties would focus and provide federal law enforcement incentives. Quantities reflecting the differentiation of major and serious dealers were established for all drugs. The amounts were calibrated based on information from federal law enforcement agencies. Compared to all other drugs contained on the schedule, crack cocaine had a very limited historical record on which to construct these categories. Indeed, the distinction between a serious and major trafficker of crack seems driven by moral panic rather than established empirical evidence. As Congress identified what were subsequently criticized as very small quantities to trigger mandatory minimums, Senator Lawton Chiles justified the action, offering the following statements:

> This legislation will . . . decrease the amount for the stiffest penalties to apply. Those who possess 5 or more grams of cocaine freebase will be treated as serious offenders. Those apprehended with 50 or more grams of cocaine freebase will be treated as major offenders. Such treatment is absolutely essential because of the *especially lethal charac-*

teristics of this form of cocaine (132 Cong. Rec. 26, 447, Sept. 26,1986, emphasis added).

[T]he carnage [that] the crack is going to leave in its path is something I don't know if this nation can literally survive (132 Cong. Rec. § 8091, Daily ed. July 15, 1986).

Historically, the more harmful nature of certain drugs has been recognized in sentencing policy. For example, heroin is perceived as a more serious (harmful) drug than marijuana, and, as a consequence, the maximum punishment for possession and/or sale of heroin is greater. However, any difference in punishments, within a single drug type, was determined solely by weight. It would not matter if one chooses to inject or smoke heroin; users' preferences of ingestion were irrelevant to punishment. With the differentiation between crack and powder cocaine, for the first time ever a distinction with dramatic consequences was made between different forms of the same drug. Specifically, five kilograms of powder cocaine and 50 grams of cocaine base (crack) were established as equivalent, each meriting a 10-year mandatory minimum sentence. A five-year mandatory minimum was established for 500 grams of powder cocaine and five grams of crack. This constructed equivalence established the 100:1 ratio between powder and crack cocaine that remains within the structure of the federal sentencing guidelines.

The Anti-Drug Abuse Act of 1986 was not the product of lengthy deliberation and careful evaluation of research evidence. This point is acknowledged in the recent U.S. Sentencing Commission report on crack cocaine and in the popular media. For example, the following statement in a magazine article: "[w]e didn't have hearings on this, which is really extraordinary," says Eric Sterling, then counsel to the House Judiciary Committee. "The bill passed without careful consideration of the issues involved" (*Time*, July 19, 1995:45). In fact, it moved through Congress on the heels of several sensational media stories concerning the horrors of crack cocaine (Gest, 1995). The most prominent of these stories and one close to Congress, both emotionally and geographically, was the death of University of Maryland basketball star Len Bias in June 1986. The Act was initiated and eventually passed without the usual committee hearings, debate and reports (U.S. Sentencing Commission, 1995). As a result, there is no specific or detailed historical record revealing the thinking and justifications to support the 100:1 ratio. There is evidence that during this period of time and in formulating other pieces of legislation, different ratios were proposed that included 20:1 and 50:1 (U.S. Sentencing Commission, 1995:117). The legislative evidence is not clear on why the 100:1 ratio was established. However, inferences can easily be drawn from the general discussions within Congress concerning the perils of crack cocaine. The notion that crack cocaine was significantly more dangerous than powder cocaine was based on five assumptions: crack was more addictive; crack was associated with serious crimes; crack had more negative physiological effects leading to death; crack was appealing to young people; and finally, the cost of crack was low and the purity high, encouraging widespread use.[1] As a new war on drugs was constructed in 1986, crack cocaine was portrayed as the very heart of the spreading evil. Other drugs more familiar to the public and whose mysteries were dispelled during previous "drug wars" could no longer capture media attention and stimulate public fear. Characterizations of "reefer madness" or hallucinating killers on LSD were discredited to a degree that they could no longer serve as the focal concern. A new threat was necessary to gain public support for a war on drugs of unprecedented dimensions (Currie, 1993).

First Congress, and then the U.S. Sentencing Commission, responded to the "plague" of crack cocaine by selecting its users for particularly harsh punishment. The disparity in sentences was initially established by a statute (Narcotics Penalties and Enforcement Act of 1986) creating various mandatory minimums for certain drug types and weights. The sentencing guidelines were subsequently adjusted to be consistent with the statute. Formally, the U.S. Sentencing Commission can make arguments against such statutory overrides of their general mandate to establish sentencing guidelines for all federal crimes. In the extreme case, it is possible that the U.S. Sentencing Commission could fail to adjust the specific guidelines and allow the statute to determine the sentence. This would largely be a symbolic protest because if the guidelines and a statute are in conflict, the statutorily determined sentence must be applied when longer. Formally, the U.S. Sentencing Commission had little choice and could not prevent the implementation of the new penalties for crack. However, there is no evidence to suggest that the U.S. Sentencing Commission mounted any strong objections to the sentencing differential established by Congress. The lack of critical comment or objection suggests at least a tacit acceptance of the statute and surrounding arguments. The media, public, politicians, and the federal agency charged with creating sentencing guidelines were all elements in the social construction of the crack problem.

1988 Anti-Drug Abuse Act

The media, political, and public concern with crack cocaine did not lessen between 1986 and 1988. The hysteria and mounting moral panic resulted in an escalation in the war against crack cocaine. Among other changes, the Act amended 21 U.S.C. 844 to make crack cocaine the only drug with a mandatory minimum penalty for a first offense of simple possession (U.S. Sentencing Commission, 1995:123).

> Section 404(a) of the Controlled Substances Act (21 U.S.C. 844(a)) is amended by inserting after the second sentence the following new sentence: 'Notwithstanding the preceding sentence, a person convicted under this subsection for the possession of a mixture or substance which contains

> cocaine base shall be fined under title 18, United States
> Code, or imprisoned not less than 5 years and not more
> than 20 years, or both, if the conviction is a first conviction
> under this subsection and the amount of the mixture or sub-
> stance exceeds 5 grams. . . . (102 Stat. 4370 P.L. 100-690,
> Nov. 18, 1988, § 6371).

In addition, the five-year mandatory minimum sentence was set at three grams for the second crack possession conviction and at one gram for the third crack possession conviction.

As the war on drugs escalated between 1986 and 1988, the concern with crack became acute. The media discovered and presented new revelations about crack including: increasing violent gang activity and the discovery of crack-exposed infants (i.e., crack babies) (Beckett, 1995a). These images expanded public perceptions of the spreading destruction of crack. Belenko, in summarizing the media coverage of the "New Hysteria" period of 1988-1989 stated:

> First, the coverage associates crack with terrible violence
> that is portrayed as overwhelming our cities. Second, crack
> use is presented as being out of control and extending its
> reach into white middle America. The subtext to such
> rhetoric is that only drastic or dramatic government action
> might stem the tide of crack abuse. Third, crack is present-
> ed as the worst drug plague in history, with America
> quickly succumbing to this 'plague' (Belenko, 1993:27).

The underlying logic of the mandatory minimum sentences had been to create an incentive for law enforcement to focus on dealers and to differentiate serious from major traffickers. The 1988 revisions extended these efforts to users. It seemed, given the increased public concern, that more stringent measures were necessary. The 1986 mandatory minimum penalties, focused primarily on traffickers, had not controlled the crack problem. The new mandatory penalties, focused on users, would perhaps provide adequate general deterrence and stem the spread and destruction of crack. These expanded penalties at least gave the appearance of concern and offered a new strategy aimed at solving the problem. The increased penalties focused on users, along with civil fines and asset forfeiture directed at dealers, and largely symbolic for poor users, were part of the new strategy to create accountability (Belenko, 1993:16; Zimring & Hawkins, 1991).

Some investigators have labeled this time as the aftermath or postcrisis period, but with an enduring siege mentally (Reeves & Campbell, 1994), or the new hysteria (Belenko, 1993). Several factors and critical events came together at this time elevating the war on drugs to new levels. The 1988 presidential election identified new problems, offered additional promises, and renewed media interest—much of which focused on the failures of the war on drugs during the previous two years. These issues, combined with a more violent and threatening crack plague, produced greater public concern and fear. In the late 1980s, the war on drugs, animated by the special threat of crack, was politicized and moved to the top of the social problems/policy agenda. This process created a level of public concern extremely disproportionate to the extent of use. This process occurred in spite of the fact that the use of crack has always been limited and highly concentrated (Lockwood et al., 1995).

OPERATION OF THE SANCTION

Federal Sentencing Guidelines for Cocaine

The sentencing guidelines became law in November 1987, but constitutional challenges prevented full implementation until January of 1987 (U.S. Sentencing Commission, 1991). The five- and 10-year mandatory minimum sentences created in the 1986 Anti-Drug Abuse Act established the basic penalty levels for crack and powder cocaine. Using these as the anchor points, the sentencing guidelines were "expanded proportionately . . . upward and downward, to address trafficking in larger and smaller quantities of crack and powder cocaine. The 100:1 quantity ratio was maintained throughout. . . ." (U.S. Sentencing Commission, 1995:126).

Consequences of 100:1 Ratio: Distribution of Offenses and Offenders

The number of drug cases within the federal system has been steadily increasing since approximately 1987. Unfortunately, the U.S. Sentencing Commission monitoring data did not initially distinguish crack and powder cocaine with all cocaine cases coded into a single category. Not until the 1992-1993 data was it possible to distinguish crack and powder cocaine cases.

Available federal data indicate that for the year 1993, 19.4 percent of the drug trafficking cases were for crack cocaine and 34.5 percent were for powder cocaine. Crack and powder cocaine taken together accounted for more than 50 percent of the drug cases sentenced in federal court during this time period. This distribution more likely reflects the concentration of federal law enforcement resources rather than the prevalence of use ("Crack and Punishment: Is Race the Issue?" New York Times, October 28,1995).

The more interesting and disturbing outcome is the distribution of cases by race/ethnicity. For the same time period, the race of drug trafficking defendants for powder cocaine is almost evenly distributed with 32 percent white, 27 percent black, and 33 percent Hispanic. However, the distribution of cases by race for crack cocaine indicates that 88 percent are black, with only four percent white, and seven percent Hispanic (U.S. Sentencing Commission, 1995). How to account for this disparity became of critical concern to many both inside and outside of the criminal justice system.

VOICES OF CONCERN: JUSTIFIED PUNISHMENT OR INSTITUTIONALIZED RACISM?

Judicial

As information concerning the unintended consequences of the crack guidelines began to emerge in the early 1990s, various legal challenges were presented. Stimulated by the emerging federal sentencing data, arguments of institutional racism and unwarranted sentence disparity appeared in the popular media (*Washington Post,* August 1993; Criminal Justice, 1993; *USA Today,* May, 1993). During this time period numerous states created the same or similar distinction between crack and powder cocaine in their criminal codes (U.S. Sentencing Commission, 1995). At the federal level, various legal challenges to the statute and related crack guidelines have been uniformly unsuccessful. Constitutional challenges argued that the distinction violates due process and the equal protection rights of African-Americans. An Eighth Amendment challenge of cruel and unusual punishment was also put forth and rejected. Subsequent legal challenges focused on the definition of cocaine base, claiming that it was not clearly defined within the federal guidelines and that the differentiation had no rational basis and a discriminatory impact on African-Americans (see Shein, 1993 for a concise summary of the case decisions; also Wytsma, 1995; and U.S. Sentencing Commission, 1995). To this time, all legal challenges to the crack provisions of the federal sentencing guidelines have been rejected.

To some extent, the specific rejection of constitutional challenges helped fuel public dismay and media attention. In many case decisions, it was difficult for organized opposition groups to comprehend the explicit acknowledgment— that although the crack guideline (and other state statutes) had a differential negative impact on African-Americans, it was not unconstitutional. Increasing the tension of this apparent contradiction was the widely publicized Minnesota decision (*Minnesota v. Russell,* 477 N.W. 2d 887 & n. 1 1991). In this case, the Minnesota Supreme Court

> held that the evidence in the case did not establish the existence of a *rational basis* for the statutory sentencing distinction between the quantity of powder cocaine possessed and the quantity of crack cocaine possessed. Therefore, because of its discriminatory effect on blacks and the lack of a rational basis for the disparity in sentencing, the statute violated the equal protection provisions of the Minnesota constitution (Shein, 1993:31, emphasis added).

The Minnesota statute was identical to the current federal guideline. A critical issue in the various legal and constitutional challenges to the distinction between crack cocaine and powder cocaine is the acceptance of a rational basis. At least one critic identified the constructed nature of the rational basis in writing:

> Several judges have upheld the ratio, finding that Congress had a rational basis for imposing more severe penalties for crack than for powder cocaine, and that there was no evidence of a discriminatory purpose in passing the guidelines. Congress, according to these judges, *believed* that crack was more dangerous to society because of its potency, its affordability, its highly addictive nature, and its increasing prevalence (Elden, 1995:250, emphasis added).

The arguments put forth to justify the federal statute and subsequent guidelines for crack cocaine are reified in these various federal court decisions and become the "rational basis" justifying the punishment differential. The early assumptions of increased violence, or that the more intense, immediate high produces greater levels of addiction, were now explicitly accepted as part of the rational basis for the continuation of the sentencing differential. The putative rational basis, like the earlier supporting arguments, was accepted without substantial empirical evidence to support the claims.

The claims-making power of the political and policy elite is starkly evident in these developments. This particular case seems to turn on its head the ideal rational policy-making process. Initial claims that were put forth and uncritically accepted defined the social reality of crack cocaine. Rather than requiring a new policy to demonstrate the ability to accomplish stated goals or to offer convincing evidence supporting assumptions, it becomes necessary for critics to disprove asserted claims that have been institutionalized in the law.

Media

Negative reports pertaining to the war on drugs increased beginning in the early 1990s. Many of these focused on the social and economic costs to urban minority communities (Mauer, 1990; Tonry, 1995). The dramatic increase in the rate of incarceration, both its cost and connection to the war on drugs were also explored (Currie, 1993; Irwin & Austin, 1994). In this context the specific consequences of the federal sentencing guidelines for crack, particularly the 100:1 ratio, suddenly received substantial media attention. A front page story in *U.S.A. Today* captured public attention with the headline, "Sentences for Crack called Racist" (Cauchon, 1993). A previous but less visible news article in the *L.A. Daily Journal* (Sept. 16, 1992:4) had suggested this possible unintended outcome. A series of editorials in *The Washington Post* ("Same Drugs, Different Penalties," 1993; "Two Penny-Weights of Crack," 1994)[2] decried the unfairness of the distinction and called for the U.S. Sentencing Commission and then Congress to correct the injustice. The editorial attack was blunt, implying both unwarranted disparity and selective prosecution. For example:

> [t]his sentence disparity, mandated by Congress in 1988, is even more egregious than it appears. Crack is the preferred form of the drug in the black communities, while powder is more widely used by whites. Three times as many Americans use cocaine in its powder form as use crack, which is smoked, but there are far more prosecutions for the latter (*Washington Post,* August 4, 1993).

Societal

Through these reports and other media coverage, information concerning the unintended consequences of the crack cocaine sentencing guideline slowly filtered out to the general public. Obviously, those individuals and families affected directly were well aware of the disparity in punishment. However, as is now recognized, the weight of the sanction falls on poor, urban minorities, a group that does not instantly elicit widespread public concern in the current political context. In response to the increasing evidence of racial disparity and media attention, various groups were formed to address the perceived unfairness of the punishment for crack cocaine. Initially, these groups formed within the affected communities (e.g., Families Against Mandatory Minimums), but soon spread and gained public visibility (e.g., Jesse Jackson and The Rainbow Coalition).

Media attention, implications of racism, and limited research evidence to justify the sentence disparity began to alter the ideas about crack as a social problem. Specifically, both the definition of seriousness and the consequent policies of the criminal justice system were challenged. Congress was sensitive and responded to this public criticism, but was unable to reconstruct clear evidence to support the assumptions underlying the mandatory minimums for crack cocaine. Consequently the 100:1 ratio held.

POLICY RE-EVALUATION

U.S. Sentencing Commission Review

> The U.S. Sentencing Commission ('Commission') is an independent agency in the judicial branch. . . . Its principal purpose is to establish sentencing policies and practices for the federal criminal justice system. . . . The Commission has the authority to submit amendments each year to Congress between the beginning of a regular congressional session and May 1. Such amendments automatically take

> effect 180 days after submission unless a law is enacted to
> the contrary (U.S. Sentencing Commission, 1991:1).

Acknowledging that political interests may intrude on criminal justice policies, particularly in the controversial area of sentencing and punishment, the U.S. Sentencing Commission was created to provide a substantial degree of independence. Specifically, the U.S. Sentencing Commission was structured as an independent agency to allow state actors a high degree of autonomy in the formation of sentencing policy (Lofquist, 1993).

On December 31, 1992, the U.S. Sentencing Commission opened the door for comment on whether it should recommend to Congress that the sentencing distinction between crack cocaine and powder cocaine should be changed or eliminated (U.S. Sentencing Commission, 1995:207). The majority of organizations, criminal justice professional associations, and general citizen comments (approximately 2,000 letters) were strongly in favor of substantial changes to the current cocaine sentencing structure. For example:

> [f]amilies Against Mandatory Minimums wrote that the
> ratio was 'racially discriminatory,' and urged a one-to-one
> ratio for powder and crack cocaine penalties to be imple-
> mented retroactively. And the National Association of Crim-
> inal Defense Lawyers characterized the current ratio between
> powder cocaine and crack cocaine penalties as 'grossly
> unfair, illogical, and racially biased' (U.S. Sentencing Com-
> mission, 1995:210).

Congressional Directive

To preserve their overall "get-tough on crime posture," Congress reacted cautiously but with a public appearance of concern about the possible racial bias in the operation of the sentencing structure for cocaine. In 1994, as part of the Omnibus Violent Crime Control and Law Enforcement Act (Public Law 103-322-Sept. 13, 1994), Congress directed the U.S. Sentencing Commission to study the current sentencing policy pertaining to cocaine. Their cautious, almost deferential tone, is evident in regard to these three general issues in the following statement:

> The absence of firm answers does not mean that the per-
> ceptions are necessarily wrong. However, gaps in the data
> make it difficult to draw precise conclusions about the mer-
> its of existing congressional distinctions in cocaine sentenc-
> ing policy. Further, to the extent that Congress has created
> a sentencing system that so disparately and substantially
> punishes crack cocaine over other forms of the same drug,

> the absence of comprehensive data substantiating the leg-
> islative policy is troublesome (U.S. Sentencing Commission,
> 1995:180).

In one area, the accumulated evidence does appear to support the observa-
tion that the marketing and distribution of crack cocaine is surrounded by higher levels of systemic violence (Inciardi & Pottieger, 1991). However, this is not
the drug-induced violence or economic criminality of individuals that was most
often presented by the media and feared by society. Indeed, many analysts have
attributed the increased systemic violence to the newness of the crack cocaine
market with the associated expansion of distribution networks. This general
expansion produced increased violence as groups vied for control of specific
market areas (Goldstein et al., 1989). As noted by several commentators, a similar phenomenon occurred in Miami during the early 1980s as groups fought
for control of the distribution of powder cocaine (Inciardi, 1990).

The final summary in the U.S. Sentencing Commission report is judicious
and recognizes the special circumstances of crack cocaine, including the perceived greater harmfulness, but refuses to endorse a specific penalty differential.

In the end, to avoid the task of specifying an acceptable quantity ratio, the
U.S. Sentencing Commission recommended revisions to the guidelines system to
address the particular offender and offense characteristics associated with crack
cocaine. The special report to Congress: *Cocaine and Federal Sentencing Policy*,
made this broad recommendation, concerning the troublesome quantity ratio:

> . . . until the possibility has been thoroughly explored of
> using specific guideline enhancements to account for the
> more significant societal harms associated with crack, the
> Sentencing Commission cannot state definitively that some
> base differential is warranted and whether that differential
> should be guideline-based or statutory (U.S. Sentencing
> Commission and Cocaine Sentencing Policy, 1995:xvi).

Congressional Action

In the amendment cycle (May 1995) following submission of the special
report in a four to three vote, the U.S. Sentencing Commission provided its
final recommendation to Congress. Based firmly on the logic developed in the
earlier report and review of current research, a recommendation was presented
to equalize the penalties for the distribution of crack and powder cocaine and
treat possession of either in the same manner. At first blush this may appear to
be a bold action, but in fact it would have firmly maintained the potential for
offenders convicted of crack offenses to be punished more harshly than similar
offenders convicted of powder cocaine offenses. Although the base penalty
would be equalized under this proposal, specific offender and offense guideline
adjustments could substantially increase the sentence length for crack cocaine

offenses. The notion that equalizing the quantity ratio for crack and powder cocaine would, in fact, equalize the punishment severity, was more appearance than practical reality.

Congress Rejects the U.S. Sentencing Commission Guideline Revision

The degree of trouble and specific issues of concern emerged during the Senate Judiciary Committee hearing on "Examining U.S. Sentencing Commission Recommendations for Cocaine Sentencing," held on August 10, 1995.

Five concerns, some vague and others specific and practical, are discernible in these discussions. First, equalization of penalties would send the wrong message to society (Hearing Before the Committee on the Judiciary, United States Senate, 1995:9, 52, 55); second, it would reduce the general deterrence of the existing harsh punishment and possibly encourage more people to use and sell crack cocaine (Hearing Before the Committee on the Judiciary, United States Senate, 1995:9, 43); third, retroactive application may create inmate litigation (Hearing Before the Committee on the Judiciary, United States Senate, 1995:7); fourth, the necessity of a statutory change in the mandatory minimum penalties that must occur prior to or simultaneous with any guideline changes; and fifth, the changes would make it more difficult to prosecute cases because they must prove each of the individual sentence adjustments (Hearing Before the Committee on the Judiciary, United States Senate, 1995:8). Throughout the hearings, these and other general concerns were put forth without any supporting evidence. Few of the comments attempted to address the specific details of the U.S. Sentencing Commission guidelines amendment. In several instances, the statements sounded more like ideological pronouncements reflecting concern for the symbolic value of sentencing policy. The practical and real consequences, however unintended of the crack and powder cocaine disparity, are easily dismissed, while the symbolic message is privileged and preserved (Gordon, 1994). For example, specific evidence of unintended consequences (minorities in prison), selective prosecution (movement from state to federal court), and public attitudes (perception of unfair punishment) were offered during testimony and commentary. Each of these issues was dismissed or unacknowledged when offered and the focus of concern immediately shifted to the symbolic message of the sentencing policy.

Negative Reaction

Public attention, interest and concern over the perils of crack cocaine had begun to decline in 1991 (Belenko, 1993). Federal prosecutions of crack cocaine in many urban areas had stabilized, or, in some instances, declined (U.S. Sentencing Commission, 1995). It seemed that by many indicators the crack plague was on the wane. In this context, Congress, during the fall 1995, finalized legislation rejecting the USSC recommendation to equalize the quantity ratio for crack and powder cocaine. In rejecting the amendment to the cocaine guideline the legislation stated:

> [w]hile the evidence clearly indicates that there are signifi-
> cant distinctions between crack and powder cocaine that
> warrant maintaining longer sentences for crack-related
> offenses, it should be noted that the current 100-to-1 quan-
> tity ratio may not be the appropriate ratio. The goal must
> ultimately be to ensure that the uniquely harmful nature of
> crack is reflected in sentencing policy and, at the same
> time, uphold basic principles of equity in the U.S. Code
> (104-272, Sept. 29, 1995:4).

Addressing the issue of racial disparity, the report concludes that "[T]here is no evidence that Congress or the Sentencing Commission acted with any dis-criminatory intent in setting different statutory guideline penalties for different forms of cocaine" (104-272, Sept. 29, 1995:3). This conclusion is perhaps will-fully naive and surely begs the fundamental question, to which evidence was offered, of how the guideline is applied and not the issue of to whom it applies. In policy terms, this represents a problem of implementation and not one of intent. The assumptions employed to justify the quantity differential are not required to have unambiguous empirical support. Indeed, the untested assump-tions subsequently form the "rational basis" of the policy and are used to refute charges of racist intent. This logic seems to prevent reform based on evaluation of policy implementation. In this circumstance, it appears that accumulated evi-dence of consequences is ignored in favor of specious denials of intent.

> Republicans said that the tougher sentence for crack has
> nothing to do with race. Sponsor Dill McCollun, R-Fla.,
> said any bias in the system is caused not by the guidelines,
> but by people who are not enforcing them properly (*Con-
> gressional Quarterly*, October 21, 1995:3212).

SOCIAL CONSTRUCTION AND SOCIAL CONTROL: THE ROLE OF FEAR AND IDEOLOGY

How is the congressional rejection of the U.S. Sentencing Commission rec-ommendation explained? Was this an unexpected outcome? Did this event sug-gest a different model for policy creation and subsequent public policy revision?

The rejection of the U.S. Sentencing Commission amendment to the sen-tencing guidelines for cocaine raises many important questions concerning the-oretical models of social problems creation, the politics of social policy formulation, and the relationship between the two processes.

The early stages of the crack phenomenon, particularly the discovery and crisis phases, have been analyzed and are well explained from the social constructionist perspective (Reinarman & Levine, 1989). The increasing importance of the media is dramatically evident in creating, shaping, and expanding the dimensions of the crack plague (Reeves & Campbell, 1994). Certainly, public understanding, knowledge, and fear seems driven primarily by the dominant media images. The elaborated public arenas version of the social constructionist perspective explains the increased role of the media in the creation of social problems.

How are policymakers and policy formation influenced by the changed environment of social problems creation? Policymakers appear to both influence and be influenced by the media portrayals of specific social problems (Scheingold, 1991). The dominance of political elites to frame or define social problems and justify social policies appears diminished. In addition, the nature of this relationship is clearly influenced by individual (e.g., ideology) and structural (e.g., economic conditions) factors. In some cases, political elites define social problems, and the media reflect this construction. In other cases, the media may present a social issue as a developing problem stimulating political interest. In such cases the media may dominate. In many, if not most cases, a reciprocal process seems to best characterize social problems creation and policy formation. Objective qualities of social problems are secondary to ideology and political concerns. The dominance of ideology in the formation of criminal justice policy is clearly revealed in the debate over the punishment for crack and powder cocaine. Sending the appropriate message is considered more important than the actual consequences of criminal justice policy. Rigid adherence to ideology and the fear of seeming soft on crime now dominate political discourse and direct criminal justice policy formation.

NOTES

[1]   132 Cong. Rec. § 8092 (June 6, 1986). 132 Cong. Rec. § 14, 293 (Sept. 30, 1986). See specifically the statements of Senator D'Amato and Senator Bumpers. As cited in U.S. Sentencing Commission, 1995:118.

[2]   A general overview of media attention and useful summaries of newspaper and magazine stories are available in Belenko, 1993; Reeves and Campbell, 1994.

7

Crack Babies, Moral Panic, and the Criminalization of Behavior During Pregnancy

Inger J. Sagatun-Edwards
San Jose State University

Illegal drug use by pregnant women and mothers of young children has become a focal point in the media coverage of the war on drugs and a key issue in raising the moral panic over substance abuse. With the emergence of heavy cocaine abuse in the 1980s, and especially the use of crack cocaine, thousands of articles on the effects of crack use by pregnant mothers on their offspring appeared in the popular media during the last decade. A dramatic description of the crack-baby crisis included the following passage: ". . . babies born months too soon; babies weighing little more than a hardcover book; babies that look like wizened old men in the last stages of terminal illness; babies who do not cry because their mouths are full of tubes . . . The reason is crack" (Quindlen, 1990). Early medical studies did indeed conclude that crack cocaine had very negative effects on the fetus (Chasnoff et al., 1989), findings that soon were picked up and exaggerated by the media. As summarized by Goode (1994) in his analysis of the social construction of drug babies as a major social problem, the common wisdom that sprang up in the late 1980s and early 1990s was that crack cocaine addiction among pregnant mothers causes serious, often irreparable, medical problems in their babies; this condition is extremely widespread and extremely costly to our society. Early hospital studies, for example, estimated that about 375,000 drug-exposed infants are born each year, at least one of every 10 births in the United States (Dixon, 1989), and a federal study in 1991 found that the number of young foster children who had had prenatal exposure to drugs grew from 17 percent in 1986 to 55 percent in 1991 (United States General Accounting Office, April, 1994). Most states also reported dramatic increases in the numbers of children victimized by parental drug involvement (Daro & McCurdy, 1992). However, later critics of these numbers have noted that the early hospital estimates were based on a survey of 36 hospitals, accounting for only five percent of all United States births in 1989 (Farr, 1995), that the women surveyed had used a number of different drugs, and that the incidence of fetal exposure in different hospitals varied substantially (Gustafson, 1991).

Based on the numbers described above and the resultant alarm in the media, the response to prenatal drug-use, especially the use of crack cocaine, has in turn been largely punitive. This was driven both by the construction of drug use by mothers as an immoral and negligent choice and an emerging "fetal rights" movement (Beckett, 1995a). According to Beckett, the construction in the current war on drugs of drug use as a criminal choice rather than a public health or socio-economic problem has had particular consequences for pregnant women. Women who use crack cocaine have been portrayed as selfish, negligent, and criminal. Class and racial biases in the war on drugs have insured that poor African-American and Latino women have been particularly singled out for testing (Chasnoff, Landress & Barrett, 1990) and for prosecutions (Paltrow, 1993; Roberts, 1991). Similarly, the "fetal rights" movement that seeks to define the fetus as a person grew out of the attempt to hold women liable for prenatal conduct that may cause harm to the fetus (Beckett, 1995a; Roberts, 1991). Within this movement, drug babies are seen as separate entities from their mothers and in need of protection from their substance abusing parent.

In the last decade, a heated legal and social policy debate has developed over the issue of "crack babies" and how to respond to pregnant substance abusers. This chapter will provide an overview of the types of legal responses to the moral panic raised in the media, as well as discuss newer medical evidence on the effects of prenatal substance abuse and the constitutional rights of those affected.

THE LEGAL RESPONSE TO THE "CRACK BABY EPIDEMIC"

Criminalization of Drug Use During Pregnancy

Proponents of criminalization argue that there are three compelling interests that should be met: (1) the state's interest in protecting the fetus' right to potential life, (2) the state's interest in protecting the newborn's right to be born healthy, and (3) the state's interest in protecting maternal health. This latter interest is rooted in the nexus of concerns linked to the war on drugs. From this perspective, there is also a fourth compelling state interest in the criminalization of fetal injury by pregnant drug users; (4) the state's interest in protecting society from the burden of providing for injured newborns (Wright, 1990).

Based on these arguments and the public perception of "crack babies" as a major criminal problem, at least 167 women in 24 states have been prosecuted for taking illicit drugs while pregnant (Beckett, 1995a). These prosecutions have typically involved creative applications of existing statutes such as (1) delivery of a controlled substance to a minor, or (2) some form of child endangerment or abuse. Most prosecutions under both types of existing law have ultimately been unsuccessful. The courts have concluded that these laws were not meant to apply to the situation of drug use during pregnancy, and all but one of the successfully prosecuted cases at the trial level have been thrown out by either the appellate or superior court of the relevant state. Many of these attempts to prosecute women criminally for illicit drug use during pregnancy have foundered on the question of nonrecognition of fetal personhood by the law (Chavkin, 1991). Traditionally, the nonrecognition of a fetus as a legal entity is embodied in the "born alive" rule, that states that the fetus has to be born alive as a precondition to legal personhood. Underlying this rule is the presumption that the mother and the fetus constitute a unit whose legal interests are coextensive (McNulty, 1987-1988).

Prosecution under Controlled Substance Statutes

As stated above, many criminal prosecutions have been based on existing criminal laws that were never designed or intended to govern prenatal conduct. These include statutes that prohibit drug use, sale, possession, or delivery of drugs to minors, and apply to all adults—males and females. *Johnson v. Florida* (1992) was the first case of this kind that was successfully prosecuted at the trial level, using a "delivery of drugs to a minor" statute to apply to drugs being transferred through the umbilical cord at birth. The mother appealed and the appellate court affirmed her convictions. The Florida Supreme Court, however, reversed the convictions on a variety of grounds, including legislative intent. The court held that the legislature did not intend the word "deliver" to include the passage of blood through the umbilical cord. The Florida Supreme Court adopted the language of the justice who dissented in the lower appellate court decision when she wrote that:

> . . . The Legislature never intended for the general drug
> delivery statute to authorize prosecution of those mothers
> who take illegal drugs close enough in time to childbirth
> that a doctor could testify that a tiny amount passed from
> mother to child in the few seconds before the umbilical

> cord was cut. Criminal prosecution of mothers like Johnson
> will undermine Florida's express policy of 'keeping families
> intact' and could destroy the family by incarcerating the
> child's mother when alternate measures could protect the
> child and stabilize the family.

Although the Florida Supreme Court reversed the trial court conviction, this decision also illustrates that courts were not immune to the perception of "crack babies" as a major societal problem. The Florida Supreme Court noted that drug abuse is a serious national problem and that there is a particular concern about the rising numbers of babies born with cocaine in their systems as a result of maternal substance abuse. But the court pointed out the negative aspects of prosecuting pregnant substance abusers, stating that women who are substance abusers may simply avoid prenatal care for fear of being detected when the newborns of these women are, as a group, the most fragile and sick and most in need of hospital neonatal care.

Decisions from higher courts since the Florida Supreme Court reversal in *Johnson* have followed the same path (i.e., the courts have consistently refused to apply drug delivery statutes to pregnant women).

Prosecution under Child Abuse and Neglect (Child Endangerment Statutes)

Prosecutions based on criminal child abuse statutes have also had infrequent success. Courts have repeatedly held that a fetus is not a "child" within the meaning of statutes prohibiting acts endangering the welfare of children. An example of such a decision is a case from the Supreme Court of Kentucky, *Commonwealth of Kentucky v. Connie Welch* (1993), where the high court reversed the trial court that had found Welch guilty of a criminal child abuse count. The court of appeals affirmed her convictions for possession of a controlled substance, but vacated her conviction on the criminal abuse charge. The Supreme Court affirmed the decision of the court of appeals by noting that

> . . . the mother was a drug addict. But, for that matter, she
> could have been a pregnant alcoholic, causing fetal alcohol
> syndrome; or she could have been addicted to self-abuse by
> smoking, or by abusing prescription painkillers, or over the
> counter medicine; or for that matter she could have been
> addicted to downhill skiing or some other sport creating
> serious risk of prenatal injury, risk which the mother wantonly disregarded as a matter of self-indulgence. What if a
> pregnant woman drives over the speed-limit, or as a matter
> of vanity doesn't wear prescription lenses she knows she

needs to see the dangers of the road? The defense asks where do we draw the line on self abuse by a pregnant woman that wantonly exposes to risk her unborn baby?

. . . it is inflicting intentional or wanton injury upon the child that makes the conduct criminal under the child abuse statutes, not the criminality of the conduct per se. . . . In short, the District Attorney's interpretation of the statutes, if validated, might lead to a 'slippery slope' whereby the law could be construed as covering the full range of a pregnant woman's behavior—a plainly unconstitutional result that would, among other things, render the statutes void for vagueness.

The Supreme Court of Kentucky concluded that their state drug delivery statutes and child endangerment statutes did not intend to punish as criminal conduct self-abuse by an expectant mother that is potentially injurious to the baby she carries. However, this decision also neglected all the other social conditions that might have contributed to the health problems of a "crack baby" in referring to "self abuse by a pregnant woman that [who] wantonly exposes to risk her unborn baby."

In a departure from the above conclusions, a recent case from the Supreme Court of South Carolina, *Whitner v. State of South Carolina* (1996), upheld the prosecution of a woman who ingested crack cocaine during the third trimester of her pregnancy under child abuse and endangerment statutes by concluding that a fetus does have legal rights on its own. The Court noted that South Carolina law has long recognized that viable fetuses are persons holding certain rights and privileges for purposes of homicide laws and wrongful death statutes, and that it would be absurd to not recognize a viable fetus as a person for the purposes of statutes proscribing child abuse. The Court argued that "the consequences of abuse or neglect which take place after birth often pale in comparison to those resulting from abuse suffered by the viable fetus before birth," relying on the harms reported by early articles in the *New England Journal of Medicine* (e.g., Chasnoff et al., 1985; Volpe, 1992). The perception that the defendant endangered the "life, health and comfort of her child" through ingesting crack cocaine led the court to upheld the prosecution under the criminal child neglect statute. In contrast, the dissent argued that a "fetus" is not a person, and that the distinction of a "viable fetus" is absurd in that it would then be legal for a woman to ingest cocaine early on in the pregnancy when presumably the fetus is most at risk for harmful substances.

Attempts to Criminalize Failure to Seek Treatment

Some proponents of criminalization have argued that prosecutions will help women seek much needed medical treatment. An example of this approach was the Interagency Drug Policy Project at the Medical University of South Carolina, that was in effect from 1989 to 1994 and was designed to protect the babies of mothers who used controlled substances during their pregnancy. Under this policy, pregnant drug users were required to enter treatment programs, and patients who refused to cooperate were treated as criminals, subject to arrest and jail. A first offense resulted in an arrest warrant. The second offense resulted in immediate police custody. If the child was born testing positive for drugs, the patient was arrested immediately and the child removed by the Child Protective Services. These pregnant women who were mostly poor and African-American were subject to arrest simply for failure to attend either drug therapy appointments or prenatal appointments.

During the time that the policy was in place, a total of 42 women were arrested. The policy was discontinued in 1994, after the university responded to pressure from the Civil Rights Division of the Department of Health and Human Services, and the Federal Office of Protection from Research Risks deferred renewal of government funding (Jos, Marshall & Perlmutter, 1995). There was also no evidence that this policy had saved any babies or improved the health care of the mothers. The South Carolina experiment is an example of how a rigid, simplistic policy failed to correct a complex social problem (Pearson & Thoennes, 1996).

New Legislation to Criminalize Use of Drugs During Pregnancy

Even though prosecutions both under delivery to minor statutes and criminal child abuse statutes, as well as attempts to compel women into treatment programs, have mostly failed at the court of appeals and state supreme levels, some prosecutors favor bringing actions against pregnant drug users to encourage legislatures to address the issue in specific legislation. Because prosecutions under existing criminal statutes have not been successful, many states have considered new legislation, and several states have proposed statutes designed to protect the unborn child from prenatal harm. Proposed bills in some states would make it a felony to give birth to a drug addicted child (e.g., Georgia, Louisiana, Ohio, Colorado). Several members of Congress have supported such legislation. However, in spite of the moral panic created by the sensationalized media reports on "crack babies," neither the Senate bill nor any of the state bills have yet been enacted (as of this date). This may be because there are serious social policy concerns and constitutional difficulties with such bills, and because many medical and legal scholars have strongly criticized the use of any criminal sanction to address the problem of prenatal drug use. Indeed, several important medical, legal, and civil rights groups have voiced their opposition to policies aimed at the criminalization of pregnant drug users.[1]

JUVENILE COURT (CIVIL COURT) INVOLVEMENT

Although criminal prosecutions of pregnant drug users have been largely unsuccessful, thousands of women have had their children removed from their custody as a result of prenatal use of drugs (Paltrow, 1993). While the stated purpose of the criminal court is to punish the offender, the stated purpose of the juvenile court is the protection of the child. Until recently, juvenile law and the jurisdiction of juvenile court did not extend to unborn children. In *In re S. Stevens* (1981), the court of appeals in California overturned a juvenile court decision, finding that an unborn fetus was not a person within the meaning of the child-abuse or neglect statutes. However, in Michigan (*In re Baby X,* 1980), an appellate court reasoned that since prior treatment of one child can support neglect allegations regarding another child, prenatal treatment can be considered probative of child neglect. In *In re D. Troy* (1989), the California Supreme Court let stand an earlier appellate decision that the use of drugs during pregnancy is a sufficient basis to trigger a child abuse report and to support juvenile court dependency jurisdiction. This decision was later negated by the passage of the Perinatal Substance Abuse Services Act in California that does not endorse the view that prenatal substance abuse is, by itself, indicative of future child abuse and neglect (see description later in this chapter). However, several other states have passed civil child abuse and neglect statutes that declare drug and/or alcohol use during pregnancy to be predictive of child abuse (Paltrow, 1992). Issues of concern for juvenile court or family court jurisdiction are the criteria for testing, whether positive tests should be included under mandatory reporting laws for child abuse and neglect, and the criteria used to remove a child from the mother.

Testing

The first point of entry of drug exposed infants and their families into the juvenile court system is often right after birth. Many hospitals now perform neonatal toxicology screens when maternal drug use is suspected. Typically, hospital protocols dictate that such screens are performed when the newborn shows signs of drug withdrawal, when the mother admits to drug use during pregnancy, or when the mother has had no prenatal care (Robin-Vergeer, 1990). Based on a positive toxicology test, the hospital may report the case to the Child Protective Services, which in turn may ask the court to prevent the child's release to the parents while an investigation takes place. If further investigation reveals a risk to the child, the court may assume temporary custody of the child, and in the most serious cases, parental rights may be terminated (Sagatun-Edwards, Saylor & Shifflett, 1995).

There are several problems with testing mothers and children for the presence of illegal drugs. First, there is the invasion of privacy problem. Second, such testing is notoriously unreliable, and the results may depend on what type of drug was ingested and how soon after the ingestion the drug test was administered (Gomby & Shiono, 1991). Thirdly, there may be both racial and social class biases in both the testing procedures and the reports of the testing. A study by Chasnoff et al. (1990) found that African-American women were almost 10 times as likely to be reported to county health authorities for alcohol and drug use during pregnancy as Caucasian women. This occurred in spite of the fact that urine samples of the pregnant women collected at their first prenatal visit revealed no significant differences between black and white patients and between low-income and upper-income women.

As of this date, no states require mandatory testing for drugs of all pregnant women. Minnesota is one state that has chosen to universally screen neonates, while limiting maternal testing to women with pregnancy complications that suggest drug use (Sagatun-Edwards, Saylor & Shifflett, 1995). Most states condition testing on a physician's suspicion of prenatal drug use, based on obstetric complications or assessment of mother and baby. Such discretionary testing is, however, most often conducted in public hospitals on poor and minority mothers. If routine testing is to be conducted at all, it should be universal testing of all newborns, thus negating the criticism of bias against minorities and the poor. However, compelling arguments against universal screening include cost, lack of informed consent, lack of reliability, and overemphasizing illegal drugs over equally dangerous drugs, such as alcohol. Most importantly, the threat of screening may influence a woman's decision to seek prenatal care.

Mandatory Reporting Under Child Abuse and Neglect Reporting Laws

Since 1974, most states have instituted mandatory reporting laws that require health-care professionals, teachers, day-care providers, Child Protective Services agencies, and other professionals dealing with children to report any reasonable suspicion of child maltreatment to the authorities. Failure to do so is typically a criminal offense at the misdemeanor level. These statutes traditionally had not included the concept of "fetal abuse," but many states have in recent years passed legislation to include "fetal abuse" under mandatory or discretionary reporting laws. Minnesota's legislation appears to be the most far-reaching. Its definition of child abuse has been amended to include prenatal exposure to drugs (Minnesota Statutes Annotated, 1990; MN Stat. 626.5561). If the results on a toxicology screen of either mother or child are positive, the physicians are required to report the results to the Department of Health, and local welfare agencies are then mandated to investigate and make any appropriate referrals (MN Stat. 626.5561). If a woman is still pregnant and refuses to cooperate, civil commitment is authorized under Minnesota Statute 253B.05. However, a recent study of the actual implementation of the Minnesota law concluded that Minnesota, in effect, has eschewed the punitive provisions embodied in the law (Pearson & Thoennes, 1996).

Other states such as Florida, Massachusetts, Oklahoma, Utah, and Illinois have also included fetal abuse under their mandatory child-abuse reporting laws (Sagatun, 1993). Florida responded to the crack/cocaine hysteria of the late 1980s by amending its child abuse laws to underscore the specific risks associated with maternal drug use. Simultaneously, the Department of Health and Rehabilitative Services issued a policy requiring reports of newborn drug dependency and created a specialized unit to investigate drug-affected infants. While these laws and policies established Florida's reputation as being tough on maternal substance abuse, many Child Protective Services workers and legal personnel in the Pearson and Thoennes study (1996) characterized Florida as being a lenient climate due to gaps in the law, treatment voids, and court backlogs. Child Protective Services workers reported that most drug-affected infants were released to their mothers with a voluntary treatment contract and with no penalty for failure to comply. Lack of resources for case supervision, court oversight, and treatment also contributed to limited interventions. However, Child Protective Services workers also reported that due to the discretionary testing law in Florida, testing occurs only in publicly-funded health-care facilities among poor and nonwhite populations, thus mirroring the earlier race and social class bias reported by Chasnoff et al. (1990).

Illinois amended its child abuse reporting laws in 1989 so that any child born with any illegal drug in his or her system would be defined as a "neglected child." This eliminated the need to prove any harmful effects of maternal cocaine use and created the legal basis for filing a neglect petition. However, the Pearson and Thoennes study (1996) reports that these statutory changes did not revolutionize case handling. Administrators said that while reports of positive toxicology were routinely indicated by the Child Protective Services agency, such reports were often perceived to be racist and not acted upon unless there was other evidence of parental insufficiency. Most cases reported to Child Protective Services were not opened for services, and mothers were urged to explore drug treatment sources on their own. When placement was made, it tended to be with relatives. Finally, there was a perceived lack of treatment resources and an underuse of existing ones. Similar relative placements were made in the large majority of cases in a large urban county in California, often with the mother residing in the same house (Sagatun-Edwards, 1996).

In California, the Perinatal Substance Abuse Services Act of 1990 emphasizes the desirability of medical services and drug treatment, and it does *not*
endorse mandatory reporting of positive toxicology screens. This law modified
the existing child abuse reporting laws in California to specify that a positive
toxicology screen at the time of delivery of an infant is not in and of itself a
sufficient basis for reporting child abuse or neglect. Instead, any indication of
maternal substance abuse shall lead to an assessment of the needs of the mother and her infant. Any indication of risk to the child, as determined by the
assessment, shall then be reported to county welfare departments (Perinatal
Substance Abuse Services Act of 1990, 1991; California Senate Bill, 2669).

The state of Washington treats perinatal substance abuse as a public health
issue. The state has eschewed legislation requiring routine testing of babies,
relying instead on hospitals to flag, test, and report cases to Child Protective
Services where the risk of child abuse is high. As a result of the Omnibus
Drug Act of 1989, Washington made pregnant women a priority for treatment
of chemical dependency (Pearson & Thoennes, 1996). Drug-exposed infants
are referred primarily when other children and the family have already been
referred to Child Protective Services for other reasons.

Legal Criteria for Removing a Child from the Parents

In determining what to do with a child, social services and juvenile courts
in all states must follow the directives of Public Law 96-272 or the Adoption
Assistance and Child Welfare Act of 1980 which requires states to exercise
reasonable efforts to avoid out-of-home placement (Adoption Assistance and
Child Welfare Act, 1980). Under this law, it is assumed that children develop
best in their own families and that most families are worth preserving. State
welfare agencies are mandated to make reasonable efforts to prevent a child's
placement in foster care; and if foster care is necessary, the state must make
efforts to reunite the family during specified time periods. If such reunification
is not possible, the law further requires permanency planning for the child,
which may include termination of parental rights to make adoption possible.
The juvenile courts are required to determine whether the agency has made
these efforts (McCullough, 1991). In addition to the federal law, many states
have passed their own reasonable efforts and family reunification requirements. This reasonable-efforts requirement has great significance for drug-
exposed infant cases. It means that the state must provide reunification
services for a period up to at least 12 months (unless the risk to the child is
determined to be so great that reunification is not viable, or if the parents vol-
untarily relinquish the child) in order to try to reunite the child with the parent. In a longitudinal study of cases where the child is now five to six years
old, it was not uncommon for such reunification to be attempted more than
once (Sagatun-Edwards, 1996).

In spite of the mandated reunification policy, however, drug-exposed cases tend to show a higher risk of removal (Leslie, 1993), court involvement (Sagatun-Edwards, Saylor & Shifflett, 1995), and foster care placement (Feig, 1990). Taylor (1995) found that it was much more common for a drug-abusing parent to lose the right to visitation and custody than for non-abusing parents. The assumption that drug use during pregnancy causes "imminent" danger to the fetus reinforces the perception of pregnant women's drug use as child abuse and neglect (Pollit, 1990). According to Beckett (1995a), the majority of the lower and appellate civil court rulings have supported the state's removal of infants from their mother's custody based on a positive drug toxicology.

MEDICAL TREATMENT:
VOLUNTARY OR COMPULSORY?

Very few adequate drug rehabilitation services are available for pregnant substance abusers or for mothers with young children; and the ones that are available may not serve their particular needs. Opponents and proponents of criminalization and/or juvenile court involvement alike agree that the most effective solution to the problem of prenatal drug abuse is drug treatment and rehabilitation. The major problem here is that appropriate drug treatment programs are often unavailable or unaffordable, and when they are available there are long waiting lists.

Existing treatment programs often discriminate against pregnant women. In a survey of 78 drug treatment programs in New York City, Chavkin (1991) found that 54 percent refused to treat pregnant women; of those that treated pregnant women, 67 percent refused to treat pregnant women on Medicaid, and 87 percent had no services available for Medicaid patients who were both pregnant and addicted to crack. Although this survey is now several years old and more treatment facilities have become available to pregnant women, the situation is still much the same. The financial cost involved alone is one reason that court ordered drug rehabilitation services through the juvenile court may currently be the only way that a mother can afford to undergo drug rehabilitation programs (Larson, 1991). Ideally, what is needed are free prenatal care and drug counseling in a non-punitive setting, available to all, and geared to different ethnic and cultural subgroups.

NEW MEDICAL EVIDENCE

Early medical research concluded that maternal substance abuse causes a wide range of health complications for the infant, including withdrawal, physical and neurological deficits, low birth weight, growth retardation, cardiovascular abnormalities, spontaneous abortion, premature delivery, as well as long-term developmental abnormalities (Chasnoff et al., 1985, 1989; Howard, Kropenske & Tyler, 1986; Petitti & Coleman, 1990; Weston et al., 1989). However, the extent to which these problems are actually due to illegal drugs is difficult to determine. Many drug users are polydrug abusers, mixing illegal drugs with legal drugs such as nicotine and alcohol, all known contributors to poor fetal outcomes. Often such factors are compounded by family poverty, poor nutritional status and general health, sexually transmitted diseases, and little or no prenatal care (Lutiger et al., 1991). When the lifestyles, social background, and other covariants of cocaine use are taken into consideration, it becomes clear that cocaine use per se may not affect infant outcomes (Richarson & Day, 1991). While the initial paper by Chasnoff et al. (1985) had pointed to the many medical problems of drug-exposed infants, a later paper found that babies exposed to cocaine only in the first trimester of pregnancy weighed the same as babies from a control population (Chasnoff, Landress & Barrett, 1990). A problem with the early studies on the babies of mothers who used powdered cocaine and crack was that there were no control groups. The effects of cocaine are particularly difficult to identify because of the high probability of a total lack of prenatal care (Inciardi, Lockwood & Pottieger, 1993). Clearly, the impact of prenatal drug use on fetal health is mediated by diet, prenatal care, and other factors associated with social class (Bingol et al., 1987; Mathias, 1992). A more recent study gives support to this view. Hurt et al. (1995) studied 105 cocaine users and their infants of 34 weeks gestation or more at an urban hospital in Philadelphia. While cocaine-exposed infants had an increased incidence of congenital syphilis, increased admission to the neonatal ICU, and lower birth weights and head circumference, the data showed that these children did not differ from the controls in the incidence of severe growth retardation. The researchers concluded that the data did not support the theory that cocaine alone increases the risk of growth retardation. Nicotine, a legal drug, was found to be an independent predictor of small head circumference. Thus, the effects often attributed to fetal exposure to illegal drugs may as likely be due to a host of other factors. Goode (1994), in fact, concludes that by the early 1990s there was enough medical evidence assembled to indicate that the "crack-baby syndrome" was, in all likelihood, mythical in nature.

VIOLATION OF CONSTITUTIONAL RIGHTS

Prosecution of pregnant substance abusers violates the constitutional rights of those affected. Farr (1995) argues that prosecuting women under laws that were not intended for the prosecution of substance abuse during pregnancy violates the due process clause of the Fourteenth Amendment. This clause guarantees a person the right to fair notice that his or her conduct is criminal. Thus, prosecuting women under existing laws, such as delivery of drugs to a minor which do not specify the delivery of drugs to a fetus, violates the due process clause. Additionally, criminal laws require that punishment be imposed when there is both a criminal act and a culpable mental intent. Assuming that the state has a right to maintain a reasonable standard of fetal health, it seems logical that the state could punish only those women that willfully, intentionally, or knowingly create a substantial risk of harm to their fetus. The fact that the harmful effects of drug use alone have been called into question, as well as the fact that many women may not even know that they are pregnant when they ingest the drugs, are arguments against such prosecutions.

The criminalization of substance abuse by pregnant women also amounts to an unconstitutional invasion of a woman's right to privacy. In *Roe v. Wade* (1973), the Supreme Court found that a woman's right of privacy to decide whether to abort was protected within the personal liberty guarantees of the Fourteenth Amendment's due process clause. Every woman, regardless of her marital status, has a constitutional right in the first trimester of pregnancy to decide privately with her physician whether to have an abortion or to carry the baby to term. The creation of "fetal rights" mandating state intrusions in regulating a woman's conduct during pregnancy would necessarily intrude in the most private areas of a woman's life. Ironically, however, *Roe v. Wade* has also been used to argue in favor of the "fetal rights" movement. The Supreme Court held in this decision that after the first trimester of pregnancy, the interests of potential life become important, and that after viability, the state has a legitimate and important interest in the unborn. After viability, the state may protect fetal life by prohibiting all abortions that are not necessary to protect the life and health of the mother. Thus, both proponents and opponents of the criminalization of "fetal abuse" can draw on different parts of *Roe v. Wade* to support their cause. *Webster* (1980) subsequently rejected the rigid trimester scheme for establishing viability, thus giving ammunition for those who argue that states may constitutionally criminalize pregnant women who abuse substances known to harm fetuses (Wright, 1990).

Criminalization of maternal conduct during pregnancy also violates a woman's rights to equal protection under the law. Because evidence of a newborn's positive toxicology screen is used only in cases against women, women would be punished because of their drug use and their ability to get pregnant. A statutory requirement that women resolve all health-care decisions in favor of the fetus would hold women to a much higher standard of self-care than men.

Paltrow (1990) argues that no criminal statute could be tailored narrowly enough to protect a woman's right to privacy or her due process rights. Even if a narrowly tailored statute could be drawn, such a statute would deter a significant number of pregnant substance abusers from seeking prenatal medical care, thereby increasing rather than decreasing the harm to be avoided. At all stages of pregnancy, the fetus is completely dependent on the woman. Recognizing "fetal abuse" as a crime moves us toward criminalizing pregnancy itself because no woman can provide the perfect womb, as noted in the "slippery slope" arguments of the court decisions against prosecution. Extending the scope of pre-existing laws to include fetal protection will render these laws too vague to pass constitutional muster.

CONCLUSION

As shown in this chapter, criminalization of substance abuse during pregnancy is a failed policy. Again and again, the courts have thrown out such cases, warning that prosecution of behavior during pregnancy leads us down the "slippery slope" to an invasion of women's constitutional rights and statutory vagueness. Courts have declined to find women guilty under statutes not intended for this use (with the exception of South Carolina), and no state or federal legislatures have so far been able to overcome the constitutional and other legal obstacles (such as the problem of recognizing a fetus as a person) to enact new criminal code legislation. Criminalization of conduct during pregnancy is simply a wrong policy; it is unconstitutional, sexist, and serves no social policy purpose. The threat of such prosecutions alone would lead women away from prenatal care, worsen the risks for the fetus, and make interventions less likely.

It is also true, especially in the past, that newborns who tested positive for drugs were too often reported to the Child Protective Services while children born with more severe symptoms, such as the fetal alcohol syndrome, were not reported simply because alcohol use is legal. The best policy to be followed is the one in the state of Washington that treats perinatal substance abuse as a public health problem. The next best policy is the one in California that dictates that additional risk factors must be present before drug-exposed infants are reported to the social welfare system.

It has been demonstrated that punishing women for their behavior during pregnancy is not an effective deterrent to addiction problems. What is needed from the parents is the ability to provide good parenting to the child, whether drug use is involved or not. In many cases, court-ordered counseling and parenting programs may be necessary both to pay for such programs and to persuade the parents and other relative caretakers to attend the programs. Only when parents are unable to care for the child at all should the juvenile court take custody away from the parent. Such indicators that the mother may be able to care properly for the child might include the mother's attentive care of siblings, her willingness and ability to participate in drug treatment and parenting classes, and the availability of a support system. The goal should be to provide pregnant women and mothers of young children with effective treatment, comprehensive prenatal care, and contraceptive help, so that they may maintain custody of their own children and manage their own lives. Juvenile court intervention should be limited to protect children who are at great risk, so that loss of constitutional rights and societal costs may be prevented, and criminal court intervention never used.

NOTE

[1] These organizations include the Children's Defense Fund, the American Public Health Association, the American Medical Association, the American Nurses' Association, the Center for the Future of Children, the National Association on Alcoholism and Drug Abuse, the National Black Women's Health Project, and the National Association for Perinatal Addiction Research.

8

Drug Testing in the Rehnquist Era

Donald W. Crowley
University of Idaho

Testing a wide range of federal and state employees, student athletes, truck drivers, and numerous others for drugs is a policy option that has become increasingly popular in the most recent version of the war against drugs. Such tests have been supported by three consecutive presidents, many corporations, numerous editorial columnists, and apparently public opinion (Latessa, Travis & Cullen, 1988). In an earlier time frame, such policies, when ordered or carried out by public officials, would have violated the Fourth Amendment's prohibition against unreasonable searches and seizures. However, the demand for forced disclosure of urine or blood specimens as a check on illegal drug usage came at a time when the Supreme Court had seriously weakened Fourth Amendment protections against unreasonable search and seizures. Examining how political and social developments have joined with shifts in judicial philosophy to lead to the legitimization of drug testing will be the focus of this chapter.

WAGING WAR ON DRUGS

As others have illustrated, the war on drugs can be usefully analyzed as a socially constructed crisis (Jensen, Gerber & Babcock, 1991). To paraphrase Mark Fishman's analysis of crime waves, drug crises may be "things of the mind," but they have real consequences (Fishman,1978:31). One of those consequences has been the call for drug testing and the narrowing of constitutional protections against such invasions of personal privacy. This chapter views the war on drugs as an extension of what Scheingold (1984) termed the "politics of law and order." The politics of law and order revolves around a complex pattern of interactions. As the media give extensive coverage to a "crime wave," the public perception of being in jeopardy increases. Public officials running for reelection are quite eager to suggest ways to alleviate those fears. However, simple proposals that play to the punitive instincts of the general public and American culture are far more likely than complex discussions of social factors and individual rights to provide the symbolic reassurances that voters seek. "Certainly the politician who, in a climate of fear, champions due process, redemption, or rehabilitation faces an uphill struggle. Thus politicians are more or less forced to promise [a] simple punitive solution to complicated and intractable problems" (Scheingold, 1984:87).

In such a political climate, a concern with civil liberties and personal privacy is likely to get lost in the rush to obtain urine samples (Weisman, 1986). Thus, it was not surprising when President Reagan announced a policy aimed at testing a wide range of federal government employees. Little attention was paid to questions about how effective such tests were likely to be, what government interests were being protected, and what individual rights were threatened by such a proposal (Levine & Reinarman, 1987). The president apparently saw no conflict between his frequent assertions of the importance of limited government and his endorsement of a proposal to expand the power of government over people's private lives. With public opinion on his side, the President issued Executive Order #12564 on September 15, 1986, authorizing the heads of every executive agency to establish a plan for achieving a "drug free" workplace (51 F.R. 32889). Such a plan would include a drug testing program for all employees in "sensitive positions" (51 F.R. 32889). All other employees would be subject to drug testing if they were involved in an accident or "unsafe practice" or if there was "reasonable suspicion" to believe that they used illegal drugs (51 F.R. 32889). Any applicants for new positions would also be subject to drug testing.

The problem at which this plan for extensive drug testing was directed was not entirely clear. The order itself mentioned several possible goals. Reagan suggested that the federal government ought to be concerned with drug usage by its employees because it "is concerned with the well-being of its employees, the successful accomplishment of agency missions, and the need to maintain employee productivity" (51 F.R. 32889). The President also asserted the need to maintain public confidence, protect the public from health and safety violations, and in general, protect national security from irresponsible actions by public officials (51 F.R. 32889). It also seems likely that the development of policies aimed at achieving "drug-free workplaces" was designed to legitimize and encourage private employers to develop similar drug testing programs and thereby help to combat what Reagan termed the "billions of dollars of lost productivity" attributed to drug use (51 F.R. 32889).

DRUGS, PRODUCTIVITY, AND SAFETY

The attempt to turn the question of drug use into one of job performance was made most explicitly by then-Vice President George Bush who stated that "drug use is job abuse" (Husak, 1992:185). Irrespective of the confidence with which the Reagan Administration asserted a relationship between drugs and lost productivity, there is very little information on the extent to which the use of drugs by individuals actually results in a decline in worker productivity (Morgan, 1988). Clearly, the American economy had witnessed a decline in productivity since the early 1970s, but solutions to a problem of this nature must be located in the more complex patterns of world trade, investment, and retraining rather than in the simplistic scapegoating of American workers and their alleged drug habits. What little information is available on the relationship between drug usage and lost productivity is not terribly convincing and suggests that President Reagan's program was not even aimed at the most costly forms of substance abuse.

Although advocates of drug testing asserted a clear relationship between drug use and efficiency, it still remains beyond the ability of modern social science to sort out the various influences that may contribute to making a person somewhat less than the ideal worker. Even those few studies that have made an attempt to arrive at some estimate of the relationship between drug use and lost productivity end up making assumptions about cause and effect that are far from obvious. Indeed, one critic of many of such studies accused "the proponents of testing of zealotry and improper use of statistics and data to support a moral cause" (Morgan, 1988:697). Attributing lost productivity to drug usage seems to assume that if a worker with a high absentee rate admits to recent drug use then the latter is responsible for the former (Morgan, 1988). While having engaged in drug use may contribute to such results, it need not be the case. If a worker smokes some marijuana on the weekend, has an argument over finances with his or her spouse on Tuesday, gets little sleep on Tuesday night, and then has an accident on Wednesday, can one reasonably associate the accident to illegal drug use? As a Department of Health and Human Services report concluded, "The fact is, very little is known about the complex relationship which undoubtedly exists between drug abuse, worker performance and productivity or lack thereof, and how the work setting influences or is influenced by drug abuse" (Felman & Petrini, 1988:258).

When Reagan issued his call for drug testing, the most frequently cited study on drug abuse and productivity was conducted by the Research Triangle Institute. This study estimated that in 1980, drug use cost the American society $46.9 billion, including $25.7 billion in costs to industry (Felman & Petrini, 1988:258). The Institute's study was widely quoted as evidence of the economic cost of drug use although one scholar characterized the study as a "litany for the promoters of urine testing" (Felman & Petrini, 1988:258). While it seems plausible to acknowledge that illegal drug use results in some social costs, either in terms of lost productivity, health risks, or increased susceptibility to accidents, we really do not possess the information to sort out the costs of illegal drug use from the costs of legal use of prescription drugs or the widespread use of alcohol. Even the Research Triangle study placed the costs of alcohol abuse at almost double the cost of illegal drug abuse. Nevertheless, this finding did not keep President Reagan from ignoring the estimated cost of alcohol abuse while more than doubling the estimated cost of drug abuse (Felman & Petrini, 1988:258). If the purpose of the widespread use of drug testing was really to promote efficiency and safety in the workplace, then ignoring the effects of alcohol abuse seems particularly nonsensical. As one critic of drug testing argued, "it would take transcendental creativity to conclude that programs of testing for illegal drug use that exclude alcohol are really directed toward policing the productivity and safety of workers" (Wisotsky, 1987:769-770).

A related problem is that advocates of drug testing seem to assume that a positive result somehow tells us something about impaired functioning on the job. Even assuming the accuracy of the testing methods, which in some cases is a big assumption, testing one's urine for drugs at best only tells us that an individual had some traces of the drug in his system. The test, by itself cannot tell us anything about whether an individual was impaired or whether the drug contributed to some work related problem. Among the many problems associated with drug testing, one of the biggest is the false inferences people are likely to make after an employee tests positive for drug use. It does not take a great imagination to anticipate how the press would treat an employee who tested positive for drugs after an accident. If the drug use was days before, or even if the test rendered a false positive, it would not matter much. Indeed, few would take the time to note that in some contexts the possibility of a false positive is fairly high (Wells, Helperin & Thun, 1988). The use of drug testing may help identify those who have engaged in illegal behavior; whether it helps enhance productivity or public safety is a different question entirely.

> The zeal to condemn and isolate the bad—those who take illegal drugs—should not be mistaken for a rational response to a clearly defined social goal of promoting productivity and safety in the workplace. That would require a reasoned assessment of the subtle interrelationship of a particular job task, a particular drug, and the time and occasion of its use (Wisotsky, 1987:778).

Along with productivity arguments, drug testing in the workplace is frequently defended as helping to protect the safety of workers and the public. As we will see, this was ultimately the grounds upon which the Supreme Court justified the testing of many federal workers. However, as John Gilliom (1994) points out, many of those who advocated the use of testing on safety grounds were reluctant to accept other safety methods that might have greater impact. This is illustrated by the fact that while drug testing was being advanced by the Reagan Administration, the enforcement of existing workplace safety laws by Occupational Safety and Health Administration (OSHA) was being scaled back (Gilliom, 1994:45). Gilliom suggests that this anomaly is explained by the fact that many safety regulations undercut managerial prerogatives and control while drug testing increases such control (Gilliom, 1994:44-45). To him, arguments about the use of drug testing to enhance productivity and safety miss the point since the real purpose is to enhance bureaucratic control and create the "perfect worker" who fits well within such a system (Gilliom, 1994:51). In this sense, advocacy of drug testing by political leaders may serve largely symbolic goals, but the acceptance of such policies by employers serves their goals of creating employees who fit more readily inside a system of bureaucratic control.

Ascertaining the relationship between drug use, productivity, and safety does not seem to have been a major motivation for those promoting the widespread use of drug testing. Indeed, there has also been little interest in utilizing methods, like video tests, that would be less intrusive than drug testing while helping to ascertain whether someone is functioning up to normal levels that day (Fine, 1992). It is equally clear that excluding alcohol use from testing makes little sense if the reason to conduct testing is worker efficiency and safety. However, such an exclusion makes perfect sense if the real purpose of the program is to send symbolic reassurance to the public that something is being done about the use of illegal drugs without disturbing the more socially acceptable consumption of alcohol. Testing for illegal drugs may or may not reduce the drug problem but as Lance Bennett (1980) has argued, a successful policy may not be the point.

Policies become means of affirming the larger images of the world on which they are based. In most policy areas, it is more acceptable to suffer failure based on correct theories than it would be to achieve success at the price of sacrificing social values (Bennett, 1980:397).

PRIVACY AS A SOCIAL VALUE

No doubt many would claim that the widespread use of drug testing certainly does sacrifice important social values. Still, even if privacy and human dignity are values deeply rooted in our constitutional tradition, they seem to be values that many Americans are ready to dismiss in the face of the widely held perception of a drug epidemic. Even though drug testing raises issues central to our sense of the proper limitations on the power of the state, such technological assaults on privacy are relatively new and not as firmly entrenched in the public mind as a search of a person's home without a warrant. In their study of tolerance, McClosky and Brill (1983) noted that

> popular support for civil liberties tends to be greater when the norms are clear and well established and weaker or more uncertain when the norms are newly emerging, still unfamiliar to many members of the mass public, and not yet firmly fixed in the body of constitutional principles endorsed by the courts (McClosky & Brill, 1983:185).

Also, given the manner in which the court has systematically weakened basic Fourth Amendment protections in recent years, it appears that the social learning necessary to maintain public support for civil liberties protection in this area may be lacking. Rather than demand that their right to personal privacy be respected, many seem inclined to say that they don't mind if they are tested since they have nothing to hide. This tends to imply that if one says "no" to drug testing they must be guilty. In this sense, drug testing has become the 1990s equivalent of the loyalty oaths of the 1950s; refusing to cooperate seems to suggest guilt.

The complex interactions between a public convinced of a rising drug threat, fueled by a media that plays to the most sensationalized aspects of the problem, and further exacerbated by public officials eager to reassure the public that something is being done, created a climate where drug testing could be offered as a simple solution to our problems. One might hope that the courts would resist the popular tide and act to insure that drug testing is conducted only under proper judicial constraints. However, Fourth Amendment pronouncements by the U.S. Supreme Court over the last decade have articulated a methodology under which courts are far more likely to bow to public concern about criminal activities and governmental assertions of the need to gather evidence. A close look at recent trends in the Supreme Court's Fourth Amendment decisions should make it clear why they did not resist the call for the widespread use of drug testing of public employees.

THE FOURTH AMENDMENT IN DECLINE

President Reagan's program may have been proposed as a model for both public and private workplaces, but it is worth stressing that drug testing conducted by government raises different issues than drug testing by private employers. The most important difference lies in the limitations placed on government action through the Fourth Amendment. Thus, at least theoretically, there are limitations on the degree to which government agencies may order drug testing. There are no constitutional limitations on what a private employer may require although such tests may be subject to collective bargaining and other legal considerations (Hogler, 1988).

Historically, judicial enforcement of the Fourth Amendment has sought to ensure that government officials may only "search" or "seize" an individual's personal effects when such a search is deemed reasonable. The obvious way that searches become reasonable is if those wishing to search convince a judge that probable cause exists before a warrant is issued. However, under certain carefully defined circumstances, a search can be conducted without a warrant. As Justice Stewart explained:

> . . . over and again this Court has emphasized that the mandate of the Fourth Amendment requires adherence to judicial processes, . . . and that searches conducted outside the judicial process, without prior approval by Judge or magistrate, are per se unreasonable under the Fourth Amendment—subject only to a few specifically established and well-delineated exceptions (*Katz v. United States*, 1967).

When Justice Stewart made this comment more than two decades ago, the list of exceptions to the warrant requirement was short and narrowly defined, usually related to considerations of time and mobility. Thus, if the police possessed probable cause to search, but time considerations prevented them from seeking a warrant, the search could be conducted as an exception to the warrant rule. For instance, in a 1960s case raising issues related to blood and urine testing, the Court allowed a blood test to be administered without a warrant on a person involved in a traffic accident, because in the Court's view probable cause clearly existed and there was not sufficient time to obtain a warrant (*Schmerber v. California*, 1966). However, Justice Brennan's majority opinion made it clear that such intrusions beyond the body surface were searches that could be allowed only if probable cause existed and not simply "on the mere chance that desired evidence might be obtained" (1966:770). In seeking to reiterate the limited scope of the Court's ruling, Brennan emphasized the importance of the values of human dignity and privacy:

> The integrity of an individual's person is a cherished value of our society. That we today hold that the Constitution does not forbid the State's minor intrusions into an individual's body under stringently limited conditions in no way indicates that it permits more substantial intrusions, or intrusions under other conditions (1966:772).

Given the careful way the Court justified this exception to the warrant rule and the fact that four dissenters found even this exception too great to tolerate, the *Schmerber* decision gave little comfort to advocates of drug testing in the absence of probable cause. However, the *Schmerber* decision was three decades ago and the Court has changed considerably since then. In the 1970s, Richard Nixon's four appointments began to incrementally expand the list of exceptions. Reagan's appointments of Justices O'Connor, Scalia, and Kennedy, along with Bush's appointment of Justice Thomas, accelerated this trend to the point that the exceptions have, it appears, overwhelmed the general rule. Without going into a detailed description of the ways in which the Court has expanded the exceptions to both the warrant and probable cause requirements, a short analysis of the Court's basic methodology will help explain how the constitutional case for widespread drug testing without a warrant, probable cause, or even reasonable suspicion became easier to make in the Rehnquist era.

In recent Fourth Amendment cases, especially those that involve what the Court has termed "the special needs of government," the Court has increasingly used a balancing approach in determining the degree of protection offered to the individual. The initial step is to claim that the Fourth Amendment does not require warrants or even probable cause. What is required is that a search be reasonable. To determine whether a search is reasonable, the Court balances the nature and quality of the intrusion on the individual's Fourth Amendment interests against the importance of the governmental interests alleged to justify the intrusion" (*O'Connor v. Ortega*, 1986:719). Balancing allows the Court considerable room for discretion, since justices alone determine the weights that are applied to either side of the balance.

EXPECTATIONS OF PRIVACY

In order for an individual to receive protection, he or she must first demonstrate that he or she possesses a "legitimate expectation of privacy" that he or she seeks to keep private. After one has demonstrated a legitimate expectation of privacy, then that expectation must be balanced against the governmental need for the search. However, the Court has frequently argued that one has a "legitimate expectation of privacy" only in circumstances that "society is prepared to recognize as reasonable" (*Katz v. United States*, 1967:361). This allows for two basic ways in which the Court can reject an individual's claim that a search violates the Fourth Amendment. First, the Court can argue that one does not possess a legitimate expectation of privacy; or it can assert that, even though one possesses a legitimate expectation of privacy, such an expectation is outweighed by a pressing societal purpose.

The Court's attempts to discern what constitutes a reasonable expectation of privacy have been problematic at best and totally confused at worse. Indeed, the Court's "expectation of privacy" concept has been so poorly articulated and justified that one begins to suspect that its main function has been its ability to serve "as a rhetorical shield which allows the majority a method to balance away traditional Fourth Amendment protections, claiming that little social value is gained by paying attention to them" (Crowley & Johnson, 1988:341-342).

Occasionally, the Court has been willing to reduce Fourth Amendment protections even when the majority acknowledges that a person possesses a legitimate expectation of privacy. In a 1985 case that had significant overtones for drug testing (*New Jersey v. T.L.O.*, 1985), six justices agreed that school officials could conduct a full search of a student's purse even though they possessed neither probable cause nor a warrant. Concern with the presence of drugs in the public schools animated Justice White's plurality opinion that seemingly endorsed a totally open-ended balancing formula (Johnson & Crowley, 1986). Despite a young girl's significant expectations of privacy in her purse, such expectations were overwhelmed by the greater need of school administrators to "maintain discipline in the classroom and on school grounds" (1986:339). White's approach demonstrates the ease with which the balancing formula can lead to an erosion of privacy interests. All that is necessary is for the Court to make general references to the widespread existence of a drug and discipline problem. This expression of a special governmental need is then seen as outweighing the individual interest in privacy and therefore justifying a relaxation of Fourth Amendment protections.

New Jersey v. T.L.O. (1985) illustrates the effect that a balancing methodology can have on constitutional rights. Even though a careful balancing of competing principles may sometimes be a necessary or even desirable mode of decisionmaking, the type of ad hoc balancing increasingly employed by the Court is, in Justice Brennan's phrase, "destructive nihilism" that ultimately undermines the very notion of a constitutional right (*New Jersey v. T.L.O.*, 1985). Such a formula manages to rig the scales and undercut the meaning of a constitutional right while it maintains the illusion of a neutral and careful consideration of the competing claim (Aleinikoff, 1987).

WASTE PRODUCTS AND GOVERNMENT EMPLOYEES

Under a balancing approach, if the Court wished to uphold the governmental power to drug test, it simply needed to argue that the individual's expectation of privacy had been reduced or that the government's interest in protecting public order is greater than the privacy interest asserted. One method of reducing the individual's interest in privacy is to argue that conducting a urinalysis is not really a search, or at least is so minimally intrusive that no important privacy interests are compromised. Indeed, one federal appeals court judge made the argument that urine is simply a waste product, like garbage, and thus one has no constitutionally protected interest in keeping it private (*National Treasury Employees Union v. Von Raab*, 1987).

The problem with this argument is that even though urine is obviously a waste product, urinalysis demands that an individual provide a urine sample at a time and place of government's choosing. Even in allowing garbage to be searched after it has been put out for collection, (*California v. Greenwood,* 1987) the Court never claimed that a person could be ordered to provide certain garbage from the house for inspection (Joseph, 1987). Not only is the process of demanding a urine sample an invasion of one's privacy, but, like a bug placed on a telephone, it yields information far removed from the apparent reason for the search. As one chemist associated with drug testing has asserted, a urinalysis "can tell a company whether an employee is being treated for a heart condition, manic-depression, epilepsy, diabetes or schizophrenia" (Joseph, 1987:621). Any search that can reveal this type of information can hardly be called minimally intrusive.

While in the 1980s a wide variety of scholars criticized the weakening of traditional Fourth Amendment protections, prior to the drug testing cases, the Court still required that some degree of suspicion be focused directly on the individual before a search could be conducted. However, a crucial point to remember is that under the methodology of balancing, if the government need is considered important, not only can the requirements for warrants and probable cause disappear, but so can the need for individualized suspicion. The Court's use of balancing made it easy to respond to governmental claims that the public safety was so threatened by drug use that previously existing constitutional requirements were unnecessary luxuries in the fight against drugs

DRUG TESTING IN THE REHNQUIST COURT

There had been numerous cases testing the constitutionality of drug testing heard by lower courts in the 1980s. The majority of these decisions ruled against the use of drug testing in the absence of at least reasonable suspicion directed at the individual (*McDonell v. Hunter,* 1985). However, the U.S. Supreme Court had been silent on the issue until the 1988 term when the Court heard two cases that dealt directly with the question of the degree to which federal agencies could require drug testing. The cases came to the Court with conflicting decisions from the appellate courts. In *Skinner v. Railway Labor Executives Association* (1989), the Court reviewed a policy of the Federal Railway Administration that required both alcohol and drug testing of train crews after an accident or when operating rules were violated. A refusal to submit to such a test would result in a nine month suspension. The federal appeals court (9th Circuit) ruled that this policy was a violation of the Fourth Amendment. Even though the appeals court used balancing, it argued that without some degree of particularized suspicion, accidents or rule violations by themselves did not create reasonable grounds for suspecting drug usage (*Rail-*

way Labor Executives Association v. Burnley, 1988). The appeals court also noted that urinalysis cannot demonstrate that an individual was impaired at the time of the accident and thus such tests are not reasonably related to a legitimate government objective. In contrast, a federal appeals court (5th Circuit) upheld the use of drug testing for Custom's Service employees who are selected for promotions. In *National Treasury Employees Union v. Von Raab* (1987), the Fifth Circuit balanced the interests involved and concluded that considering the need for "public confidence in the integrity of the Service," the risk to public safety from employees that use drugs, and the "limited scope of the search" drug testing even in the absence of "individualized suspicion," was not unreasonable (1987:178).

These cases illustrate how little guidance is received from the Supreme Court's reliance on balancing. The open-ended style of balancing practiced by the Rehnquist Court can lead to any result depending upon the personal preferences of those doing the balancing. While the government argued that the tests are limited in scope, the opponents claimed that drug testing amounted to having a "periscope into the private lives of the employees" (*U.S. Law Week*, 1988:3327). The government asserted vital interests in public safety and job performance, while the opponents noted the lack of evidence relating to private drug use and safety problems, and emphasized that drug tests would not demonstrate that a person was under the influence of any drug while on the job. All of these are important considerations, but without any principles to help determine relative values or give substance to the purpose of the Fourth Amendment, the Court is left adrift in a sea of competing claims.

More central to the theme of this volume, the Court's unbounded balancing makes it possible to become highly affected by the mood and fears of the general public. When the mass public becomes frightened by a "crime wave" or "drug epidemic," public officials frequently advocate policies that endanger civil liberties while seeking to reassure the public. Although the effect of public opinion on the Court is difficult to demonstrate, public concern and the pronouncements of public officials make it easier for some justices to balance an individual's "expectation of privacy" against the need for public order and conclude that either the expectation is not legitimate or is simply outweighed by the competing government interests. An individual's expectation of privacy can be swept away under a generalized fear that a person might have taken drugs sometime and this occurrence might contribute to some workplace related problem. Thus Reagan's Solicitor General Charles Fried, who once wrote a scholarly defense of privacy as essential to human dignity (Fried, 1968), could, without apparent irony, argue before the Court that drug testing was justified because it would act as a deterrent and would occasionally catch a drug user (*U.S. Law Week*, 1988:3327). In this type of environment, pointing out that testing urine for drugs does not reveal any information that demonstrates impairment on the job is of less value than simply reassuring the public that something is being done.

In March of 1989, the Supreme Court upheld the use of drug testing as practiced in the previous two cases discussed. While the cases did not deal directly with the even more extensive drug testing plans proposed by President Reagan's executive order, the Court's ruling was broad enough to justify most of the proposed. Writing for a seven person majority in the railroad case and a bare five-person majority in the custom's officer case, Justice Kennedy engaged in a balancing analysis to further restrict the protections offered by the Fourth Amendment. In *Skinner v. Railroad Labor Executives Association* (1989), Kennedy and six other justices found that even though the Fourth Amendment applied to the employees in question, and blood and urine testing constituted a search and seizure, the workers' expectation of privacy was diminished by the fact that they were employed in a highly regulated industry. This diminished expectation of privacy must then be balanced against the significant government interests in ensuring a safe transportation industry. In applying its balancing formula, the Court reached the predictable result that drug testing under such circumstances was not unreasonable.

The Court's willingness to abandon both probable cause and the warrant requirement was not surprising; but the ease with which they dispensed any need to show some degree of suspicion focused on the individual was striking. Previously, the Court had abandoned individualized suspicion only for routine administrative searches or border stops (*Camara v. Municipal Court*, 1967 and *United States v. Martinez-Fuerte*, 1976). Here the Court evaded what some had thought to be the absolute baseline constitutional requirement by "minimizing the invasion of privacy and emphasizing the importance of the information to be obtained" (Crowley, 1995:113). From the Court's perspective, in special circumstances "where the privacy interests implicated by the search are minimal, and where an important governmental interest furthered by the intrusion would be placed in jeopardy by a requirement of individualized suspicion, a search may be reasonable despite the absence of such suspicion. We believe this is true of the intrusions in question here" (*Skinner v. Railway Labor Executives Association*, 1989).

The Court argued that the invasion of privacy was minimal. Since the tests were similar to other types of medical screening already required of employees, there was no administration discretion and the required monitoring was discreet. On the other hand, the testing for drugs and alcohol was reasonable because the Court accepted the Federal Railroad Administration's claims that the tests would help to make railroad transportation safer. The government's "interest in ensuring the safety of the traveling public and of the employees themselves plainly justifies prohibiting covered employees from using alcohol or drugs on duty, or while subject to being called for duty" (1989:621). It seems unlikely that anyone would take exception to the claim that individuals can be prohibited from using alcohol or drugs on the job. However, the Court avoided the question of the degree to which a urinalysis for drugs would provide meaningful information about an employee's job performance. Instead the Court argued that

> positive test results would point toward drug or alcohol impairment on the part of members of the crew as a possible cause of an accident, and may help to establish whether a particular accident, otherwise not drug related, was made worse by the inability of impaired employees to respond appropriately (1989:630).

In addition, the Court noted that the existence of such tests would serve as a deterrent to the use of drugs by railroad personnel. In short, the use of the tests might have a positive effect; the invasion of privacy is minimal and requiring reasonable suspicion is too burdensome. Thus drug testing under such circumstances is constitutional.

The Court's approach undermines traditional understandings of the Fourth Amendment by allowing the obviously important government goal of safety to outweigh all competing claims. The Court does not make a persuasive case that the use of urinalysis will actually provide convincing evidence about whether the job performance of someone who tests positive was actually negatively affected. The unarticulated assumption seems to be that since drugs are bad, if the use of such tests will help deter someone, then little is lost and much is gained.

The Court's asserted connection between drug testing and public safety may not have been persuasively made in *Skinner*, but public fears of being left at the mercy of a drug impaired train operator provide the decision with a cloak of respectability. Certainly the argument in *Skinner* is easier to comprehend than the similar argument made for customs officials. Here the symbolic nature of the policy becomes more readily apparent. In the companion case of *National Treasury Employees Union v. Von Raab* (1989), a narrow majority of five justices upheld the implementation of drug testing for Customs Service employees seeking transfer or promotion to positions having direct involvement with drug interdiction or requiring the carrying of weapons. Once again Justice Kennedy wrote the majority decision that essentially tracked the *Skinner* decision's emphasis on the special needs of government overriding the privacy interests of Customs Service employees. In *Skinner*, the Court couched their arguments in terms of the specific safety interests of the railway industry, but in *National Treasury Employees Union v. Von Raab* (1989), the Court relied on generalized references to "the veritable national crisis in law enforcement caused by the smuggling of illicit narcotics (1989:668). Thus, in the majority view the country's "interest in self-protection could be irreparably damaged if those charged with safeguarding it were, because of their own drug use, unsympathetic to their mission" (1989:670).

Apart from the continued lack of concern with the need for suspicion focused on the individual, the Court's *ad hoc* balancing allowed them to undermine privacy claims by simply referring to the possibility that the public's confidence in the "integrity of our borders" might be compromised by the mere chance that some Customs Service employees might not be drug free (1989:672). The fact that the commissioner of the Customs Service had stated that his employees were "largely drug free" did not affect the way the Court weighed the competing claims (1989:660). Even Justices Scalia and Stevens, who joined in the *Skinner* decision, could not support drug testing here. Interestingly, Scalia argued that the Customs Service policy was "a kind of immolation of privacy and human dignity in symbolic opposition to drug use" (1989:681).

Justices Marshall and Brennan, dissenting in both cases, insisted that the Court should have, at the very least, required that the programs be justified by reasonable suspicion focused on the individual. In words that suggest that Marshall and Brennan were sympathetic to a social constructionist view of the drug crisis, they accused the majority of the Court of having been "swept away by society's obsession with stopping the scourge of illegal drugs " (*Skinner v. Railway Labor Executives Association,* 1989). In this light they feared "that the first, and worst, casualty of the war on drugs will be the precious liberties of our citizens" (1989:636).

IMPACT AND IMPLICATIONS

Along with the Drug Free Workplace Act (1988) that required that companies receiving federal contracts to establish a drug free awareness program, these decisions provided impetus and a degree of legitimacy to the drug testing movement. However, the more difficult question to answer is what are the limits on government's power to drug test. Some scholars read the decisions narrowly and suggested that the Court would only endorse drug testing if a significant safety issue was presented (Fine, Reeves & Harney, 1996). Thus, they argued that government agencies would need to demonstrate "that the public good might be irreparably damaged, the national security threatened, or disaster or great tragedy could result from momentary inattention" to justify drug testing without individualized suspicion (p. 32). Some federal and state courts took such an approach (*American Federation of Government Employees v. Sullivan,* 1992 and *University of Colorado v. Derdeyn,* 1993). This interpretation, while plausible, underestimates the ease with which the balancing style and a perceived national crisis can combine to justify drug testing even when public safety is not at issue. This is illustrated most clearly by the Court's 1995 endorsement of random drug testing for student athletes in *Vernonia School District 47J v. Acton* (1995). Here the Court upheld random drug testing for student athletes even where the case for the protection of public safety was clearly lacking. Demonstrating the flexibility of balancing and ignoring his own words about the symbolic nature of testing in *Von Raab*, Justice Scalia found that the government interest in testing student athletes to be the equivalent of the government interest in *Skinner* and *Von Raab*. "Deterring drug use by our Nation's schoolchildren is at least as important as enhancing efficient enforcement of the Nation's laws against the importation of drugs, . . . or deterring drug use by engineers and trainmen" *Vernonia School District 47J v. Acton*, 1995:2395). After weighing the significant government interest in deterring students from drug use against the diminished expectation of privacy available to students (especially athletes) in public school, the Court had no difficulty justifying this vast expansion of the social control role of our public schools (Crowley, 1995).

In the future there will be much public and scholarly debate about the extent to which the *Acton* decision limits drug testing to athletes or whether all students might be included (Rosenberg, 1996). On this point, Scalia's majority argument is ambiguous since some of his justification rests on the particular circumstances of student athletes and his assertion that "school sports are not for the bashful," while other aspects of his argument emphasize that government may exercise a greater degree of control over students than adults (*Veronia School District 47J v. Acton*, 1995:2392). Even though it remains unclear where the Court will draw this line, there is no doubt that balancing allows them to justify drug testing anytime the perceived public interest is regarded as sufficiently important.

After Reagan's call for widespread use of drug testing of federal employee's was legitimized by the Supreme Court, most federal agencies created plans to implement such testing. Many federal agencies adopted testing plans that went well beyond any reasonable connection between the testing and public safety. For instance, the Justice Department's original plan included testing "stenographers in the Anti-Trust Division on grounds that the result of drug abuse by these workers could well be 'higher prices, lower quality of goods and services, and decreased competitiveness of American business in world markets'" (Thompson, Riccucci & Ban, 1991:519). Prior to *Acton*, some federal courts rejected such plans that did not demonstrate a clear connection between the tests and a significant safety issue (*American Federation of Government Employees v. Sullivan*, 1992). Others have accepted the broader logic implied in *Von Raab* and accepted more generalized claims of the need to protect public safety and governmental integrity by testing those who come into close contact with drug traffic. For instance, one federal appellate court accepted the need to test county corrections officers on the grounds that great harm might come from drug-impaired correctional officers who come into regular contact with prisoners or who have opportunities to smuggle drugs to prisoners (*Taylor v. O'Grady*, 1989:1199). Of course, not all programs get challenged and, at least according to one recent study, 81 percent of the cities responding had drug testing programs that did not fit a clear safety rational (Fine, Reeves & Harney, 1996:33-34). The authors of this survey described these policies as not in compliance with Supreme Court guidelines, but given the vagaries of balancing and the *Acton* decision, this is far from obvious.

Beyond what courts might accept as constitutionally justified lies the equally important question of whether the tests work. On many issues, Americans tend to be rather pragmatic—if it works then we do not concern ourselves too much with the niceties of the constitutional debate. However, given the various and ambiguous ways that drug testing programs have been justified, it is not easy to determine the extent to which they work. In *Skinner*, the Court assumed that one benefit of the tests would be the effect they would have in deterring future drug use. Interestingly, much of the testing of populations like government employees or even student athletes have fairly consistently failed to turn up the number of positives that the pretesting rhetoric would have led one to suspect. In one study of federal employees, only 51 out of 12,427 tested positive in random tests, a positive rate of 0.4 percent (Thompson, Riccucci & Ban, 1991:520). While not all testing programs have such a low positive rate, the numbers in this study were not atypical. The National Collegiate Athletics Association (NCAA) has been testing college athletes since 1986 and less than one percent have tested positive (Crowley, 1995:98). Surely, testing certain populations can result in far more positives. For instance, a review of persons arrested in 23 major cities showed positive rates ranging from 50 to 80 percent (Maguire & Pastore, 1995:415); but the high rate of positives in such a selective population tells us virtually nothing about the effectiveness of drug testing within in a more typical setting.

The low rate of positives has been subjected to vastly different interpretations. To proponents of testing, the low rate of positive tests illustrates the success of the programs and their powerful deterrent effect. One high school principal, reflecting on the fact that in 10 years of testing his school had never had a positive result, states that "it is absolutely a deterrent" (*U.S.A. Today*, June 25, 1995). In a similar vein, a legal scholar commenting on the low numbers of athletes who tested positive claimed that "it does not require a great leap of logic to conclude that the reason there is little evidence of drug use is because of the regulatory efforts, not despite them" (Cochran, 1990:548-549). This view is typical of proponents of testing, but it suffers from the logical flaw of assuming what is needed to be proved—that there was extensive drug use before the testing started. Since we do not know how many used drugs before the tests, or would continue to use drugs in the absence of the tests, we really have no way of determining whether drug usage declined or how much of the alleged decline can be attributed to drug testing. Thus, one study of drug testing of federal employees concluded "no firm evidence exists concerning the deterrent effect of drug testing in the federal civilian workplace" (Thompson, Riccucci & Ban, 1991:520). Much the same can be said for the alleged positive benefits of drug testing on safety and productivity. Since we did not know what the relationship was before, those attributing such positive benefits to the use of drug testing are doing it more on faith than any meaningful empirical assessment (Husak, 1992:205).

So why the continued push for such programs? This chapter has argued that the reasons for the expansion of drug testing had little to do with real developments in the use of drugs. Rather, the rise of drug testing was a policy developed largely for symbolic reasons in response to a socially constructed problem. As Scheingold (1991) argued with respect to much public policy aimed at crime, such policies have more to do with reassuring the public that something is being done than in addressing real underlying problems. However, arguing that drug testing developed for symbolic reasons does not mean that such policies do not have real consequences. In particular, symbolic solutions to socially constructed problems help to "signify who are virtuous and useful and who are dangerous and inadequate, which actions will be rewarded and which penalized" (Edelman, 1988:12).

One important consequence of drug testing, with the help of the Supreme Court, has been to undermine long-held values regarding the importance of bodily privacy and the limitations of government in requiring that people reveal information about their bodies. To create wholesale exceptions to the basic principles of the Fourth Amendment by relying on generalized speculations of public need undermines values central to our concept of limited government. Historically, drug testing has been a tool used by the criminal justice system to monitor and control convicted law violators. Indeed, it is still used extensively in that regard. Only recently has the sanction been expanded into the civil realm to monitor and control employees and students. Even when not used as a criminal sanction, drug testing "threatens millions of Americans with the speedy, inexpensive infliction of a sanction—unemployment—that has far more sting than the criminal penalties usually imposed for casual drug use" (Gilliom, 1994:132). Justice William O. Douglas once warned about the "powerful hydraulic forces throughout our history that bear heavily on the Court to water down constitutional guarantees and give the police the upper hand," (*Terry v. Ohio*, 1968:39). Today, the courts along with presidents, school boards, and city councils seem compelled to water down constitutional guarantees to reassure the public that something is being done about the drug problem. Such policies, while probably not having much effect on actual social problems, vastly expand administrative control over the lives of American citizens. The long-term damage done to the principles embodied in the Fourth Amendment by the latest drug war seems a heavy price to pay for symbolic reassurance that something is being done about the nation's drug habit.

9

Globalizing the Problem: The United States and International Drug Control

Kevin F. Ryan
Norwich University

As the thesis of this book states, society "constructs" its own problems through a process of definition and redefinition (Best, 1987; Gusfield, 1963, 1981; Schneider, 1985; Spector & Kitsuse, 1987). On one level, this constructive process involves the selection of certain sets of circumstances and the treatment of them as problematic while other sets of circumstances are ignored. A large body of research explores the dimensions of this "picking out" process (see, e.g., Best, 1987, 1989; Conrad, 1975; Gusfield, 1981; Pfohl, 1977).

On another level, the constructive process means that a problem, such as the "drug problem," can take many forms and meanings, with each form and meaning implying a particular set of policy solutions. Seen as a medical problem, for example, as it primarily has been in England (Pearson, 1990; Rouse & Johnson, 1991), the drug problem involves persons who suffer from illnesses or from ill-advised, unsupervised self-medication. Once "medicalized" (Conrad, 1975; Conrad & Schneider, 1992), the problem becomes one best addressed by the medical and scientific communities, and calls are made for "control" (Gusfield, 1981) over the problem by medical professionals. The opportunity for a medicalization of the drug problem existed in the United States during the early years of the twentieth century, but was lost due to a combination of factors; including the rise of a federal law enforcement community eager to claim certain issues as their domain, and the concomitant desire of the medical profession to claim higher status and distance itself from drug users and other "undesirables" (Granfield & Ryan, 1996).

Instead of taking on a medical meaning, the drug problem in the United States has most commonly been understood in terms of the "prohibition model." This model starts from a belief that drug use is immoral, extremely harmful to both users and others, or in some other way deeply wrong. The proper role of government is thought to be the elimination of the cause of the harm and the source of the immorality. Hence, government policy should be designed to prohibit citizens from possessing, using, or trafficking drugs. The primary vehicle chosen for prohibition policies (though not the only logical possibility) has been the criminal law; making crimes out of possessing, using, and trafficking. Once criminalization has taken place, law enforcement agents are called in to police drug-related activities, and criminal court and corrections systems are expanded (or overloaded) to punish violators. Operating within the prohibition model, then, United States drug policy has been characterized by: (1) a belief that drug users and sellers are bad; (2) a criminalization of drug-related activities; and (3) a reliance on the mechanisms of the criminal justice system to solve the perceived "drug problem."

The processes of social problem construction usually take place on a local or national level, as is implied in the writings of Blumer (1971) and Spector and Kitsuse (1987). Nevertheless, at times the process of negotiation and renegotiation spills over, crossing the borders into other social orders, where it merges with similar processes. Social actors redefine the problem as a transnational or "global" problem requiring a global solution; they seek legitimation for the problem, mobilize action to address it, and form and implement official plans of action (Blumer, 1971) involving international and regional organizations, as well as treaties and other forms of cooperation.

As ambiguous as the notion of "the drug problem" has always been (Ryan, 1994), it has had, almost from its "emergence" in the late nineteenth century, a global dimension. American drug problem "entrepreneurs" (Becker, 1963) have regularly asserted that much of the problem lies outside our borders, in those other areas of the world (always less developed nations that have been viewed as "less civilized") where these "evil" substances are cultivated, manufactured, and shipped into the United States. For example, despite the existence of a northern European tradition of opium use, the use and importation of opium in nineteenth century America was traced to Chinese immigrants (Musto, 1973). These early attributions of the real evil to "foreigners" and foreign lands parallels the way in which drug use inside the United States was associated with fringe, deviant, and usually "foreign" groups—the Chinese with the opium problem, Mexicans with marijuana, Southern blacks with cocaine, Irish and Italian immigrants with alcohol (Bonnie & Whitebread, 1974; Himmelstein, 1983; Levine, 1984; Musto, 1973; Peele, 1989).

Having defined the problem as a global one, policymakers have sought international solutions to it by carrying it into the discussions of international bodies, seeking to convince other nations of the seriousness of the "global" drug problem, mobilizing international resources in the fight against drug use and drug traffic, and sponsoring and pushing through various action plans designed to address the problem. In particular, the United States has sought to extend its drug agenda outside its own borders in two complementary ways. First, it has broadened the sphere of law enforcement activity and authority by permitting domestic law enforcement agents to operate abroad and by enlisting the armed forces in domestic and foreign drug enforcement actions. Second, it has sought to tailor international law to fit the prohibition model, playing a leading role in drafting and gaining approval of international agreements that reflect United States policy interests and orientations. This chapter provides a brief overview of these two tactics.

LAW ENFORCEMENT OUTSIDE THE UNITED STATES

The United States has sought throughout this century, but especially during the 1980s, to extend the long arm of its domestic law across international borders, erasing to a great extent the boundary between domestic and foreign affairs (Gibney, 1990; Nadelmann, 1993). The aim has been to expand the scope of United States law to cover actions undertaken, and persons residing, in other nations or on the high seas. The increased range of domestic criminal jurisdiction has been justified by reference to the "fact" that most drugs come into the United States from other countries, coupled with a belief that once the suppply is shut off the problem will go away. But while "blaming the U.S. drug problem on external sources has historically been the politically popular thing to do . . ., foreign policies derived from that dubious position suggest that on occasion the United States has put the sovereignty of other nations at risk in order to avoid dealing with the vexing issue of domestic demand for drugs" (Walker, 1992:275).

The global extension of the United States law enforcement policy has taken several forms. One manifestation of this "globalizing" of domestic solutions involves what Walker (1992:274) has called a policy of "coercive bilateral diplomacy": the attempt to compel foreign nations to change their domestic drug policies to fit better with United States interests, policies, and priorities. For example, since the 1940s, Mexico has been the object of intense pressure to tailor its drug policies and drug enforcement activities to fit the aims of the United States government (Toro, 1992; Walker, 1989, 1992). In perhaps a more significant and serious attempt to bend foreign governments to the dictates of the United States drug policy, the Reagan and Bush administrations sought to dictate the response of the governments of Colombia, Bolivia, and Peru to the difficult national problems associated with coca growing and cocaine production and trafficking. Through a combination of threats and offers of military and economic assistance, the United States sought to force the Andean governments to crack down on domestic growers, manufacturers, and shippers, even in the face of significant domestic opposition (Lee, 1989; Malamud-Goti, 1992a, 1992b; McCoy & Block, 1992; Smith, 1992, 1996; Walker, 1992).

As might have been predicted, these efforts backfired. Attempts to crack down on drug producers and traffickers have subjected these countries and their people to unprecedented levels of violence, intimidation, and rights violations (Lee, 1989; McCoy & Block, 1992; Smith, 1992, 1996). Further, the increased stakes of the drug traffic have created innumerable and highly lucrative opportunities for corruption among poorly paid or greedy public officials (Andreas et al., 1991-1992; Nadelmann, 1988; Smith, 1996). The enlistment of the armed forces of these countries to fight the drug war internally has significantly increased the power and autonomy of already brutal and authoritarian military establishments (Andreas et al., 1991-1992; Malamud-Goti, 1992a, 1992b). In addition, the destruction of crops, laboratories, and other facilities further impoverished rural peoples who had come to rely on illicit income to make ends meet (Andreas et al., 1991-1992; Lee, 1989; Tarazona-Sevillano, 1990). One result of the combination of these factors has been the creation of fertile ground for revolutionary movements, destabilizing the governments the United States seeks to push around (Lee, 1989; Smith, 1992, 1996; Tarazona-Sevillano, 1990). Indeed, revolutionary groups, such as the Shining Path in Peru, have found themselves allied with drug traffickers, for both are resisting the government and both claim to be working in the interests of poor, rural populations (Andreas et al., 1991-1992; Malamud-Goti, 1992; Tarazona-Sevillano, 1990; Walker, 1992).[1] And in the end, the production of illicit drugs in the Andean countries actually increased (Andreas et al., 1991-1992; Reuter, 1992).

An extreme example of coercive diplomacy is provided by the enlistment of the United States military in fighting the drug war abroad. The most noteworthy military action undertaken in pursuit of domestic law enforcement goals was the invasion of Panama in 1989 (Gibney, 1990). With little or no international legal justification, United States troops invaded a sovereign nation in order to arrest Manuel Noriega for drug trafficking. Though other justifications were offered for the invasion—justifications drawn from generally recognized grounds for the use of force in international law—few observers failed to see through the smokescreen set up by the state department's official statement. To most it was clear that the primary motivation for the invasion was the desire to bring Noriega to justice in the United States (Gibney, 1990; Johns, 1992; Nanda, 1990).

The use of United States military forces has been facilitated by a reversal of a long-standing policy against the use of the armed forces for law enforcement purposes. The Posse Comitatus Act (1877) imposed a criminal penalty on the use of the armed forces for domestic or foreign law enforcement, and for a century constituted a significant barrier to military involvement in such activities. That Act was effectively amended by the Defense Authorization Acts of 1982 and 1988 which, while they did not directly change the language of the Posse Comitatus Act, did authorize use of United States military personnel and equipment for domestic drug enforcement and for a growing list of enforcement activities in other nations (Note, 1990).

The globalization of United States law enforcement policy has also entailed the abduction of fugitives from abroad to stand trial when an asylum nation refuses an extradition request. Such abductions are justified by the United States under the *Ker-Frisbie* Doctrine (*Frisbie v. Collins,* 1952; *Ker v. Illinois,* 1886) that states that courts are generally not interested in how a defendant was brought into their jurisdiction; an illegal arrest, regardless of how it is carried out, does not void a subsequent conviction. While previous administrations at least paid lip service to the idea that abducting people to bring them to court in the United States was an unsavory practice, the Bush administration reversed this tradition. A secret Department of Justice (DOJ) opinion dated June 21, 1989, argued that the president and the attorney general have inherent executive power to order, without the consent of a foreign government, an extraterritorial abduction of a fugitive in that nation (Isikoff, 1991; Note, 1991). While recognizing that such abductions violated international law, the DOJ seemed essentially untroubled. Arguing that the president has the authority to override customary international law, Assistant Attorney General Barr assured members of the Subcommittee on Civil and Constitutional Rights of the House Judiciary Committee that the administration would engage in such abductions "only in the most compelling circumstances" (Lowenfeld, 1990:486). Speaking to the same audience, the legal advisor of the state department, while recognizing the principle of territorial integrity, insisted that the principle "is not entitled to absolute deference," and claimed that nations have the right to defend themselves against the harms threatened by drug traffickers even if that defense means violating the territorial integrity of another nation (Lowenfeld, 1990:487). In effect, the courts have sanctioned the practice of abduction of drug defendants (Abramovsky, 1991). While recognizing that such actions "may be in violation of general international law principles," the U.S. Supreme Court held in *United States v. Alvarez-Machain* (1992) that "the power of a court to try a person for a crime is not impaired by the fact that he has been brought within the court's jurisdiction by reason of a 'forcible abduction.'"[2]

DEA agents have also conducted searches of the foreign dwellings of suspected foreign drug traffickers. Again, attesting to the success of domestic legitimation and mobilization efforts, the courts have winked at this practice, permitting the admission of evidence derived from such searches, and softening Fourth Amendment search and seizure restrictions with the implication that constitutional rights only apply to law enforcement activity conducted in the United States or involving United States nationals (Gibney, 1990). In the absence of "substantial connections" with the United States, foreign nationals do not have Fourth Amendment rights against unreasonable searches and seizures (*United States v. Verdugo-Urquidez*, 1990).

Finally, the United States Coast Guard has stopped, boarded (often covertly and at night), and searched numerous private vessels in international waters, and has seized many such vessels (French, 1991). The Maritime Drug Law Enforcement Act of 1988 provides statutory authority for this assertion of extraterritorial jurisdiction. Such actions, though highly questionable under both customary and conventional international law, have been held constitutional by United States courts (*United States v. Davis*, 1991). The United States seeks to justify its actions by reference to the so-called "protective" and "effects" principles (*Rivard v. United States*, 1967). Under the "protective" principle, a nation may prescribe laws against extraterritorial criminal behavior that threatens a nation's security. United States legal officials seem little troubled by the fact that this principle has not traditionally applied to standard criminal acts, but only to acts such as espionage, counterfeiting a state's official seal, falsification of official documents, violation of immigration laws, and perjury before consular officials (Restatement [Third] of Foreign Relations Law sec. 402, c f. [1987]). Under the "effects," principle jurisdiction is supported when criminal acts outside the nation's boundaries produce an effect within the nation. While drug trafficking fits this definition, there has traditionally been a strong presumption against the use of this principle when the acts are predominantly those of nationals of other states (Restatement [Third] of Foreign Relations Law sec. 403 [1987]). Nevertheless, United States courts have frequently relied upon these principles when asserting jurisdiction over foreign drug traffickers (Neumayr, 1988). Indeed, United States courts have stripped away most of the Fourth Amendment restrictions on boarding and searching vessels on the high seas (*United States v. Villamonte-Marquez*, 1983). Further, international law clearly requires that before boarding a foreign flag vessel, law enforcement agents must have the consent of the flag state (Restatement [Third] of Foreign Relations Law secs. 432, 433, reporters' note 4 [1987]). Both the 1982 Law of the Sea Convention and its predecessor, the 1958 Convention on the High Seas, specify that consent to board can only be given by treaty between the flag state and the state of the boarding party. The United States has ratified the 1958 Convention. While the United States has not signed the Law of the Sea Convention, citing disagreements over the seabed mining provisions, it has indicated that the LOS Convention generally reflects international customary law (Sohn, 1984). Despite the clear voice of international law, however, current Coast Guard practice permits the boarding of vessels after receiving consent over the telephone or radio (Innis, 1990).

THE GROWTH OF THE INTERNATIONAL DRUG CONTROL REGIME

Considerable scholarly attention has been devoted to these extensions of United States law enforcement activities outside the United States territory (Nadelmann, 1993; Note, 1990). Significantly less attention has been focused on the complementary attempts by the United States to tailor international law concerning drugs and drug trafficking to reflect and support a particular vision of the drug problem and of the proper ways to solve it.

Prior to the twentieth century, little international concern existed about drug abuse or trafficking. Indeed, Great Britain and Asian colonial powers derived a considerable portion of their imperial incomes from the drug trade (Donnelly, 1992). The opium wars of the mid-nineteenth century reflected, among other things, a belief on the part of Western imperial powers that the profits of the drug trade should be protected from national governments concerned about the effects of that trade on domestic populations (Adams, 1972).

By the beginning of the twentieth century, Western powers began to be concerned with the effects on their own populations of drug abuse. In response to these concerns and at the instigation of the United States, 13 states met in Shanghai in 1909 to discuss ways to regulate opium. The result of this meeting was the International Opium Convention, signed at The Hague in 1912. One aim of the convention was the gradual elimination of the Far Eastern opium trade, and an attempt was made to set up limitations on the manufacture, sale, and use of manufactured opium (especially morphine) and cocaine. Despite the refusal of certain key countries (e.g., Germany, a major manufacturer, and Turkey, a major producer) to accept it, the Convention set the terms of future international discussions of the "drug problem."

Subsequently, under the auspices of first the League of Nations and then of the United Nations, a series of multilateral conventions created a complex world system to supervise and regulate the production, control, and shipment of narcotic drugs for licit (i.e., medical and scientific) purposes, as well as to prohibit illicit trade in such substances. The League of Nations produced three conventions related to the drug traffic. The first, the 1925 International Opium Convention, provided for annual submission by each party of extensive statistical information on the production of and trade in opium and coca to a Permanent Central Opium Board. When a group of nations led by the United States sought to strengthen the provisions of the 1925 Convention, however, the limits of international consensus were quickly reached. The 1931 Convention for Limiting the Manufacture and Regulating the Distribution of Narcotic Drugs, an attempt to find some middle ground between those desirous of much tougher international drug control and those suspicious of such a policy, lacked broad support: numerous nations refused to sign, some (e.g., China and the United States) because the Convention was not strict enough, others (e.g.,

Turkey and Switzerland) because it was too strict (McAllister, 1991). The final drug treaty produced by the League, the 1936 Convention for the Suppression of the Illicit Traffic in Dangerous Drugs, came to nought when the onset of World War II made effective enforcement of international drug controls both difficult and less pressing to the nations of the world (McAllister, 1991).

The task of developing drug policy—under the United Nations—fell to the newly established Commission on Narcotic Drugs (CND). In general, the United Nations, under the CND, pursued the same supply side—regulatory policies sponsored by the League of Nations. But by the late 1950s, the United States and many of its allies had concluded that the system was too complex, too cumbersome, and too toothless to be an effective barrier to the use and distribution of "dangerous drugs." By 1960, six separate drug control treaties and two amending protocols were in force. Consequently, a new convention was proposed to consolidate and strengthen the international control regime. The Single Convention on Narcotic Drugs, as its name suggests, was designed to pull the provisions of existing treaties into a single document, as well as to strengthen the existing drug control regime by eliminating the array of agencies charged with oversight and replacing them with a single body, the International Narcotics Control Board (INCB). The Single Convention extended international control to include the cultivation of plants grown as the raw materials of natural narcotics drugs, thus putting cannabis and coca, as well as "narcotics" properly so-called, under a single set of rules and guidelines. Although Article 38 of the Convention called for efforts, including education and treatment, to prevent drug abuse, the placement of this provision near the end of a document focusing almost entirely on prohibition and control, suggests the lack of importance these measures had in the minds of the drafters. While the Convention received more support from member states than any previous or subsequent treaty, only slightly more than one-half of all member states (126 nations) ratified it. Almost immediately, critics attacked the Convention as too narrow and weak to cope with what was perceived to be a growing international drug menace.

As had been the case under the League of Nations, however, discord prevailed over the viability and justifiability of extensive international drug control. Subsequent to the Single Convention, a series of agreements expanded and sought to strengthen the international drug control regime. The 1971 Psychotropic Substances Convention, for example, enlarged the list of controlled substances to include 32 substances having hallucinogenic effects, including LSD, mescaline, and various stimulants and depressants, using a classification scheme remarkably like the four schedule approach of the Comprehensive Drug Abuse Prevention and Control Act of 1970 in the United States. But the growing reach of the international drug control regime seemed to disturb many members, and only 87 nations ratified the 1971 Convention.

The 1972 Geneva Protocol amended the Single Convention, strengthening its control provisions and recognizing a need for treatment and rehabilitation services for drug abusers as an alternative to imprisonment. Again, however, in the context of a document designed to bolster the criminal control apparatus of international drug law, the reference to treatment and rehabilitation sounds less like a legitimate alternative and more like an offhand remark, aimed perhaps at those nations who do not share the strong prohibitionist orientation of the United States. In fact, as had been the case with the 1971 Convention, the expanding control regime laid out in the Protocol prompted many nations to withdraw their support from the international drug control effort: only 94 nations had ratified the Protocol by 1989.

From the late 1970s to the mid-1980s, the United States and some of its allies reinvigorated international concern about drug trafficking; successfully constructing it as a major international problem (Nadelmann, 1990). To an extent, the increased concern about trafficking was due to the very success of the regulatory regime that had been emerging since the 1909 meeting in Shanghai, which had made diversion from licit international shipments extremely difficult, forcing trafficking for the purposes of illegal drug use into "patently illicit channels" (Donnelly, 1992:287). The 1981 International Drug Abuse Control Strategy, hailed as a "master plan" for increased international cooperation to fight the war on drugs (Stewart, 1990:390), reflected American interests in attacking drug-related problems through the mechanisms of criminal law. With the minor exception of a passing reference to treatment and rehabilitation, the Strategy was almost entirely focused upon criminal control of what was perceived as the heart of the international drug problem: supply of desired substances by traffickers based outside the countries of final destination.

In response to the Strategy, the United Nations Commission on Narcotic Drugs, consulting a bevy of American "experts" (including representatives of the United States Coast Guard), began work on a draft convention aimed at curtailing international drug traffic. The United States successfully pushed for a strong, prohibitionist convention obligating states to take affirmative steps toward the *elimination* of drug trafficking and writing current United States practice into international law. The final draft of the Convention, as adopted, "reflect[ed] most if not all of the Coast Guard's goals" (Innis, 1990:118).

In 1987, an International Conference on Drug Abuse and Illicit Trafficking convened in Vienna, charged by the General Assembly "to generate universal action to combat the drug problem in all its forms at the national, regional and international levels." The Conference developed a set of regulations and recommendations concerning drug abuse and trafficking titled the Comprehensive Multi-Disciplinary Outline of Future Activities in Drug Abuse Control (CMO). Designed as a font of ideas and recommendations rather than a formal legal instrument, the CMO indicated a shift in emphasis by the international community in regard to perceived drug problems. In particular, the document gave a much more significant place to treatment, rehabilitation, and other forms of demand reduction, giving these topics as much attention (and seemingly as much importance) as supply control and trafficking. In addition, previous calls for forced eradication of illicit drug crops were replaced by a recommendation for financial incentives for the production of legal crops. As Donnelly (1992:290) has put it, "the package as a whole represents a serious effort to see drug abuse as a complex and multifaceted problem that requires national and international attention focused not merely on production and trafficking but also on consumption and rehabilitation."

The new emphasis of the CMO, however, was to have limited influence on the 1988 United Nations Convention Against Illicit Traffic in Narcotic Drugs and Psychotropic Substances, which went into effect in 1990. Whereas the CMO agreements had given greater prominence to treatment and demand reduction, the Convention took up only the CMO recommendations concerning illicit trafficking. As befits a product of the late 1980s "war on drugs," the convention focused entirely on criminal control, emphasizing customs, extradition, law enforcement, and penalties. Essentially, the Convention urged other nations to adopt policies already being employed by the United States and Western European nations. The document elaborated specific law enforcement measures designed to enable states to identify, arrest, prosecute, and convict drug traffickers. Further, the Convention tightened the international control regime over chemicals, equipment, and other materials used in drug processing. It strongly encouraged party states to cooperate in suppressing illicit traffic by sea or through the mail, obliged states to monitor private transportation by commercial carriers to end the underground trafficking in drugs, and required states to suppress illicit trafficking in free trade zones and free ports. In addition, and again in line with United States policy goals, states must take strong action to prevent illicit cultivation of plants containing narcotic or psychotropic substances, to cooperate in crop eradication programs, and to take *forceful* action to reduce, if not eliminate, the demand for drugs.

By 1990, however, while 89 nations had entered into the agreement, only nine countries had ratified it. While nations appear willing to sign on to a general declaration of the evils of drug abuse, there is some question about the depth of the commitment of non-Western (and even some Western) nations to the growing international war on drugs (Bassiouni, 1990; Donnelly, 1992; Falco, 1996; Stares, 1996). It is also possible that even the commitment to general declarations is more coerced than voluntary, reflecting a need for foreign aid from the larger drug-consumer nations who do not hesitate to threaten severe cuts for failure to fight the drug war vigorously enough (witness the United States policy of "aid leveraging," linking continued aid to vigorous prosecution of the drug war [Note, 1990]).

In 1990, a special session of the United Nations General Assembly produced the Political Declaration and Global Programme of Action, which reaffirmed the directives set forth in the Single Convention and its successors, and gave top priority to international efforts to control drugs. In general, while the Programme used language that suggests a more complex understanding of the dimensions of the drug economy (for example, calling for "comprehensive and multidisciplinary" strategies and encouraging programs creating viable alternative means of income for those involved in illicit drug production), the primary focus was still law enforcement.

Those working within a view of the "drug problem" as a global problem, calling for international solutions, of course, seek to obtain international recognition of "their" problem as significant enough to rest at the top of the international agenda and thereby command extensive resources. Internationalists hailed the Programme as "an important 'consciousness-raising' exercise, a major effort to move drugs to a higher place on international agendas" (Donnelly, 1992:292). In opening the special session, the secretary-general insisted that "drug abuse is now right at the top of the list of priorities requiring urgent attention from the international community. . . . Very considerable additional funding will be required," both in the regular budget and in contributions to the United Nations Fund for Drug Abuse Control (United Nations, 1990a:9,13). This view was reiterated in the Commission on Narcotic Drugs' report to the special session. Interestingly, the nation most involved in the effort to create an understanding of drugs as a global problem calling for global solutions—the United States—indicated a lack of willingness to increase its contributions to the United Nations drug control effort (United Nations, 1990b:34).[3]

In response to new concerns over money laundering associated with drug trafficking, the United Nations International Drug Control Programme was established, combining several United Nations drug agencies and boards into a single agency, reducing duplication, and increasing coordination of United Nations efforts. In 1993, the United Nations General Assembly reaffirmed its previous drug-control efforts and adopted Resolution 48/112 that emphasized the necessity for international cooperation in the war on drug production and trafficking. The Resolution called upon the secretary-general to promote and monitor the United Nations Decade Against Drug Abuse, 1991-2000, under the theme "A global response to a global challenge."

THE UNITED STATES CONSTRUCTION OF INTERNATIONAL DRUG CONTROL POLICY

Several observations can be made from the study of the history of international drug regulation. One overarching theme of that history is the operation of the not-so-hidden hand of Western nations, and especially the United States —what Bruun, Pan, and Rexed (1975) have called the "gentlemen's club." A small number of nations, led by the United States and the United Kingdom, have been the driving force behind calls for additional legislation and have played a leading role in the drafting of conventions and protocols. These nations have been longer-standing members of, and have had more delegates on, the various international drug control agencies, boards, and bureaus than have other nations (Bruun, Pan & Rexed, 1975; Nadelmann, 1990). Further, the majority of the top staff members of the various international agencies and organizations set up to implement international drug policy have come from these same few nations (Bruun, Pan & Rexed, 1975).

The United States, in particular, has been a major force behind the creation of most of the control apparatus and has dominated that apparatus by providing many of the personnel and key figures (Bruun, Pan & Rexed, 1975), as well as by contributing huge amounts of money to the drug control regime, even while it has refused to make its required contributions to the United Nations (Donnelly, 1992). In the 1920s, the key players in international drug control agencies tended to be British or French diplomats or domestic officials. United States dominance of these agencies began in the 1930s when Herbert May became president of the Board and Harry Anslinger joined the Advisory Committee. Anslinger, the long-time commissioner of narcotics of the Federal Bureau of Narcotics, is generally acknowledged to have been the most important figure in the Commission for many years after World War II, and several of his close friends also played prominent roles (Bruun, Pan & Rexed, 1975).

The United States has, from the beginning, been a prime mover behind the design of international drug law. The United States has initiated the majority of international drug conferences, including those in Shanghai (1909) and The Hague (1912) that laid the foundations for the essentially "criminal" construction of the international drug problem that still guides international deliberations today. While the early goals of the United States were more economic than moral (Taylor, 1969), American policymakers were disturbed by a growing addict population in the United States, and saw the source of and solution to the problem as lying outside United States borders (Musto, 1973).

During the 1920s, while the United States continued to call for increased international control over narcotics in line with the regulations laid down by the Harrison Narcotics Act of 1914 and the interpretation of the Act by the courts (Granfield & Ryan, 1996; Musto, 1973; Taylor, 1969), leadership in international drug policy was forfeited due to the failure of the United States to join the League. Nevertheless, American dissatisfaction with the League prompted the United States to support the creation of the Permanent Opium Control Board, and, although the members of the Board were supposed to be independent experts unbeholden to their respective governments, the American chair, Herbert May, had close ties with the U.S. State Department and federal drug control authorities (Musto, 1973; Taylor, 1969). By the 1930s, the United States had regained its leadership role in international drug policy, despite its refusal, at the instigation of Harry Anslinger, to sign the 1936 Convention on illicit trafficking because it was too soft on traffickers and paid insufficient attention to marijuana. (Recall that Anslinger was, at that time, in the midst of a powerful anti-marijuana campaign that would result in the Marijuana Tax Act of 1937.)

Within the United Nations framework, the United States has continued to be the key player in international drug policymaking. Much of the structure of the Single Convention owes its existence to the desire to see American drug policies written into international law. The United States led the movement to amend that convention to "beef up" its control apparatus and to include psychotropic drugs within the control umbrella (Bruun, Pan & Rexed, 1975). Finally, it was the United States that lobbied hard for a recognition of the dangers of drug trafficking in the 1980s, and the "official plans" (Blumer, 1971) that emerged from international bodies to cope with trafficking strongly reflected American goals and tastes.

Indeed, throughout the century the United States has set many of the goals of the control regime and determined the appropriate means to achieve these goals. Several major goals of international drug control reflect strong United States influence. In the 1920s and 1930s, domestic drug policy focused primarily on the attempt to limit the production of narcotics and other drugs to medical and scientific needs (Musto, 1973). The same focus characterizes the League of Nations and early United Nations drug control policy. In an effort to facilitate attempts to control the supply of illicit narcotics in the United States, international law was developed to prohibit medically dispensable drugs and to prevent export of drugs to countries prohibiting their entry. Much of the momentum for international control of psychotropic drugs came from the "moral panic" (Ben-Yehuda, 1986; Cohen, 1980) in the United States in the mid- to late-60s (Stevens, 1987). Finally, the goal of eliminating drug trafficking, which has waxed and waned as the heart of international drug prohibition efforts, has from the beginning been a major plank of United States international drug policy; and its return to prominence in the 1980s paralleled a similar re-emphasis on trafficking in American domestic policy and drug control debates.

Most importantly, international drug policy has, since its origins, been shaped by the prohibition model, reflecting the preferred means of control of the United States. While some conventions and protocols contain reference to less punitive approaches (e.g., treatment and rehabilitation), these references have been confined to the margins, coming at the end of documents otherwise entirely devoted to various control techniques (much as references to treatment appear in United States domestic drug legislation). Though the CMO suggested a shift in international focus from criminalization toward rehabilitation, that shift simply had no impact on subsequent international legislation. In the most recent international agreement, the Drug Trafficking Convention of 1988, concern for the complex problems lying behind demand for drugs is simply submerged beneath a strong criminal approach to shutting off supply—the approach that has characterized international policy from its inception.

Of course, drug prohibition systems are never pure, primarily because of the recognition that most of the drugs people take for pleasure also have medical utility. As a result, the practical (as opposed to the rhetorical) object of prohibition systems has seldom been to eliminate these drugs completely, but to restrict their use to medical purposes. The international control regime has been no exception to this pattern. The aim of the system has been to find ways to produce some of these substances while at the same time strictly limiting their production and use. The result has been an indirect prohibition system in which each nation is encouraged to develop its own criminal control system, and in which international organizations supervise a regime of production quotas, estimates of the amount of drugs a given nation will need for a given year, and import-export certification. Nevertheless, the sort of control system encouraged by the international agreements has been at its heart one based primarily on the prohibition of non-medical use of drugs, and those who have criticized it have argued that its control measures are too weak to combat the "menace" of drugs.

Finally, the drugs included within the umbrella of international regulation generally reflect American prohibitionist attitudes and tend to mirror United States drug laws. The prohibition of heroin, cannabis, and LSD on the international level are all directly attributable to United States influence. Virtually no international agreements seek to control the production, use, or distribution of alcohol or tobacco, despite the strong scientific evidence that these drugs are at least as dangerous as, if not more dangerous than, some of the proscribed substances. The single exception is an agreement that focuses on alcohol control in Africa between the two world wars; efforts to extend this control to other regions have failed (Bruun, Pan & Rexed, 1975). The exclusion of alcohol and tobacco from drug control policy has been a defining feature of the American approach since the failure of alcohol prohibition. This same focus has been written into international law, providing a powerful example of the dominance of Western nations (who generally approve of the use of alcohol and tobacco) over Third World nations (who often strongly disapprove of these substances, particularly alcohol, while being indifferent to the use of cocaine, heroin, marijuana, and LSD) (Nadelmann, 1990). Further, the evaluation of dependence-producing drugs by experts, the standards used to evaluate them, the schedules into which controlled substances are placed, and the effects of such placement all mirror United States domestic legislation.

RECONSTRUCTING THE
INTERNATIONAL DRUG PROBLEM?

Critics of the prohibition model, as practiced both domestically and internationally, contend convincingly that it simply does not work. The United States has pursued a domestic drug policy built almost entirely around prohibition since the early years of this century, and yet there is every indication that drug problems have, if anything, gotten worse (Currie, 1993; Duke & Gross, 1993; Falco, 1996; Kleiman, 1992; Ryan, 1994). Further, prohibitionist policies have been extremely costly and have generated a stream of unintended negative consequences, including much of the violence now associated with drug distribution and the overwhelming of the criminal justice system with drug offenders (Belenko, 1990; Kleiman, 1992; Nadelmann, 1989; Ryan, 1994).

The prohibition approach has not had any great success in the international realm either. A well-known RAND Corporation study concluded that despite the United States government's very expensive attempt to close its borders to drugs, the problem only grew worse: despite massive seizures of drug shipments, the amount of drugs flowing into the country actually increased and the price of the drugs on the street went down (Reuter, Crawford & Cave, 1988). Further, the extension of prohibitionist law enforcement outside of United States borders has been seriously counterproductive, as other nations have come to look upon the United States as a "loose cannon" ready to violate or manipulate international law whenever the mood strikes (Nadelmann, 1988; Smith, 1996).[4] The level and extent of drug trafficking has undoubtedly increased since the passage of the 1961 Single Convention; indeed, a perception of this boom in the trafficking industry provided the major motivation for the 1988 Vienna Convention. While it is too early to tell whether that Convention will have any significant impact on drug trafficking, there is little reason to be hopeful: international efforts at drug control have, in general, been noticeably ineffective (Stares, 1996). Even those who once supported prohibitionist approaches of drugs in the international realm, have concluded that all previous efforts to control drugs have failed and the prospects for future effectiveness are remote (Bassiouni, 1990). Significantly, the lack of success exhibited by international prohibitionist policy has prompted the Clinton administration to adopt a drug strategy de-emphasizing international criminalization and placing new emphasis on domestic prevention and treatment programs (Perl, 1993-1994).

The growing perception that prohibition has failed has produced a call for new ways of understanding and coping with the drug problem—new constructions of the problem. In particular, much evidence suggests the growing appeal of regulatory policies rooted in the "harm reduction" or "public health" model (Bertram et al., 1996; Duke & Gross, 1993; Nadelmann, 1992). Proponents of this view see drug users as a heterogeneous group, ranging from persons (children, addicts) who become problem users to those who use occasionally in a controlled, nonharmful manner. Policy, then, should be designed to *reduce the harms* caused by the problem users and yet permit other, nonproblematic uses. Government, on this view, should pursue various forms of regulatory activities, ranging from taxes, to licensing users, to time-place-manner restrictions on use and sale (Kleiman, 1992; Nadelmann, 1992). Proponents of the harm reduction model seek to legitimate a new construction of the universally acknowledged "drug problem." In a few nations and localities (notably The Netherlands, Liverpool, Zurich, and Canberra), advocates of harm reduction have been successful not only in legitimating their view of the drug problem, but in writing harm reduction approaches into official policy (Fox, 1994; Fromberg, 1994; Leuw, 1991; Marks, 1994; Pearson, 1990). As this alternative construction gains legitimacy around the globe, we can expect that its proponents, appreciating the transnational dimensions of the problem, will seek to develop international action plans designed to minimize harms rather than punish and prohibit.

NOTES

[1]   Of course, these alliances are fragile, in part due to the fact that the great wealth of traffickers permits them to enter the socioeconomic establishment, giving them a stake in the status quo inconsistent with revolutionary goals (Smith, 1992; Tarazona-Sevillano, 1990).

[2]   Other examples are found in *United States v. Verdugo-Urquidez,* 856 F.2d 1214 (9th Cir. 1988), *rev'd* 110 S. Ct. 1056 (1990); *United States v. Zabaneh,* 837 F.2d 1249 (5th Cir. 1988); *United States v. Cordero,* 668 F.2d 32 (1st Cir. 1981); *Matta-Ballesteros v. Henman,* 697 F. Supp. 1040 (S.D. Ill. 1988), *aff'd,* 896 F.2d 255 (7th Cir.), *cert. denied,* 111 S. Ct. 209 (1990).

[3]   Donnelly (1992:292) points out that the total budget for United Nations drug control programs ($37 million) is not only small (compared to the size of the global drug market), but suggests that drug control does not rank any higher on the international agenda than do the functions of the Universal Postal Union, the World Intellectual Property Organization, and the International Maritime Organizations, whose budgets are roughly the same. Indeed, the United Nations financial crisis in the late 1980s, triggered in large part by the failure of the United States to keep up with its required contributions, led to a reduction in both the budgets and the staffs of United Nations-sponsored boards and agencies responsible for the international drug control system.

[4]   Of course, other actions by the United States have contributed to this image, not the least of which were the arming of the Contras, the mining of Nicaraguan waters and the subsequent refusal to accept the jurisdiction of the International Court of Justice, and the invasion of Grenada.

10

Prohibition as the Art of Political Diplomacy: The Benign Guises of the "War on Drugs" in Canada

Benedikt Fischer[1]
University of Toronto

THE ORIGINS OF PROHIBITION IN CANADA

The foundations of the Canadian prohibitionist approach to select psychoactive substances—in general the ones that today fall under the category of "illicit drugs"—were laid around the turn of the century (Cook, 1969; Solomon & Madison, 1977). During the period of expansive social and economic development of Canada's West in the latter part of the nineteenth century, many Asian, in particular Chinese, immigrants entered the country and constituted a substantial part of the country's cheap labor force (Comack, 1985; Giffen, Endicott & Lambert, 1991). By 1882, the proportion of Chinese in British Columbia's population had risen to about 20 percent (Giffen, Endicott & Lambert, 1991). This labor force, much of which was Chinese, was used on such projects as the Canadian Pacific Railway that moved toward completion quite quickly around 1885 (Comack 1986).

However, a number of critical social and economic developments caused growing anti-Chinese sentiments while the numbers of immigrants from Asia kept increasing. Because of the processes of full-scale industrialization and the completion of the Canadian Pacific Railway, the once rapidly expanding mining and construction work declined and Western Canada's economic growth stagnated, sharply decreasing the demand for industrial labor. Employment became increasingly scarce around 1900, but the available labor force kept growing. While large numbers of Asians kept arriving, the supply of Chinese labor peaked, resulting in a disadvantage for traditional Caucasian workers to compete for employment (Comack, 1986; Solomon & Madison, 1977).

The Caucasian population perceived that Asian immigrants were endangering the wealth of the Euro-centric segment of society. They were also concerned that their cultural and moral predominance and norms were becoming undermined through the increasingly diverse ethnic mix in the province, and that an "immoral" or lax lifestyle was spreading in British Columbia. Subsequently, a struggle for moral hegemony and reform started to emerge in Western Canada that was primarily aimed against Asian culture or forms of deviant behavior that were associated with Asian immigrants, mainly gambling, prostitution, and heavy drinking. Calls for "moral reform" against all forms of "cultural deviance" spread rapidly in social and political circles (Cook, 1969; Giffen, Endicott & Lambert, 1991). In the meantime, the Canadian government tried to restrict the growing influx of Asian immigrants by imposing an immigration tax. However, the immigration levy remained ineffective, and in the year 1900 alone more than 20,000 Asians entered the country (Cook, 1969; Giffen, Endicott & Lambert, 1991).

Finally, when the growing anti-Chinese campaign peaked in 1906, a number of severe riots erupted in Vancouver. These riots, protesting against Chinese immigration and businesses, involved thousands of demonstrators, and caused substantial material damage to business owners. In an effort to restore order, the federal government sent its deputy minister of labor, Lyon MacKenzie King, to British Columbia to find solutions for the contended issues of ethnic values, immigration, and labor economics (Cook, 1969; Comack, 1985).

Added to and becoming increasingly the focus of the growing list of putative Chinese "vices"—including gambling, prostitution, and leprosy—was opium smoking. Opium smoking had not been an issue in the province before, but the Christian churches, medical organizations, and the police with media support now increasingly asserted that it was a source of crime, deviance, and cultural degeneration. A few select moralist publications in the 1920s colorfully described the crime and disease potential of opium and cocaine, allegedly posing a substantial threat to civilized Caucasian norms (Carstairs, 1995; Murphy, 1922). On the international level, the United States and Canada were already part of negotiations for transnational control of the opium trade (Musto, 1973).

The federal government "discovered" the opium issue as a potential solution to the socio-economic and immigration problems in Western Canada. As the political conclusion to his British Columbia investigation, MacKenzie King thus quickly proposed prohibitionary legislation outlawing the opium trade in Canada (Fischer, 1995a; Giffen, Endicott & Lambert, 1991; Solomon & Green, 1988). He assumed that this move would be effective in keeping new Chinese businesses, merchants, and especially immigrants out of the country, that it would make professional and social lives less comfortable for Asian residents in Canada, and that the law would also appease the moral crusaders by aiming against Chinese habits and culture. The prohibition statute was a very short, quickly drafted and swiftly passed piece of legislation—the 1908 "Opium Act"—that was to become Canada's first drug law. It was only a few lines long, generally prohibiting the importation, manufacture, and sale of opium (Cook, 1969).

In the following years, the much more complex 1923 "Opium and Narcotic Drugs Act" was enshrined. This act significantly expanded the scope of offenses prohibiting opium supply to include punishment provisions as well as enforcement powers. Since 1911, the drug law included in its prohibitive scope the possession of cocaine, after a cocaine scare was launched in Montreal newspapers. The new 1923 statute also criminalized the possession of opium for personal use as well as mere presence in an opium den, thus laying the foundation for drug-user criminalization in Canada (Giffen, Endicott & Lambert, 1991; Solomon & Green, 1988). The act widened the enforcement powers of the police; they were granted drastically extended rights to seize, confiscate, and destroy drugs. In addition, the general "presumption of innocence" was reversed with drug defendants and now laid the "onus of proof" on the accused. Finally, a newly created offense of drug "possession for the purpose of trafficking" resulted in aggravated punishments. Interestingly, in terms of its socio-economic context, its original aim against Chinese immigrants and opium as well as the historical timing, the launch of opium prohibition in Canada reflects many of the themes of the origins of drug prohibition in the United States (Fischer, 1995a; Musto, 1973). However, an anti-Chinese and anti-opium crusade in the United States had materialized already starting in the 1870s, and almost a dozen Western American states had opium laws in place by 1890 (Helmer, 1975; Morgan, 1978). While there is only limited evidence that the Canadian version of the anti-opium crusade was directly influenced by the American models, it can rather be argued that the socio-economic conditions—domestic economic and labor pressure, moral and cultural conflict, and racial hostility—were quite similar in the Western United States and Western Canada, and that the political leadership in both jurisdictions "discovered" opium prohibition as the most promising instrument of intervention and control to deal with all these challenges at the same time.

DEVELOPMENTS AND CHALLENGES DURING MID-CENTURY

Between the 1920s and 1940s, a coordinated central prohibition apparatus was established in Canada that expanded the scope and rigor of the legal campaign against scheduled drugs. Police made increasingly more use of the drug laws. Convictions under the anti-drug statutes had quadrupled by 1922. The enforcement focus, however, quickly shifted from Chinese to other groups, and Asians basically disappeared from the lists of drug offenders by the mid-1930s (Giffen, Endicott & Lambert, 1991).

Around 1925, the Royal Canadian Mounted Police (RCMP) assumed the primary jurisdiction of drug enforcement. This mandate was hailed as an opportunity of institutional survival, and taken on with the full vigor of a nationwide organized, paramilitary institution (Fischer, 1994a). The RCMP increased the scope of enforcement, and effectively cooperated with local and provincial police forces. The enforcement apparatus—which was later coordinated by the "Division of Narcotic Control" (DNC) under its crusading leader Colonel Sharman—requested significant enhancements to the prohibition system that were granted quickly by the bureaucracy; the need for search warrants for drug raids was eliminated, and specialized drug offense prosecutors were hired. Mandatory imprisonment, minimum sentences (including "whipping"), and the deportation of foreigners were introduced widening the severity and scope of enforcement (Solomon & Green, 1988; Solomon & Madison, 1977).

In 1923, cannabis and codeine had silently been added to the schedule of the new "Opium and Narcotic Drug Act", despite the fact that both substances had not been particularly prevalent until then (Cook, 1969). In particular, the inclusion of cannabis into the new 1923 drug law raises fundamental questions with regard to the American influence on Canadian drug law-making. The campaign against marijuana in the United States started around 1914 on local levels in a number of southern and southwestern states, and was largely directed against Mexican minorities (Himmelstein, 1983; Musto, 1973). Marijuana was increasingly portrayed in the media as a major cause of and factor in crime, a great danger to health, as well as a source of fundamental moral decay. However, despite pressure from local enforcement and others from the mid-1920s onward, the Federal Bureau of Narcotics did not see any need for federal marijuana control legislation until the early 1930s, when the foundations were laid for the Marijuana Tax Act subsequently passed in 1937 (and thus much later than the Canadian cannabis law; see Bonnie & Whitebread, 1974; Musto, 1973). Most likely, the surprising inclusion of cannabis—which had not appeared as a social problem until then—into the Canadian law in 1923 has to be understood through the mounting American influence, although conclusive research on the issue is lacking. It is quite possible that Canadian prohibitionists and law-making reformers were looking to the United States in order to see how their neighbors were expanding prohibition. Influential in this expanding American prohibition campaign was Murphy's *The Black Candle* (1922), which described cannabis as an excessively dangerous and villainous substance—then constituting the only available hard evidence for law-makers.

A significant extent of the evolution of prohibitionary schemes, especially in regard to the expansion of the Canadian enforcement apparatus and its powers, has to be explained through the parallels between the American Federal

Bureau of Narcotics and the Canadian Division of Narcotic Control. Both of their respective long-time heads, Harry Anslinger and C.H.L. Sharman, embodied and pushed for zealous prohibition and moral reform from the 1920s to the 1940s, strategically expanding the mandate and resources of their respective agencies. It is suggested that the organization of the Canadian DNC as the strategic center of the prohibition bureaucracy and enforcement after the model of the American FBN was "no coincidence," and the two crusaders not only shared fundamental political interests but also had personal admiration for each other (Giffen, Endicott & Lambert, 1991). Cooperation between the two agencies was extremely close; collaboration occurred on a daily level with regard to information exchange or cross-border enforcement, and on the level of international drug control, Canada and the United States basically presented a united camp supporting an identical agenda of widened international drug control in the first part of the century. Through the sophisticated information network and exchange between the two national prohibition apparatuses, each side was constantly updated with regard to which enforcement priorities were set, which substances were to be newly included in enforcement activities, and which legal devices improved the efficiency of their anti-drug campaigns. This flow of information often influenced potential requests or strategies for enforcement reform on either side of the border (Griffen, Endicott & Lambert, 1991).

From 1930 on, opium offenses in Canada had basically disappeared from drug convictions, and enforcement started to focus on the growing population of opiate users, many of whom were addicted and considered ill, demonic, and dangerous individuals. One-half of all drug law convictions between 1945 and 1960 were for heroin possession (Giffen, Endicott & Lambert, 1991). In the 1950s, an emerging "treatment movement"—mostly progressive groups of physicians, psychologists, and social reformers—argued that drug use and addiction were a medical problem and should be dealt with by treatment and medical rehabilitation instead of law enforcement (Fischer, 1995a; Solomon & Madison, 1977). A number of official commissions recommended an increased emphasis on substitution and treatment programs for drug users. The spirit of "medicalization" instead of the "criminalization" of drug addiction was partly carried over into the drafting of a new drug law in the late 1950s, the proposed Narcotic Control Act (NCA). Besides the traditional repressive provisions against drug use and supply, the statute proposed that punishment for addicts could be substituted by indefinite "compulsory treatment" within a correctional facility until deemed "clean" (Fischer, 1995a; Solomon & Madison, 1977). However, this "compulsory medicalization" section of the proposed NCA was never proclaimed, and "treatment" did not become established as an alternative to criminal punishment. Instead, the NCA provided for the prohibition of opiates, cocaine, and cannabis under maximum imprisonment penalties: namely, for personal possession (seven years); and for supply offenses, like selling, trafficking, producing, and importing (life imprisonment).

When the use of cannabis substances became popular during the rise of the 1960s "counter-culture," drug enforcement quickly identified a new "target-substance" that would dominate Canadian drug control practices and debates until the present (Fischer, 1995b; Giffen, Endicott & Lambert, 1991). The number of cannabis possession offenses sharply rose from 43 in 1965 to 5,400 in 1970. The late 1970s, on average, produced 50,000 drug offenses annually; up to 90 percent of these offenses were for cannabis offenders (Bryan, 1979; Fischer, 1995a). Drug law enforcement in the United States during that time indicated a similar development.

The emerging phenomenon of young, well-educated individuals, often from middle-class or wealthy families, being criminally convicted (and often jailed) as "cannabis criminals" triggered a major socio-ideological controversy about the criminalization of drug users, also fueled by the media (Erickson, 1980). Prohibition, with its harsh and punitive effects on drug users including a criminal record, was now debated as an issue of "social harm" and an inappropriate form of social control especially for young drug-using citizens. The appellate courts tended to confirm harsh sentences (Erickson, 1980; Giffen, Endicott & Lambert, 1991), and prosecutors in the late 1960s called for prison sentences even for first-time cannabis offenders in order to emphasize deterrence principles. When a Gallup poll in 1967 indicated that Canadians favored less repressive cannabis control, the political leadership looked for a strategy to defuse the social tensions around cannabis-user criminalization (Gallup Institute, 1985). Thus, the government in 1969 installed the "LeDain Commission," an independent inquiry body to review the scope and effects of Canadian drug policy and law (Solomon & Green, 1988).

Believing that the criminal law was not the appropriate instrument to deal with drug use or even addiction (Commission of Inquiry into the Non-Medical Use of Drugs 1972 and 1973), the Commission strongly recommended that cannabis be taken out of the scope of prohibition through the criminal law, and urged that all drug possession for personal use be decriminalized and a maximum fine be imposed. The context leading to the inquiry, as well as the Commission's recommendation, presented striking similarities to the United States "National Commission on Marijuana and Drug Abuse" established by President Nixon, which in 1972 presented conclusions and recommendations very similar to the Le Dain Commission's "Cannabis report" that had been issued in the same year (Fischer, 1995b; Himmelstein, 1983).

The Le Dain Commission's rather radical recommendations opened a chapter of a long series of failed attempts of Canadian drug law and policy reform (Fischer, 1995b; Giffen & Lambert, 1988). Instead of politically reacting to the Le Dain Commission's recommendations, the government shifted the onus for policy reform to the courts, emphasizing their discretionary power to discharge offenders. The courts did not pick up on the suggested jurisprudential reform since discharges never accounted for more than ten percent of sentences imposed for cannabis possession in the mid-1970s. Convictions for cannabis possession offenses tripled to almost 30,000 between 1972 and 1974 (Bryan, 1979).

In 1974, the liberal government introduced a marijuana bill that proposed to decriminalize first-time cannabis possession to a ticketing offense with a $100 fine. The bill was passed in the Senate, but later dropped in Parliament. In the late 1970s, the Conservative opposition, the Liberal party convention, as well as the Canadian Bar Association passed resolutions calling for cannabis decriminalization, while government officials in 1979 suggested easing the severity of punishment on marijuana offenders. But in 1981, Canada set a world record in drug criminalization with 260 drug offenses per 100,000 capita (Erickson, 1992). Three years later, the rhetoric of Canadian drug policy was adjusted to its reality: both the Conservative Justice Minister as well as the Solicitor General declared that the law would not be eased, and that prohibition was there to stay.

THE LAST DECADE: RHETORIC OF REFORM, PRACTICES OF PROHIBITIONISM

After a decade of silence and "prohibition as usual" business, the Canadian drug policy arena came to a sudden wake-up in 1986 (Erickson & Fischer, 1997). The wheels were set in motion by a surprising announcement by then-Conservative Prime Minister Brian Mulroney, who singlehandedly declared that Canada was "confronted with a drug epidemic," and that serious measures had to be taken to fight the current menace of drugs (Erickson, 1992). The announcement, coincidentally, came two days after U.S. President Ronald Reagan had renewed the American War on Drugs (Fischer, 1994b). At the time, user rates for cannabis, the most prevalent Canadian illicit drug, had been decreasing for more than five years as indicated in all major surveys. Compared to the United States, Canada had continuously maintained its low level of cocaine and heroin use in the years prior (Fischer, 1994a; Jensen & Gerber, 1993).

However, the Mulroney announcement of a response to the Canadian "drug epidemic" was probably triggered by two main political factors. First, it is to be assumed that the United States had exercised political power toward support of their war on drugs campaign, since Canada had often been perceived as being too "liberal" on drug issues, and that much of the illicit American drug markets were allegedly supplied through Canada. Domestically, the Canadian Tory government was confronted with a devastating slump in popularity moving toward an election year, and was desperately looking for opportunities to prove leadership on issues of broad consensus with potential voters (Jensen & Gerber, 1993). As Jensen and Gerber (1993) have further shown, the timing and scope of the new Canadian drug campaign was certainly very much influenced by the massive American drug war, although it would be difficult to argue that the Canadian "Drug Strategy" was a well thought-out copy or strategic modification of American prohibition efforts. Rather, the drug issue seemed politically convenient and beneficial to the Canadian government for a much publicized but rather inconsistent policy campaign especially in light of the American moves, and also offered the immediate benefit of sending a sign to Washington that Ottawa took determined action against the "drug menace."

When the government tabled its outline for a new drug policy program following Mulroney's announcement, many policy analysts believed Canada would finally shift toward a "public health approach" to psychoactive substances, allowing social and medical measures priority over criminal repression, and thus eventually acting on the basic recommendations that the Le Dain Commission had put forward (Erickson, 1991; Single et al., 1991). "Canada's Drug Strategy" (CDS), as the policy program was titled, proposed a focus on "harm reduction," and thus acknowledged a new and rather controversial approach urging for pragmatic, public health, effectiveness- and humanism-oriented measures that were being sharply rejected (for example as being a disguised rhetoric for "legalization") especially among traditional ideological circles in the United States (Fischer, 1994a; Government of Canada, 1991). The CDS suggested converting Canadian drug control into a "balanced approach between supply and demand reduction," and thus alluded to the intention of a "separation of markets" with respect to the policy and control instruments used in distinguishing between drug users and suppliers (Fischer, 1994a; Government of Canada, 1991).

In terms of its operational scope, the CDS featured a policy program fund of $210 million years over the first five years (1987-1992). Because 70 percent of the program funds were spent on "demand reduction" initiatives, while the remainder was devoted to "traditional" supply reduction or enforcement initiatives, the government underlined its claims about the progressive programmatics of its "new" drug policy. Most importantly, the government also proclaimed that a new drug control statute would be drafted to constitute the "legal backbone" of this comprehensive policy initiative (Fischer, 1994b; Government of Canada 1991).

Single's subsequent analysis of the CDS, however, revealed that the policy program was more an arbitrarily assembled, incoherent, and primarily "public relations"-oriented campaign, rather than an effective "demand reduction"-based policy initiative. Initial criticism of the "drug policy program" pointed out that the initial version had disregarded alcohol and tobacco. Officials never delivered a clear-cut definition of what goals and principles the Strategy operationalized with its "harm reduction" rhetoric (a rather ambiguous exercise, since certainly none of the previous approaches had attempted to "increase harm" from their perspective) that led to substantial internal criticism of the policy program at the time (Fischer, 1994a).

The CDS spent a substantial amount of its "demand reduction funds" in so-called "community action" and education programs that were never properly evaluated in terms of input or outcome. The remaining part of the education fund was invested in a few dozen "drug educator" positions with the main drug enforcement authority, the RCMP, and thus actually flowed back to the enforcement sector. Finally, of almost $100 million allocated to expand the availability of drug treatment facilities in Canada through a cost-sharing program, less than 50 percent were actually picked up and invested by the provincial health administrations. In other words, more than $50 million of federal funds ready for increased drug treatment services as part of the emphasized "demand reduction" component of the CDS never made it to the target audience. The CDS program offered a politically progressive budget on paper, but the ideological scope and practical balances of political reality as determined by institutional enforcement budgets and resources spent on legal repression remained unnamed and unaltered following the CDS launch (Fischer, 1994a). Erickson asserts that in the early 1990s, the overall Canadian drug enforcement budget, including all criminal justice levels involved, was estimated at $1 billion per annum (Giffen, Endicott & Lambert, 1991). The annual budget of the RCMP's drug enforcement division almost equalled the size of the CDS' overall funding. Coincidentally, the patterns of declining drug use observed in select Canadian populations came to a standstill around 1992 (Adlaf, Ivis & Smart, 1994; Adlaf et al., 1995). If Brian Mulroney had seen a "drug epidemic" in 1986, his policy initiatives had certainly not accomplished much in terms of reducing it.

The critical test for the will of Canadian law-makers for drug policy reform toward the 1990s lay with the challenge of a new drug law. The then-existing Canadian drug law, the NCA, and its use by the justice authorities had traditionally set the tone of punitive drug-user criminalization in Canada. The number of drug offenses processed by the authorities during the CDS period fluctuated at a level of 50,000-60,000 annually; it thus, in international comparison, remained on a very high level per capita (CCSA, 1995b; Moreau, 1995; RCMP, 1993). The number of criminal charges for drug offenses significantly increased, indicating an even tougher line by the prosecution authorities (Fischer, 1994b). Within this continuing broad-scale drug enforcement approach, the Canadian criminal justice sector hardly implemented a "separation of markets" in regard to its operational focus: The share of drug *use* offenses (just featuring "possession for personal use" offenses, only allowing minimal amounts of the respective drug) remained at a level of two-thirds of all drug offenses until the mid-1990s. Equally important, enforcement efforts were aimed at cannabis offenders in approximately 65 percent of all drug offenses, reinforcing the fact that Canadian "drug war" was actually a contemporary version of "cannabis prohibition." While the government had communicated the message of a more health- and harm-oriented version of drug policy for the 1990s, the share of "cannabis possession" in all drug offenses remained at more than 50 percent, confirming marijuana and hashish smokers as the main target of Canadian drug repression activities (ARF, 1995; Fischer, Erickson & Smart, 1996). From 1987 to 1991, the share of inmates in Canadian prisons who were incarcerated for drug offenses rose from nine to 14 percent (Erickson, 1992).

The Attempts for New Drug Legislation

The use of the existing Canadian drug law had obviously not indicated an ideology or justice practice shift since the late 1980s, and thus stood in sharp contract to the progressive policy principles forwarded by the government. In this context, the new drug law promised as the CDS' "legal backbone" thus increasingly assumed the pivotal responsibility for possible reform in Canadian drug policy if this was to occur (Fischer, 1997). However, when the federal Minister of Health in 1992 tabled the government's new drug law proposal to replace the NCA, this latest resort of hope for reform was massively shattered. The proposal of Bill C-85, the "Psychoactive Substances Control Act" (PSCA), initiated a lengthy sequel of political attempts to establish a modernized prohibition statute in the Canadian criminal law.

The PSCA's general legal scope, offense and punishment provisions proposed a broad, and in parts even harshening, consolidation of the punitive and repressive patterns of the NCA. The bill's draft confirmed the punitive criminalization of drug use through severe punishment provisions for possession offenses with maximum penalties of seven years of imprisonment. It created a new offense aimed against potential drug buyers by criminalizing the act of "seeking or obtaining" a drug, even in cases when no "real" substances (but only ploys) were involved. The bill had not responded to any of the calls for a revision of Canadian drug law according to generally accepted standards of rational pharmacology, generally attempting to order psychoactive substances corresponding to their pharmacological nature and established harm potentials (ARF, 1995; Fischer, 1997). Thus, in terms of drug scheduling, the bill continued the traditional saga of all "vicious, bad and harmful" drugs (primarily heroin, cocaine, and cannabis) being lumped together in the most punitive schedule of the statute. The bill widened the "search and seizure" powers of the police, it criminalized the possession of "drug containers" (thus potentially threatening the legality of needle exchange programs), and it even increased the punitiveness for some offenses from previously harsh levels (ARF, 1995; Fischer, 1997). In addition to the maintenance of the repressive scope of the bill, the law was "poorly drafted, unnecessarily complex and difficult to understand" (Usprich & Solomon, 1993:240).

The initial response from the public health, drug policy research, and reform advocacy sector was dominated by astonishment and disagreement with the bill, and for a while it looked as if the government had decided to pull back the bill. However, in the summer of 1993, the government seemed determined to push the bill through the House and thus turn it into law before the upcoming election. In the evolving parliamentary hearings on the proposed Bill C-85, the government further confused lobbyists and analysts at the same time, since it sent out ambiguous messages about the intended scope and function of the proposed law, especially in the context of the CDS policy. It was a representative of the federal Department of Justice who stated in the official hearings on the bill that "there was quite an extensive consultation process" by the institutions involved in Canada's Drug Strategy, in which "the bill was included and the intent and . . . overall principles were discussed." However, according to the official, the bill was supposedly not designed as a "fundamental reassessment of Canada's drug laws," but its purpose was to "primarily consolidate existing legislation. It was not to review, reassess or undertake substantial reform" (Fischer, 1997). Government officials themselves questioned the claim of the rhetorical policy reform principles that had accompanied the CDS, which had argued that a new legislation would form the "legal backbone" of the policy initiative.

The predominant disregard of the proclaimed CDS philosophy was also expressed in the fact that the parliamentary hearing process on C-85 did not include the "Canadian Centre on Substance Abuse" (CCSA) (Fischer, 1994a). This arm's-length institution had just been created by the federal government with an explicit drug use "research and policy" department as a CDS initiative, but was not even consulted by its creators when drafting the new drug law. Though not officially asked, the CCSA sharply criticized the proposed law for its fundamental disharmony with the principles stated in the CDS. Its officials saw that the law perpetuated "the illogicality of previous legislation" providing "neither a modernization nor an enhancement of existing policy." It was stated that a "harm reduction" law would instead "aim at reducing the harmful consequences of illegal drug use," and that with the proposal for a new drug law "a complete review of Canada's drug policy was expected" (Fischer, 1997).

It was primarily the Liberal members of the parliamentary subcommittee who constituted the main political opposition to the proposed law, claiming that the law did not take into consideration any of the principles offered by the CDS, that it would ignore basic principles of "public health" but not do anything to "get people off drugs," and that is was an attempt to increase the approach of repression and deterrence as opposed to health and care for drug users (Fischer, 1997).

The hearings however, in particular on the side of governmental Members of Parliament (MPs) primarily challenged with the defense of their administration's proposed law, revealed that the politicians were predominantly in the dark about the repressive scope of drug law enforcement, and that they had naively accepted the hollow rhetoric of progressiveness claimed by the CDS. These debates were indicative of the generally popular, yet inaccurate, perception that drug laws in Canada were applied largely against traffickers, smug-glers, and dealers, and that they were not directed against "the problem with the drug user" (Fischer, 1997).

The MPs rather, ignored the central role of the criminal drug statute in determining the repressive nature of Canadian drug control acting primarily against users of cannabis, cocaine, and opiates. Instead, they saw no necessity in altering the proposed law since all the necessary "demand reduction" measures of education, public awareness, and rehabilitation seemed to be taken care of "through our national drug strategy. . . . This bill does not change our philoso-phy toward drug policy. If, indeed, we need more public awareness or . . . coun-selling for people who tend to have a health problem . . . that's different. I agree there are lots of people out there, but we can do that through another vehicle" (Fischer, 1997). This paradoxical perception of the separation of crim-inal law and social measures in policy reality was reinforced by another MP arguing that there was a possibility of "alternate forms of sentencing and deal-ing with the user and the educational role . . . and to reduce the demand side. But that's not what this bill is all about. That's another aspect of drug strategy" (Fischer, 1997).

Interestingly, it was the police (represented by the Canadian Police Asso-ciation) in the C-85 hearings who realistically assessed the relationship between drug law enforcement and the social and health principles of the CDS. Determined by the scope and use of the existing repressive law by enforce-ment, the police stated that the set of CDS principles "ends at the court room door." In order to reduce the "enormous costs" of the prosecution of cannabis possession offenders, the police went so far as to resuscitate the idea of the ticketing offense system for first-time cannabis offenders (Canadian Police Association, 1993). This proposed scheme of a civil offense through a federal law would keep cannabis possession offenders out of the criminal courts sys-tem, and also make it possible to avoid the consequence of a criminal record with offenders if fined. The police, furthermore, argued for a more rational scheduling scheme of the drugs governed by the proposed law, and argued for a more commensurate distinction within the proposed offense categories in regard to what quantities of drugs were involved.

Besides a number of professional interest groups (largely medical and pharmaceutical organizations) who were marginally affected by the provisions of the bill but did not oppose it in principle, it was largely left to the witnesses of the Addiction Research Foundation to speak out against the scope of the bill and its dissonance with basic principles of health and welfare (ARF, 1993). The ARF rejected the PSCA as not being "in keeping with Canada's Drug Strategy," and it suggested that the bill contradicted the "harm reduction" approach suggested in the CDS by actually imposing more harms and costs on drug users and the social body than it would reduce. The confusion about the proposed bill's role in the framework of Canadian drug policy in conjunction with substantial opposition and media attention on the "tough pot law" did not remain without effect in the law-making process. Because of the unexpectedly prolonged hearing process, Bill C-85 died on the order table when the Conservative government was voted out of office in the fall of 1993.

The fact that the Liberal party was being voted into government office in 1993, and that its members had been highly critical of the "resurgence of prohibition" (Erickson, 1992) approach which the Conservatives had been staging in prior years, evoked substantial hope that the new political era would produce a new and more reform-oriented drug law. The renewed surprise effect was thus substantial when just a few months after being elected into office, the Liberals basically reintroduced the PSCA under the new name of Bill C-7 (Controlled Drugs and Substances Act) (Boyd, 1994; Minister of Health, 1994).

"Liberal" Government—Liberal Drug Law?

Bill C-7 was a virtual carbon copy of C-85 (and thus also almost identical to the NCA) with a few minor modifications concerning penalties for large amounts of cannabis trafficking. It is unclear to this date which circumstances or bureaucratic forces actually pushed the bill forward after the 1993 election, except for the fact that the new Liberal government presented a politically weak Minister of Health, and the previous Liberal (opposition) critics of C-85 seemed to have become silenced on the issue.

The following parliamentary hearings presented not much more than variations on the themes introduced before when the PSCA was discussed extensively. Primarily, the government was trying to present the bill as a "house-keeping exercise," and it was staged as a legal modernization project that did not have anything to do with the overall scope or direction of public response to illicit drugs in general or within the framework of the CDS. The parliamentary secretary to the Minister of Health thus argued in defending C-7 in 1994 that this "bill is not a policy bill. It's really tidying up some of the loose ends we've had hanging around. [But] this is not a policy bill, so it shouldn't be confused with policy" (Fischer, 1997).

Another issue introduced by the government into the debate on the bill was related to Canada's obligations under the international drug control treaties. Though it was never outlined in detail what segment of the international agreements would require a completely new Canadian drug law, the government defended its proposed statute by suggesting that Canada had been attacked by the International Narcotics Control Board (INCB)—the "watchdog institution" for the international drug conventions largely driven by and enforced by the American prohibition agenda globally—for not complying with its national drug control obligations. In fact, a recent INCB report had scolded Canada for not having included benzodiazepines in its prohibition scheme (INCB, 1994). However, neither this minor issue nor the relatively limited power of the international drug control authorities seemed to necessitate such a fundamental modernization of Canada's drug law in order to "satisfy the obligations" from the treaties (Fischer, 1997).

The government's paradoxical approach to the matter of drug law modernization seemed to peak when Department of Health officials suggested that, after all the proposed amendments for modernization and housekeeping had been established as a "sort of omnibus bill," Bill C-7 (Fischer, 1997), the government would propose to go back to the drawing board and design a "substantive policy bill" that would then consider the emerging issues of drug policy reform (Fischer, 1997). The suggestion of first modernizing the prohibitionary law, and then retroactively aiming for fundamental reform, sounded as contradictory as it seemed unlikely to happen, especially since Canadian politics had expressed a strong aversion to drug law revisions. The last major revisions to the existing NCA, made more than three decades earlier, have since withstood numerous substantial reform challenges.

The lion's share of partisan opposition to Bill C-7 which now carried a Liberal flag was featured by the Bloc Quebecois, then the new opposition in the House who, in particular, questioned the perceived effectiveness and appropriateness of the proposed legislation. The response to Bill C-7 from non-governmental interest and expert groups in the new round of parliamentary hearings proved even more substance than that of its disliked predecessor, Bill C-85. A number of public health research and policy institutions, as well as legal associations, strictly opposed the proposed law, while the CCSA—this time part of the hearing process—argued for substantial revisions of the bill in regard to scheduling as well as lowering the criminal status of the cannabis possession offense. Again, the exchanges in the hearings indicated that government authorities were starkly at odds with their proclaimed drug policy principles as well as the reality of drug enforcement in the Canadian context. The committee chair's hard-line statements sent the message out that any form of marijuana control reform—i.e., the reduction of the criminal severity of cannabis use control, for example, by eliminating the criminal record or reducing the level of penalties—was not a political option (see Fischer, 1997).

When asked if marijuana had come to be treated as "more of a social problem than the justice concern it was in the past," a high-ranking health official denied the question in referring to the predominant enforcement focus on marijuana. This statement, as well as the scope of enforcement itself, was, however, bluntly contradicted by the government's justice officials. They attempted to create the impression—commensurate to what the symbolic and progressive rhetoric of the CDS had suggested—that drug enforcement in Canada had shifted its focus, since the country's "drug enforcement agencies are faced with priorities and trying to deal with the real criminal element, not with those charged with simple possession. [T]heir real thrust is toward the criminal element that is trafficking. . ." (Fischer, 1997). In 1994, the year this statement was made, Canadian police agencies enforced about 55,000 drug offenses—approximately two-thirds of which were for simple possession (Erickson & Fischer, 1997; Moreau, 1995).

The substantial resistance to Bill C-7 from external reform advocacy groups that materialized in the parliamentary hearing process during 1994/1995 forced the government into another lengthy phase of silence in regard to the pending statute. After the bill had not been touched by the committee for a few months in early 1995—a year after it had been introduced to Parliament—some policy analysts started speculating that it might have silently been dropped by the political bureaucracy. This rumor was nurtured by the apparent decisive split of the Liberal government caucus regarding the drug control scope and ideology featured in Bill C-7. These substantial concerns had culminated in an internal Liberal opposition paper to Bill C-7 that was circulated in the summer of 1995 during a critical time for the Liberal government with respect to "crime and justice" issues when it also had to deal with controversial young offenders and gun control legislation. One of the internal Liberal critics openly raised some of the issues of discontent around the law apparently shared by several Liberals. They fundamentally criticized that C-7 did not offer any "rehabilitation or treatment" (diversion) options "as an alternative" to criminal sanctions for drug offenders; that it featured pharmacologically "outdated drug schedules;" that it confirmed the "maximum prison terms" and legal status of cannabis possession offenses "in contrast to current court practices and evolved societal attitudes;" and that it generally did not attend to principles of "harm reduction" based policy (Barnes, 1995).

Coincidentally, a few months earlier in the beginning of 1995, an official governmental report of British Columbia's Chief Coroner, a former RCMP officer, investigating a dramatic provincial increase in heroin-related overdose deaths had made radical policy recommendations. It called on policymakers to assume a "harm reduction" approach to illicit substances by largely expanded methadone programs, needle exchanges, and even looking into the possibility of heroin substitution programs. On a legal side, it called on the lawmakers to "seriously inquire into the merits of legalizing the possession of some . . . drugs, such as marijuana" (Cain, 1994:91), and thus attracted substantial media attention.

The socio-political context in which Bill C-7 was bred toward the end of 1995 features an instructive example of political strategizing on the side of the federal government. The media during that period had devoted substantial attention to the apparent continuation of the "tough on drugs" stance by the Liberal government with a particular focus on the continued repression of cannabis users. In the meantime, American and Canadian student surveys suggested that the use of marijuana among high-school youth—according to the traditional prevalence indicators—had significantly increased since the late 1980s (Adlaf et al., 1995). In the context of the political confusion around an upcoming referendum on Quebec sovereignty, the government finally presented its revised version of Bill C-7 as amended by the parliamentary subcommittee.

The amendments to the revised bill were being offered by the government as critical and determined "reforms" responding to the substantial criticism launched against the bill in the parliamentary hearings (CCSA, 1995a; Hansard, 1995). The parliamentary secretary to the Minister of Health even went as far as to claim that the revised bill now "enshrined an attitude of tolerance, compassion and concern for the drug addicted person" who would now be given "the chance to rebuild and renew their lives on a healthy, law-abiding basis." The law was thus described as reflecting "a more liberal policy with regard to harm reduction, rehabilitation and societal aspects of drug use" while a few moments later, it was emphasized that "this is not a health bill," and "penalties have not been reduced" (Hansard, 1995). However, closer analysis proved that the law had not been altered in its central scope, but that all featured changes were of minor and only symbolic significance with no real effect on the punitive, drug user-oriented scope of broad repression (ARF, 1995; Fischer, Erickson & Smart, 1996). The revisions featured a form of "symbolic cannabis possession reform" that provided that first-time cannabis possession offenders under defined maximum amounts would only be charged by summary conviction, and thus not be fingerprinted for the central Canadian police data files. (In the previous legislation, the prosecution had a *theoretical* choice to proceed by indictment even against cannabis possession offenders.) Government MPs and bureaucrats, however, were quick to interpret these provisions along the lines that they had eliminated the criminal record and its negative consequences for cannabis possession offenders. This reading was simply incorrect but quickly picked up by the media wondering if the government was "going soft on pot" (ARF, 1995; Fischer, Erickson & Smart, 1996).

What the government had done in the legal text was simply to adjust the legal stipulations and punishment provisions for cannabis possession somewhat closer to existing criminal justice practices (Fischer, Erickson & Smart, 1996). No Canadian criminal court would hand down a sentence anywhere close to a six-month prison term—the suggested maximum sentence—for first-time cannabis possession. The proposed amendments, however, rather than suggesting any form of "decriminalization," maintained the legal status quo for the possession offense.

The Liberal chair of the health subcommittee, which had amended C-7, argued in his speech in the House that there had not been any reason to "decriminalize marijuana" since "no evidence was presented to us on the attitudes of Canadians" in respect to cannabis policy (Hansard, 1995). Coincidentally, public opinion data released from a Health Canada survey around the same time stated that almost 70 percent of the Canadian population favored either penalties of no more than a fine or complete decriminalization of cannabis possession as opposed to criminal prohibition (Health Canada, 1995). The suggested amendments also featured a vague general clause suggesting that "rehabilitation and treatment" for drug offenders was "encouraged in appropriate circumstances" (CCSA 1995a; House of Commons, 1995). The law, however, did not provide any specific guidelines or diversion provisions especially for drug use-related offenses (ARF, 1995; Fischer, Erickson & Smart, 1996). Arguing that the law had been comprehensively revised, and offering the paradoxical political promise that some form of governmental or independent committee would implement a fundamental review of Canadian drug policy—after the new version of criminal drug law had been anchored as the crucial policy instrument—the government reintroduced Bill C-7 for a third reading on October 30, 1995 (Hansard, 1995). It was passed the same day, coincidentally, the day of the crucial Quebec referendum that held Canadian public and politics in awe in light of the prospect of a possible break-up of the nation, with all members of the Bloc Quebecois, the only real opponents of bill C-7, being absent from the House of Commons. The bill was thus passed in silence, with a single but rather weak voice of resistance from a member of the New Democratic Party (Hansard, 1995). The ultimate paradoxical nature of Bill C-7's real features, the progressive principles of the CDS, and the way the government attempted to argue that these two contradictory concepts had been successfully merged was probably most aptly expressed by the Liberal MP who proudly claimed that the new law "will put Canada in the forefront . . . of leading the War on Drugs from a perspective of harm reduction" (Hansard, 1995).

Since the Canadian political system requires the approval of the Senate, the Bill was moved to the Senate Committee on Legal and Constitutional Affairs after its successful passage through the House. The Senate Committee experienced a reiteration of opposition to Bill C-7 by external witnesses who had testified previously on both Bill C-85 and C-7. The Committee seemed to be rather open and receptive to the criticisms raised in regard to issues of irrational drug scheduling, extensive criminalization of drug users, safety and violence issues, as well as the lack of cost-effectiveness inherent in the bill's expected practical use. It even formally requested concrete input from drug policy stakeholders on how to amend and improve the bill so that it would meet standards of public health and more cost-effective social policy. The subsequent submission by the Canadian Foundation for Drug Policy suggested a revision of the bill that would explicitly exempt drug users in possession of substances of small amounts for personal consumption from criminal punishment, and thus suggested to introduce a system of "partial prohibition" into the new Canadian drug law (CFDP, 1996). But once again, the political roller coaster temporarily stopped the bill shortly before the finish line. In February 1996, the Liberal Prime Minister prorogued Canadian Parliament, with the effect of Bill C-7 pending in the Senate Committee dying on the order table.

The bill was resuscitated, however, when in early March, the identical statute (now under the name of Bill C-8) as passed in the House in October 1995, was reintroduced and moved through Parliament in just one day. It was subsequently resubmitted to the Senate's Committee for Legal and Constitutional Affairs where it had been stopped about two months prior.

CONCLUSION

Although it has been a long and rocky way for policymakers and bureaucrats behind the attempt of establishing a new and modernized prohibition law for Canadian drug control, and some minor amendments might emerge out of the Senate hearings, it is more than likely that Canada will have its modernized prohibition law in the near future. Bill C-8, its emerging use and practice in the criminal justice system, will by and large defy central principles of public health, rational pharmacology, and a cost-effective response to issues of drug use, drug markets, and related social and health problems (ARF, 1995; Fischer, Erickson & Smart, 1996; Hansard, 1995). It will also completely ignore the drug policy lessons that other national jurisdictions such as Australia, Switzerland, the Netherlands, and Germany have learned in regard to the efficacy and negative spillover effects of legal repression on public health, safety and cost effectiveness of public policy within the last decade or so (Erickson & Butters, this volume; McDonald et al., 1995; Nadelmann et al., 1994).

It has to be speculated that the reasons for the unsuccessful efforts of law reform lay partly in the omnipresent and powerful ghost of American prohibition ideology, although a great momentum for and an organized interest in public health-oriented drug policy change in the country exists. Though many Canadian politicians, and even increasingly more law enforcement representatives, criticize current prohibition practices, it is to be expected that a major and formal move away from criminal drug use repression would have to be launched against enormous American pressure and sanctions that might far exceed the area of drug control, a rather grim prospect for Canada, a country so unilaterally dependent on the United States in socio-economic terms. The abolishment of the principles of repressive drug control including the drug *user* (as it has occurred in many European systems; see Erickson & Butters, this volume; McDonald et al., 1995; Nadelmann et al., 1994) would mean a significant erosion of traditional prohibition ideology on the North American continent, and uncomfortably fuel the many and widespread "harm reduction" movements and opposition groups to the American War on Drugs being waged in full force. It is instructive in this context to compare the history of unsuccessful Canadian drug control reform to that of Australia, which has seen a gradual shift in thinking toward a drug control rationale of "public health" and "harm reduction," but importantly having actually managed to incorporate these concepts into substantial law and policy reform measures (Erickson & Butters, this volume; McDonald et al., 1995; Nadelmann et al., 1994). It has been argued that the main reason for this fundamental difference between Canadian and Australian drug policy reality is to be found in the distance between their respective capitals and Washington, DC (Fischer, 1996).

From that perspective, Canada with its proposed new drug law is continuing an anthology of the repression of a category of "evil" and "harmful" drugs, whose mythological foundations had been successfully constructed in the early part of the century. The current Canadian developments in regard to drug policy also bear witness to the fact that the political governance of psychoactive substances has often more to do with institutional interest, bureaucratic inertia, and political scapegoating especially in socially, economically, and politically unstable times (Giffen, Endicott & Lambert, 1991). It thus seems that, unless criminal justice frontline agents such as enforcement officers, prosecutors, and judges who transform the central drug policy instruments into day-to-day practice will significantly alter their approach and rationales, the politics of drug and drug user prohibition are to stay for a while in Canada. Moreover, it is a rather disillusioning and probably adequate assessment to believe that a reasonable, public health-focused reform of the public control approach to drugs in Canada has to wait until the powerful United States neighbor has laid down its arms in the war on drugs.

Postscript

In June 1996, the Canadian Senate passed Bill C-8 without any significant changes. In April 1997, the bill was officially proclaimed, and is currently the drug law of the land.

NOTE

[1]   The author would like to thank Pat Erickson and Kim Varma for insightful and helpful comments on earlier drafts of this chapter.

11

The Emerging Harm Reduction Movement: The De-Escalation of the War on Drugs?[1]

Patricia G. Erickson
Addiction Research Foundation

Jennifer Butters
University of Toronto

INTRODUCTION: THE "SUCCESS" OF PROHIBITION

As a social policy directed at reducing the harms of drugs, prohibition is a failure. As an ideology, it must be regarded as one of the great success stories of the twentieth century.

Starting early in this century, many nations have adopted the ideology and corresponding laws of prohibition. This global movement was marked by several international treaties, culminating in the Single Convention on Narcotic Drugs (1961). Its hallmarks are the denial of any legally sanctioned supply of the drug commodity to the general public, enforced by severe criminal sanctions. Any form of self-directed use is unacceptable.

The expansion and maintenance of the prohibitionist stance to illicit drugs depended on a number of features captured in the phrase "the dope fiend mythology" (Giffen, Endicott & Lambert, 1991; Lindesmith, 1965). These include the equating of "addictive" with enslavement and the loss of free will; a preoccupation with the dangerous behavioral consequences of use, i.e., violence, crime, and sexual perversion, *not* the health of the user; the belief that users are morally reprehensible, *bad* people who will infect others; and the conviction that the threat to society justifies a severe and total repression of all expressions of use and availability.

Much legal scholarship has concentrated on the evolution of narcotic drug laws in a number of countries and the creation of an official, state-supported global prohibition regime (e.g., Ben-Yehuda, 1990; Flynn, 1993; Musto, 1973; Scheerer, 1978). We argue that a new focus of study is emerging and will dominate academic and policy discussions for this decade into the next millennium. The new focus is the *de-escalation* of prohibition.

Study in this area of law and society considers two major questions. First, how is it that countries have manifestly different drug control laws, policies, and practices, while simultaneously embracing the United Nations drug prohibition treaties? The ferocity of the U.S. drug war is matched in no other western democracy, although it resonates with the execution of drug traffickers in nations like Singapore, Malaysia, and China. Clearly the expression of prohibition has taken many forms. Second, why are significant movements toward public health regulation and control developing in some countries (e.g., Australia, the Netherlands, and Germany), while others (e.g., the United States of America, Canada, and Sweden) continue to assert allegiance to aggressive enforcement and severe penalties? Experience with prohibition appears to be conditioning different responses in utilization of the criminal justice system as the major instrument of the social control of drugs.

The experience of prohibition, however, has been relatively unsuccessful in preventing drug use and availability, and the reliance on the criminalization of drug users has come at significant costs to society at many levels. The function of the criminal law is one of deterrence through threat and application of criminal sanctions. There is a body of research, however, that indicates neither general nor specific deterrence operate with their intended consequences. Canadian and American studies of drug users find: low levels of perceived certainty of arrest or police detection; perceptions of minor sanctions if detected (fines or probation); and little evidence that threats or experience of legal sanctions contribute to reduction or cessation in drug use (Erickson, 1989; Erickson & Murray, 1986, 1989; Erickson, Watson & Weber, 1992; Waldorf, Reinarman & Murphy, 1991)

FROM PRISONS TO PUBLIC HEALTH: THE GLOBAL SHIFT TO HARM REDUCTION

While criminal approaches to illicit drug use have predominated, recent shifts toward health centered approaches have also occurred. These changes, however, have been at a different pace and emphasis in countries around the world. These various changes have resulted in a variety of programs and policies captured under the rubric of "harm reduction" (Erickson et al., 1997). Before proceeding with a discussion of specific programs and policies, we shall clarify what harm reduction is, then look at specific examples, and finally consider the prerequisites for and barriers to harm reduction.

Most definitions refer to harm reduction simply as the minimization or reduction of adverse consequences of drug use. However, as pointed out by Single (1995:288), virtually "any drug policy or program is directed toward decreasing health, social, and economic adverse consequences." Consequently, programs ranging from 12-step abstinence oriented programs, needle exchange, and even the criminalization of illicit drug users have all been labeled as harm reduction initiatives. A clear delineation between any and all drug programs and harm reduction is required if this concept is to be meaningful. Harm reduction programs and policies are unique in their design to reduce harmful consequences of drug use *while the user continues to use*. Therefore, the distinguishing feature of harm reduction is the emphasis on the reduction of adverse consequences rather than the elimination of drug use. This allows consideration of the consequences of the policy as well as the drug use behavior.

Harm reduction has been regarded as both a strategy and a goal. This duality contributes, in part, to the confusion and ambiguity surrounding the term. Therefore, to provide some conceptual clarification of harm reduction we propose that harm reduction should be conceived as a *framework*:

> Harm reduction is a *framework* from which policy and program strategies are conceptualized, developed, and implemented with the outcome goal being the reduction or minimization of harm (without requiring user abstinence or less consumption).

Harm reduction is embedded in a public health tradition and aligned with public health approaches. In 1847, Liverpool, England was the first city in the world to appoint a medical officer of health (Dr. W.H. Duncan) and has subsequently been regarded as the "cradle of harm reduction" (Ashton & Seymour, 1988).

The public health movement has passed through four phases that have in turn shaped the harm reduction movement. In Liverpool, the initial public health movement emphasized *environmental* change specifically addressing housing conditions. This phase gave way to a more *individualistic* approach with the introduction of immunization and vaccination in 1870. Following this, in the 1930s, the *therapeutic era* introduced a hospital based approach shifting power and resources away from the public health department. Finally, the emerging health care crisis, escalating medical costs, and the realization that many premature deaths and disability could be prevented ushered in the fourth phase of the public health movement: *The New Public Health*. This approach, recognizing the diversity and complexities of health issues, brings together notions of environmental change, personal preventive measures, and appropriate therapeutic interventions. The environment is social, psychological, and physical. Because harm reduction is rooted in the public health tradition, it too is multidimensional in nature.

There are five principles of harm reduction: pragmatism; humanistic values; focus on harms, not prevalence; balancing of costs and benefits; and a hierarchy of goals (for elaboration, see Riley, in press). These principles together form the basis from which goals are established and outcome measures are designed and implemented.

A schematic representation of the Harm Reduction Framework is presented in Figure 11.1. The overarching goal of harm reduction is to decrease adverse consequences of drug use without requiring decreased drug use (Riley, 1993). The notion of adverse consequences, however, needs to be further specified. As illustrated in Figure 11.1, the adverse consequences associated with drug use are threefold: health, social, and economic. Therefore, the specific goals of harm reduction are as follows: (1) to decrease the adverse *health* consequences of drug use, (2) to decrease the adverse *social* consequences of drug use, and (3) to decrease the adverse *economic* consequences of drug use.

As illustrated in the principles of harm reduction, the scope of this framework moves beyond looking at the individual. Harm reduction is designed to minimize the harmful consequences not only to individuals, but to their family, the community, and society. Harm reduction does not *require* a specific legal control regime (Erickson, 1995); it has often been defined as a policy or program. What we have illustrated here is that policy and programs emerge *from* a harm reduction framework. Each outcome strategy will have its own set of goals and targets; however, they are designed under the overarching harm reduction framework.

There are two sets of outcomes: policy and programs. Each may be independently designed and implemented. For example, there are certain policies that stand alone such as legislation directed towards advertising, legal drinking age, and drunk driving. However, it is also the case that the implementation of certain programs may require preceding policy changes. As shall be illustrated in examples described below, law enforcement plays an integral role in the implementation and success of harm reduction strategies. A central function of the police and the judicial system is to provide safety and security to citizens following the "letter of the law." To provide a user with a clean needle, to take an addict to a methadone bus, or to permit drug use in a "tolerance zone" often stands in direct opposition with the policy, guidelines, and standards the police and other law enforcement agents are expected to uphold. As such, if the message of harm reduction is to be transformed into practice, specific legal changes may be required that will provide the police and prosecutors with more discretion with respect to tolerance and *non-enforcement*. Therefore,

Figure 11.1
Harm Reduction Framework

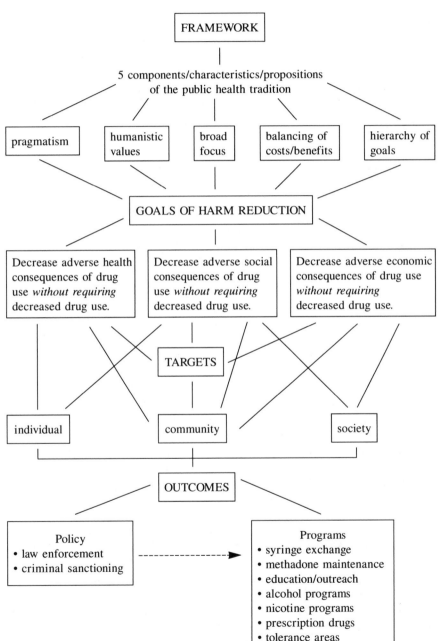

aggressive criminalization policies with punishment as their objective run counter to the aim of the harm reduction approach. Instead, laws should be used as instruments to achieve health outcomes that reduce risk to individual, family, community, and society.

Although the United States remains aggressively resistant to harm reduction initiatives (Dupont, 1996), other countries have been examining harm reduction options (Heather et al., 1993). Indeed, efforts have been made in several countries to move toward more progressive drug policies and programs. Examples of the gradual move to less punitive regulatory approaches in some countries or parts of some countries will now be presented. These focus on two areas: *injection drug user initiatives* and *police practices in law enforcement.*

Needle and Syringe Exchange

Many different harm reduction programs have been established around the world. The type of programs that most typify the harm reduction strategy are needle and syringe exchange programs. As a result of increasing awareness as to the enormous health risks associated with needle sharing by injection drug users, syringe exchange programs were established in the mid-1980s in European countries and are now operating in cities around the world, such as Amsterdam (since 1984) and Toronto (since 1987). Indeed, in Canada there are now more than 100 established needle exchange programs.

The provision of clean needles is a simple and inexpensive way to reduce the risk of HIV transmission. Following a key harm reduction tenet, the rationale behind these programs is that the injection drug user may be unable or unwilling to stop using; therefore, intervention is necessary to reduce the risk of personal HIV exposure and subsequent transmission to others. Moreover, cities like Amsterdam and Rotterdam have implemented needle exchange programs in collaboration with the police department where police stations will provide clean syringes on an exchange basis.

There is clear evidence that these types of programs have been successful in reducing risky behaviors and harm, and ongoing evaluation will highlight the long-term impact these programs have on the reduction of HIV transmission. In Montreal, Canada, the percentage of individuals sharing needles declined from 37 to 26 percent in a six month time period following implementation, and the percentage of individuals reporting that they clean their "works" with bleach rose from 83 to 93 percent (Riley, in press). While bleach is not a totally effective method of eliminating HIV, bleach kits help to reduce the likelihood of transmitting infection through needle sharing. Moreover, there is clear evidence regarding what happens when needles are in short supply or illegal. The most recent approximate figures for HIV infection among injection drug users are 60 percent in New York City, 52 percent in Geneva, 51 percent in Edinburgh, and 40 percent in Bangkok (Binder, 1994).

Methadone Maintenance

Taken orally in the form of a syrup, methadone is a synthetic opiate containing the properties of heroin and morphine. Methadone maintenance programs were established in the United States in the 1960s following the work of Drs. Vincent Dole and Marie Nyswander. It was found that methadone, could relieve the metabolic disorder created by heroin and with large enough dosages; the physical craving for heroin could be blocked making the addict immune to the euphoric effects (Rosenbaum, 1997). As such, replacing heroin with methadone allowed the individual to become a productive member of society. Thus, the initial form of drug harm reduction in the United States was methadone maintenance.

While methadone maintenance programs represent a promising step in the harm reduction armamentarium, many of these United States programs are criticized for their failure to provide the full range and flexibility of services necessary for success. Moreover, in recent years, several of the methadone clinics have been torn down displacing users either back onto the streets or to the already overcrowded, remaining clinics.

Different countries around the world have also implemented methadone programs. In the United Kingdom, other parts of Europe, and Australia, methadone is available from clinics as well as general practitioners who provide counseling and health care information. In fact, in several European cities more than 25 percent of general practitioners prescribe methadone (Riley, in press). By providing methadone without too many restrictions, larger segments of the heroin-using population can be reached. In places like Amsterdam, Frankfurt, and Barcelona, methadone is distributed via methadone buses or mobile clinics. These types of programs are referred to as "low threshold programs" and have been successful at contacting users, stabilizing their use, and detoxifying and treating users.

The success of methadone programs has also been documented in a number of ways (Drucker, 1995). For example, studies indicate a reduction in the number of offenses between the year prior to admission in the program and the most recent year in the program (Bertschy, 1995), and a reduction in the risk of arrest leading to conviction with increasing duration of methadone treatment (Chapelhorn & Bell, 1991). In addition to reductions in criminality, Ball and Ross (1991) illustrate a reduction in high risk injection behavior and a lowered risk of HIV acquisition. While 36 percent of their sample shared needles before program participation, only nine percent continued to do so (and at lower frequencies).

Methadone is the most highly regulated drug in the United States—more so than cocaine, morphine, amphetamines, and other more toxic prescription drugs (Nadelmann & McNeely, 1996). While these regulations have been effective in establishing guidelines and minimum standard levels, they have also impeded the effective delivery of programs. Many methadone programs are characterized by strict supervision and tight control: urine tests are required regardless of the client's duration in the program, patients are required to come to the clinic weekly, and in most cases, even if working a steady job, daily medication and prescriptions cannot be filled at a pharmacy (even if traveling).

Alternative "low threshold" programs have been introduced in European countries, Australia, and Asia with demonstrated effectiveness. Programs such as methadone buses operating in the United States (e.g., Baltimore, Maryland and Springfield, Massachusetts) are still following a traditional full service model. Moreover, although low threshold "interim clinics" that provide methadone without extensive supplementary services have been approved by federal regulators, many have been forced to close and none have opened anywhere in the United States (Nadelmann & McNeely, 1996). Indeed, there has been no expansion of methadone maintenance programs since roughly 1982, the beginning of the AIDS epidemic (Drucker, 1995).

If the goal of harm reduction is to reduce the harm associated with drug use, then a broader range of programs is required. Heroin addicts are not a homogeneous group and diverse programs are necessary if we are to capture and help as many users as possible. Existing methadone programs provide a base from which to work; however, layers need to be added to these programs addressing the complexities associated with drug use.

Reviving Heroin Prescription

This section will describe an innovative revival of heroin prescription. Recently, Switzerland has implemented a harm reduction program that involves prescribing and administering (on-site) either heroin, methadone, or cocaine (depending on need) to registered users. In 1989, statistics from the Federal Department of Health indicated that there were approximately 17,000 regular heroin users and 16,000 regular cocaine users in Switzerland. These numbers should be seen as rough estimates generated from official figures of *chronic users* who have come to the attention of the police and other authorities. Consequently, these numbers may be an underestimation of the prevalence of regular users. Nonetheless, the extent of regular opiate use in Switzerland is quite significant.

As of 1992, Switzerland had not only the highest prevalence of drug use and AIDS in Europe, but also the highest drinking and suicide rates (Klingemann, 1993). To make Swiss drug policy more effective, in February of 1992 the Swiss government passed new legislation. Specifically, the goal was to reduce drug-related harm and the number of users by 20 percent within five years. As such, discussion surrounding the implementation of medically supervised heroin prescription programs intensified. The larger and more problem-ridden cities such as Bern and Zurich were in favor of these projects from an early stage. Although opposition to these projects existed, in May of 1992, the government authorized the pilot prescription programs with a small number of chronic drug users to be conducted and evaluated until 1996. The provision for

these projects included voluntary participation of users who had to be a minimum of 20 years of age; they were to attend at least one consultation a week
with a counselor, and one a month with the physician in charge of the project.
At first, morphine—not heroin—was to be prescribed to a small number of
people (250). Later, the pilot projects were extended to include up to 700 drug
users, and in 1993 heroin prescriptions were subsequently allowed. To date, the
early evaluations show preliminary success on a number of different indicators
including lower unemployment and homelessness among users and lower rates
of crime (Ladewig, 1996).

In recognition that some harms stem from drug law enforcement, efforts
have been made toward developing harm reduction policy initiatives focused
on police practices.

The Netherlands and the Police

It is widely, and incorrectly, assumed that places such as Amsterdam have
legalized "soft drugs" such as cannabis—i.e. allowing legal sale to the public.
This, however, is not the policy. The Dutch Opium Act (1976) *prohibits* the
use, possession, or supply of so-called "soft" (cannabis) and "hard" (e.g., heroin, cocaine) drugs. However, the authorities have chosen to place less importance on small scale use and focus their attention on the drug trade
surrounding cocaine and heroin (Hellawell, 1995). In fact, penalties for trafficking in hard drugs have been increased (Donnelly, Hall & Christie, 1995).

The Dutch drug policy is pragmatic and guided by cost-benefit principles.
It rejects the notion that the goal of getting rid of drugs should be achieved by
whatever means. Instead, the Dutch consider it unrealistic to expect that drug
use can and will be eliminated from society. Consequently, the foremost objective of Dutch drug policy is the "reduction of harm" for both the individual
and society resulting from drug addiction. Although the risks to society are
always considered, the Dutch drug policy is also designed to ensure that users
are not harmed more by criminal proceedings than the drug itself. Indeed, the
main policy objective is the prevention of risk rather than the termination of
the addiction (Marshall, Anjewierden & Van Atteveld, 1990). As such, the role
and scope of criminal law is limited:

> The Dutch prefer a policy of encirclement, adaptation, inte-
> gration, and normalization, rather than a policy of social
> exclusion through criminalization, punishment and stigma-
> tization. . . They see the criminal law less as an instrument
> for expressing moral values and more as an instrument
> whose results, both positive and negative, must be assessed
> from case to case (Ruter, 1986:152-153).

The Opium Act of 1976 makes a distinction between "drugs representing unacceptable risks" (including heroin, cocaine, LSD, amphetamines, and hash oil) and drugs of "acceptable risk" (such as hashish and marijuana) (Marshall, Anjewierden & Van Atteveld, 1990). The intention behind this distinction was to keep the "hard" and "soft" drug markets separated, attempting to prevent young cannabis users from interacting with the "hard drug" black market.

The guidelines of the Opium Act give low priority to both the investigation and prosecution of retail dealing in soft drugs: police and prosecutors confront dealers only when their business is advertised publicly or conducted in any other provocative manner (Marshall, Anjewierden & Van Atteveld, 1990). Most of the small scale, soft drug dealing is conducted in so-called coffee shops. It is important to note that the buyer or seller of marijuana in a coffee shop *is* guilty of violating the Opium Act. However, police involvement and prosecution of the violation depends on a variety of circumstances. Set out by the Procurator-General (October, 1994), no criminal proceedings will be instituted against people involved in the sale of soft drugs if there is:

1.   no public advertising

2.   no sale of hard drugs

3.   no nuisance

4.   no sale to minors (under 18 years of age)

5.   no sale of more than 30 grams per person

6.   owner/runner of shop has no criminal record

Even if the dealing causes problems (public advertising, public nuisance, selling hard drugs), there are still a series of interventions prior to prosecution. The primary policy instruments are local administrative measures such as withdrawing permits to serve liquor or food. If these measures do not have the desired outcome, the involved parties will receive a warning, followed by the confiscation of drugs. Thus, criminal punishment is not viewed as the only alternative. In fact, very rarely is imprisonment the consequence of violating the coffee shop policy.

The strict guidelines state that a coffee shop is a catering establishment that does not sell alcohol and has no gaming machines. However, the establishments that sell soft drugs still vary considerably. In the *strict sense*, the estimated number of coffee shops throughout the country is roughly between 1,100 and 1,200 (Netherlands government report, 1995). In practice, however, soft drugs are also sold in bars, video shops, fitness centers, and in people's homes. The number of these types of selling points is estimated to be about 900 according to a Netherlands government report of 1995. Thus, in spite of tolerating coffee shops, other less condoned drug selling locations are still a reality in the Netherlands.

According to the 1995 government publication "Drugs Policy in the Netherlands: Continuity and Change," the decriminalization of the possession of soft drugs in 1976 did *not* result in increased use. In fact, the level of consumption remained stable in the first few years following the amended Opium Act. There has been a small increase in use between 1984 and 1994; however, this trend has been observed in several other countries as well. Thus, there exists in the Netherlands a system of "de facto decriminalization" of certain substances—the drug laws are retained but rarely enforced (Hellawell, 1995; Zaal, 1992). There is a tolerant attitude toward otherwise non-criminal users so that if certain rules are followed, marijuana and hash are permitted to be sold in coffee shops. Decriminalization of the sale and use of drugs, however, does not extend to acts committed by those under the influence, and enforcement is still concentrated on ensuring a safe public environment.

Throughout the 1980s and 1990s, there has been an increase in the retail trade in soft drugs. Coffee shops have proven to be of assistance in keeping the retail markets for soft and hard drugs separate. However, there are also a number of problems associated with these shops as identified by the government report of 1995: criminal organizations have gained some measure of control over some of them; neighborhood complaints about people "hanging around," litter, increased traffic; concerns about the establishment of coffee shops near schools and other youth centers; and the sale of hard drugs in or near shops. Consequently, a number of recommendations have recently been put forward by the government regarding the control of coffee shops. A number of municipal authorities in cooperation with the police and other judicial authorities are endeavoring to improve the control of the shops. Specifically, the policy of tolerating coffee shops is being tightened. For example, efforts are being made to reduce the number of shops, to refuse licenses in areas near schools, and to more strictly scrutinize those owning and/or running the coffee shop. However, given that the "bona fide" coffee shops have demonstrated the ability to keep the markets separate, these establishments will continue to be tolerated.

It is possible for these policies to exist because illicit drug use is not regarded as a law enforcement problem, but instead as a matter affecting health and social well-being (Korthals, 1987). Therefore, the "drug problem" is defined as an overall society-related problem and is not seen as being effectively served by law enforcement agencies. In Rotterdam and Amsterdam the police are part of a multidisciplinary team, actively involved in ensuring that users are "normalized" rather than "marginalized."

South Australia and Cannabis

The impetus for harm reduction programs applied to cannabis use was not the adverse consequences of use, but rather those associated with the policy of prohibition. The harms associated with criminal sanctions of cannabis use are believed by many to be out of proportion to the actual harm associated with use and have been shown to be an ineffective deterrent to drug use behavior (Morgan, Riley & Chester, 1993).

The possibility of a shift from the criminal justice to the harm reduction paradigm has been enacted in the State of South Australia. In 1987, the Cannabis Expiation Notice (CEN) scheme was introduced, decreasing penalties for personal use of cannabis. Under this program, the possession of small quantities of cannabis (less than 100 grams of cannabis or 20 grams of hashish) for personal use ceased to be a criminal offense. Those apprehended for possession are issued an infringement notice that is terminated upon payment of the fine. If the fine is paid within 60 days, the offense is not prosecuted and a record of conviction is not filed (Donnelly, Hall & Christie, 1995).

Evaluations concerning the implications of this policy change have been conducted. In the year following the introduction of the CEN scheme, there had not been a significant increase in rates of cannabis use in South Australia compared to the other states where cannabis remained a criminal offense (Christie, 1991).

Merseyside, England

A cooperative harm-reduction strategy called Response Demand Enforcement was implemented in Merseyside, England in 1986. While rigorously policing at the dealer level, less emphasis is focused on individual users. Through cooperation with local health authorities, the police are now part of an approach that refers drug offenders to services, they do not prosecute for possession of syringes that are to be exchanged, and they publicly support syringe exchange programs. A "cautioning" policy has been adopted whereby the offender is taken to the police station, the drugs are confiscated, the incident recorded, and the offender is given a warning but receives no criminal record. Cautioning also affords the officers the opportunity to distribute information packages detailing treatment services and the location of syringe exchange centers in the area.

Finally, if an addict is registered through a service agency, he or she is entitled to legally carry drugs for personal use. The overall effect of this policy is to steer users away from crime and possible imprisonment. Recently this approach was extended to cocaine, amphetamines, and ecstasy. Results indicate that there has been a decrease in drug-related crime and in the demand for street-level heroin. Moreover, Merseyside has the lowest rate of HIV cases in all of the United Kingdom (Chappell et al., 1993).

Law enforcement approaches in these countries are characterized by: selective enforcement, community policing, and officers adopting the role of referral agents. Although illicit drugs have not been legalized in any of these countries, an emphasis is placed on treatment or non-intervention rather than the punishment of drug users.

THE PREREQUISITES: A SHIFT TO HARM REDUCTION

The previous section illustrated various examples of programs and policies from countries around the world that have adopted a harm reduction framework. We next consider what conditions have fostered this shift to a harm reduction approach to the drug "problem." Glaser (1974) identifies two crucial features that distinguish, historically, successful transformations of legal and social control systems for substance use away from criminal prohibition to a more medically oriented, regulatory emphasis. The shift from criminal to health definitions of drug related problems is first, accompanied by the view of users as mainstream or potentially functional members of society rather than marginal, deviant misfits. The second and related process involves a recognition that addictive and adverse health consequences of drug use have been overstated and are not so devastating as feared. To these we have added a third: selective non-enforcement of drug laws.

For harm reduction to become a viable and accepted framework within which to construct program and policy initiatives, there must be a change in the way the "drug problem" is constructed. Drug use and drug users do not exist in isolation. Increasingly, research has indicated that most drug users do other things in their lives than seek and use drugs; moreover, the drug policies themselves, in part, dictate the ease or difficulty in which drugs can be attained and the secrecy surrounding their use (Faupel, 1991). These practices may lead to outcomes that are demonstrably more dangerous than the drug use itself. Because drug users are part of the larger society, these effects will extend beyond individuals to family and community.

The emergence, spread, and escalation of HIV infection among injection drug users has been a predominant impetus to the adoption of harm reduction initiatives. Specifically, the sharing and reuse of needles and syringes, in a climate of scarcity and protective communality among addicts, was recognized early on as a major feature of the AIDS epidemic.

Concern about HIV and AIDS in the context of drug use is driven by two factors. One centers on the humane considerations for the well-being and survival of the users, and the second on the real risks of HIV transmission to the mainstream population. In 1989, 186,803 AIDS cases had been reported to the World Health Organization with more than one-half of these reported in the United States—11.8 cases per 100,000 (Smart, 1991). More recently, studies in the United States and the United Kingdom show that 60 to 100 percent of heterosexually acquired HIV is related to injection drug use (IDU), roughly 40 percent of IDUs are in relationships with non-users, and more than 50 percent of the pediatric AIDS cases in the United States are associated with injection drug use by one or both parents (Riley, 1993).

Moreover, the ever-growing AIDS epidemic among drug users in the United States and other countries made it increasingly difficult to justify continued criminalization of users and addicts as a "preventive" health strategy. This became particularly evident in Canada, where early needle exchange programs were implemented and the legal supply of needles and syringes through pharmacies was well-established. The rates of HIV infection among drug users have been 10 to 20 times lower in comparison to the United States (Smart, 1991).

Reinforcing the pressure to shift the focus from criminal to health definitions is the issue of HIV transmission through a combination of unprotected sex and injection drug use in prisons. The rate of HIV infection in correctional systems varies geographically. For example, in the United States, the percentage of women with HIV (at admission) ranges from zero percent in Wyoming to 19 percent in New York (Hammett, Moini & Daugherty, 1991). Those who have a history of drug use often continue to use at some time during their imprisonment. A recent study indicated that on the average 33 percent of all prisoners injected themselves and about 12 percent engaged in homosexual activity (Gaughwin, Douglas & Wodak, 1991). Thus, while the majority are not sexually active nor injecting drugs, for those who do, the risk of infection is intensified because condoms and clean injection equipment are not available (Carvell & Hart, 1990; Padel, Twidale & Porter, 1992). Although there are little data on how many needles are available in prison, an analysis in South Australia on the number of syringes found in a year and former prisoners' estimates suggests a ratio of one needle for every four or five injectors (Gaughwin, Douglas & Wodak, 1991).

The rationale for a shift from criminal to health definitions is reinforced when issues of cost are considered, specifically the relative costs of caring for HIV and AIDS patients compared to the preventive measures of syringe and needle exchange. In 1989, United States statistics revealed that the average lifetime medical expenses (from diagnosis to death) per AIDS patient are estimated to be between $65,000 to $80,000 (IMNAS, 1988). In comparison, drug treatment received in a non-residential program was recorded to be as little as $3,000 per year (IMNAS, 1986).

Injection drug users are also a high risk group for overdose deaths. In fact, as of 1993 in British Columbia, Canada, the leading cause of death for both men and women between the ages of 30 and 44 was illicit drug use. Illicit drug deaths were more common than death from AIDS, suicide, motor vehicle and traffic accidents for both men and women, coronary heart disease (in men), and higher than lung and breast cancer deaths in women (Cain, 1994). Findings such as these have drawn public attention to the human and financial costs of a largely preventable outcome.

Finally, an essential element for harm reduction is to have the appropriate infrastructure to support and maintain addicts. Harm reduction is rooted in a public heath tradition and, consequently, an infrastructure that sustains adequate social and health services is necessary. Western democracies have more readily provided these types of supplements for users and communities.

When thinking about harm reduction initiatives in developing countries, the need for a broader-based approach, rooted in primary care, has been articulated (Rana, 1996; Samarasinghe, 1995). The nature of drug-related harm is different in developing countries. As illustrated in an article by Samarasinghe (1995), the differences relate to the economic impact, not necessarily dependent use, and the negative role drugs may play in the lives of even moderate consumers and their families. It is important to recognize these differences because of their impact on harm reduction implementation. Developing countries need to judge whether this "new ideology" poses significant conflict with prevailing social tenets, and whether the assumptions of harm reduction are valid from specific cultural perspectives (Samarasinghe, 1995). The argument for a shift to primary health care has also been made as a necessary context for effective needle and syringe exchange in inner cities of the United States (Woods, 1996).

This section has provided an examination of the evidence that society overall, as well as drug users and their families, are better served when users are integrated into a larger network of social and health services. As well, this approach will reduce overall costs of crisis care for an investment in better prevention and ongoing support.

The several prerequisites identified by Glaser (1974) recognize that there is a spectrum of drug users, not just addicts and non-users. Indeed, much illicit drug use is occurring in the non-deviant population, where most social-recreational use is not visible, not dependence-producing, and not harmful. This was illustrated by the spread of cannabis use in the 1970s and 1980s, to the point where whole generations have aged with regular cannabis use (Erickson, 1980).

It is no longer possible to argue convincingly that moderate cannabis use in one's youth, or even as an adult leisure activity, is incompatible with achieving conventional success (Erickson, 1989). Furthermore, even heroin and cocaine have been demonstrated to be used in a controlled and pleasurable way by those who lead otherwise normal lives. Thus, social distance between users and the rest of society has been increasingly diminished (Blackwell & Erickson, 1988).

Coinciding with the recognition of the "normalization" of use is the challenge to traditional assumptions about addiction. This distinction between myth and reality is highlighted by research on cocaine that challenges earlier assumptions embedded in the "dope fiend" mentality (Erickson & Alexander, 1989; Erickson, Watson & Weber, 1992). For example, a collection of surveys conducted in countries around the world finds that the overall distribution of cocaine coincides with the following pattern: most of the population never tries cocaine; of those who do, most use it only a few times; most do not continue use, but among those who do, frequency is low; between five and 10 percent become frequent (at least monthly) users Erickson (1993).

The "dope fiend" mythology alleges that the chemical properties of drugs cause individuals to commit crimes: that assaults, robberies, and rape results from the individual being "crazed" by the drug (Glaser, 1974). However, of the drugs most frequently abused, many actually have physiological effects that would impede both criminal and non-criminal activity. These effects include drowsiness and indifference to surroundings, needs, and desires. The physiological effects of a drug are not sufficient to cause criminal behavior. Complex social behavior requires a learning experience, so that drugs may affect crime indirectly but do not determine conduct (Glaser, 1974).

There is now quite a solid empirical foundation on which to build a more health-centered approach that recognizes a whole continuum of expressions of drug use, from the experimental and casual to the compulsive and destructive. Indeed, a series of epidemiological case control studies conducted in the United States by Anthony and colleagues (Anthony & Petronis, 1991; Ritter & Anthony, 1991) find that fluctuations in cocaine use are embedded in complex and personal social processes. This new understanding of drug use requires a variety of flexible responses, not the monolithic one inherent in the criminal justice system. In the countries that have moved toward harm reduction, some appreciation of the research evidence has been manifested, if not wholeheartedly embraced.

The role of the police is addressed separately as a third prerequisite because police officers occupy a unique position in the transformation to a harm reduction approach. For harm reduction programs and policies to be truly effective, the police must play an active role in the development and implementation of these strategies. While the criminal prohibitions remain, this approach will often result in selective non-enforcement against some expressions of illicit drug behavior. Where there is a legislative directive that provides an alternative to criminal sanction, arrests for possession of drugs will decline.

The debate over how to deal with the problem of illicit drug use has centered on the issue of demand versus supply reduction. Typically, law enforcement agencies have focused their initiatives on supply reduction and have been criticized for their failure to contain drug abuse (Wardlaw, 1992). As a result, there has been a shift in some countries to direct law enforcement activities toward demand reduction (Chappell et al., 1993). This move has involved bringing the police into a *collaborative* role with education, prevention, and treatment agencies. In general, there has been movement to remove the "soft" drug users from the criminal justice system while concentrating enforcement on the trafficking of hard drugs like cocaine and heroin (Zaal, 1992). The countries that have moved in this direction have experienced significant success in reducing drug-related harm.

The Netherlands, Britain, Australia, Germany, and Switzerland have all made efforts to incorporate the police and other service agencies in harm reduction strategy collaborations (Chappell et al., 1993; Fischer, 1995a; Fraser & George, 1992; Zaal, 1992). These integrated policies strive to create humane conditions for the user and to reduce public nuisance. In this sense, the police are not merely agents of law enforcement, but play an active role in harm reduction strategies (Zaal, 1992). For such programs to succeed, however, a whole-hearted commitment from the police and drug treatment agencies is required, along with adequate funding and provision of treatment services (Hellawell, 1995). The police are no longer seen as the "enforcer" but as a crucial service provider, an active player in harm reduction initiatives (Fischer, 1995a).

THE BARRIERS: DISCREDITING HARM REDUCTION

Resistance to change, and indeed to any willingness to consider public health alternatives, is manifested in several countries and worldwide bodies. The continued allegiance to rigorous prohibition, accompanied by increased punitiveness as found in recent Canadian legislation and the mandatory minimum sentencing in the United States, has already been explored in previous chapters. Our emphasis is on the active campaign against harm reduction as an effort to prop up the prohibitionist ideology and the drug war effort.

In the United States, the harm reduction message has fallen largely on deaf ears. For example, under the Helms Amendment, no federal funding will be provided for syringe exchange programs until the Centre for Disease Control and Prevention (CDCP) issues a report stating there will be no increase in drug abuse as a result of needle exchange (Reuter & MacCoun, 1995). The government, rejecting "harm reduction," has instead focused on a policy characterized as "use reduction." As illustrated by Reuter and MacCoun (1995), use reduction is perhaps best exemplified by examining the National Drug Control Strategy that produces each year a list of goals for decreasing prevalence and incidence of drug use. These numerical goals, however, fail to include harmful effects such as the number of birth complications associated with maternal drug use, HIV seroincidence rates among injection drug users, and number of overdose deaths.

As such, there has been a concerted effort to counter harm reduction through a global campaign emanating from the United States. One example of this was the reversal of penalty reduction initiatives for cannabis possession. In 1973, Oregon was the first state to reduce the offense of possession of less than one ounce to a civil violation with a maximum penalty of $100. By 1978, 10 other states had introduced similar legislation (Single, 1989). Initial and follow-up control studies demonstrated that the legislative change had not resulted in a significant increase in use, that certain social costs associated with enforcement had been reduced, and there had been no increase, as was feared, in "public displays" of use (Single, 1989). In addition, there was a rearranging within the health care system, allocating fewer resources to marijuana treatment and increasing those directed to treatment for the so-called "hard drugs." Moreover, the savings to the drug enforcement units also resulted in the redirection of resources to laws regarding other substances.

However, in spite of these results, these reforms were halted from the 1980s onward. In 1986, then-President Ronald Reagan stated that "Drugs are menacing our society . . . there is no moral middle ground" and declared a new crusade against drugs. The "War on Drugs" was once again crowned as the dominant ideology and approach to combating the drug issue. As suggested by Reuter and MacCoun (1995), bureaucratic and political factors may account, in part, for the emphasis on use. First, there is a noticeable separation between American drug policy and American AIDS policy. Second, Congress required the Office of National Drug Control Policy (ONDCP) to establish *measurable* goals. As such, measuring use was far easier than attempting to quantify harmful effects that proved difficult to measure.

Why does the United States drug strategy place greater emphasis on policy grounded strongly in a criminal justice and moralistic perspective (use reduction) instead of that grounded in a public health tradition (harm reduction)? One is pragmatic: if the number of users are reduced, by extension it is assumed, the number of harmful effects will also be reduced. While this may or may not be the case, by placing such a restricted emphasis on use reduction as an *indirect* means to decrease harm, this approach neglected to address opportunities of *directly* reducing harm and may have actually increased harmful effects in the process (Erickson, 1992; Reuter & MacCoun, 1995). Moreover, individuals such as Robert DuPont have spoken and written widely, portraying harm reduction as a "front" for legalization (Dupont, 1996; Dupont & Voth, 1995). This willful, misguided misrepresentation, equating a *public health approach* with legalization, contributes to the reluctance to consider harm reduction as a serious drug strategy option.

Also, the European harm reduction movement focuses most of the concern on the welfare of the drug user. However, in the United States the drug-related harm inflicted on the non-user is given precedence (Reuter & MacCoun, 1995). The current harm reduction programs appear to offer little in the way of decreasing these costs borne by others, thereby acting as an additional barrier to the acceptance of harm reduction initiatives. Furthermore, in the United States there exists a general moralistic antagonism toward "hard" drug users. "Drugs and violence" are two words commonly associated with one another and have received much attention both in the media and research communities. It is not surprising, then, that in contrast to European countries that perceive drugs as a behavioral and health problem, the United States sees drugs as only a crime problem that *must* be dealt with by harshness.

In addition, attempts have been made to reinforce the traditional "addictive" image of drugs like cocaine, as when the United States government attacked the World Health Organization report on cocaine use in 19 countries for portraying a spectrum of use patterns, most not conforming to the addictive menace required by United States drug policy officials (WHO, 1995). The very words "harm reduction" are said to be unacceptable in government grant applications or reports for mainstream United States agencies.

What is especially noteworthy about these United States attacks on harm reduction is first, their anti-empirical and anti-scientific foundation, and secondly, the extension beyond legal policy debates to the nature of society itself (Erickson, 1996). The earlier drug policy debates tended to focus on legal frameworks inherent in decriminalization or legalization arguments. The questions were about how to use the laws most effectively to control drugs, and what the impacts of any legal changes were likely to be. The attack on harm reduction is much more clearly a moral one: any sacrifice, even the health of the innocent, is preferable to accepting the reality of drug use in society. In such a moral climate, of course, facts are irrelevant.

CONCLUSION

Some drug-related harms, such as physical dependence, are indeed attributable to the direct function of the drug itself. In reality, however, much drug-related harm is attributable to the criminal distribution of drugs. The development of a criminal economy surrounding the drug market and the associated violence are *not* functions of the psychopharmacological properties of the drug, but rather have been constructed by the conditions society has created.

This chapter has portrayed the emergence of another way to address the drug "problem": reduce the harms associated with drug use. This approach is gaining adherents in countries around the world. Harm reduction is an integrative public health perspective emphasizing the achievement of pragmatic outcomes and the amelioration of the immediate harms rather than less tangible distant hazards. Moreover, harm reduction principles *can* be incorporated into many existing drug policies without the passage of major new laws or the contravention of international treaties.

This non-coercive and non-abstinence approach, however, is incompatible with that of a single-minded deterrence approach relying on punishment and threats of punishment (Erickson & Ottaway, 1994). Therefore, the full embrace of harm reduction initiatives may require, in the long run, the replacement of the dominance of the criminal justice model with explicit public health assumptions and supportive legal controls. There will always be a role for law enforcement in dealing with the broader issues of availability even in a more regulated market. A future goal should be to develop a new system that is consistent with present scientific knowledge and able to incorporate new scientific findings for effective social control of drugs (Des Jarlais, 1995).

Harm reduction provides a middle ground for the de-escalation of the war on drugs, without resorting to all-out legalization or continuing the punitive and harm-promoting practices of the war on drugs. One fear must be that the frustration with the costs and ineffectiveness of the drug war will prompt a potentially harmful abandonment of most regulatory controls along with the criminal ones. Such an outcome is unlikely to serve the interests of public health.

NOTE

[1]   Any views expressed in this chapter are those of the authors, and do not necessarily reflect those of the Addiction Research Foundation or the University of Toronto.

12

The War on Drugs Revisited: "Objective" and Socially Constructed Harm

Jurg Gerber
Sam Houston State University

Eric L. Jensen
University of Idaho

The preceding chapters have included critical discussions about the current war on drugs from the social constructionist perspective. Constructionists believe that a combination of political opportunism, media profit maximization, and a desire among criminal justice professionals to increase their spheres of influence has led to many misguided policies:

- Because crack cocaine has been treated differently from other forms of cocaine, and because crack use appears to be more common among low income African-Americans, the criminal justice system has been harsher on African-Americans for crack-related offenses than on whites.

- Prisons and jails have been overcrowded as a result of the continually increasing use of incarceration as a sentence for even possession of illegal drugs.

- Minorities, in particular, have been disproportionately sent to prison as a result of the new war on drugs.

- State intervention in the "drug crisis" has been driven by images of heavy cocaine use, crack use in particular, as "typical" drug use. In reality, the most commonly used drug is marijuana, and most users are recreational users.

- Juvenile gangs are seen as drug-driven and law enforcement has focused on this supposed aspect of gangs. In reality, drugs play a relatively minor role in gang formation and their maintenance.

- Law enforcement agencies have become concerned too much with enhancing revenues rather than with enforcing laws and protecting the public as a result of asset forfeiture laws.

- Due process protections granted to residents of the United States have been eroded during the last 10 years in an effort to fight illegal drug use and sales.

- Attempts have been made to expand law enforcement by criminalizing the health behaviors of pregnant women.

- The influence of drugs on violent crime has been overemphasized. As a result, violence has not been targeted appropriately (e.g., domestic and other forms of interpersonal violence are the result of factors other than drug use and abuse).

- Other nations have patterned their drug law enforcement after that of the United States. As a result, the problems have been globalized.

At the same time, the use and abuse of drugs themselves have led to numerous forms of harm. There is little doubt that many, though perhaps not all, illicit drugs have adverse health consequences for their users. For instance, cocaine use was mentioned as a contributing factor in an estimated 123,000 admissions to emergency rooms in 1993 in the United States (Maguire & Pastore, 1995:297). Specific reasons for seeking medical help included, among other things, unexpected reactions and overdoses. Similarly, heroin and morphine were listed a combined 63,000 times in emergency room hospital admissions during that same year (Maguire & Pastore, 1995:297).

Short-term and long-term health consequences of drug use and abuse vary among different drugs. Opiates such as opium, morphine, codeine, and heroin are believed to have toxic effects that include hypotension, allergic reaction, and insomnia; whereas an overdose may lead to convulsions, seizures, and possibly death (Fishbein & Pease, 1996). Cocaine use may lead to minor health problems including blurred vision, dry skin, and irritability, or to major consequences such as seizures, strokes, and sudden death (Fishbein & Pease, 1996). Even marijuana, an illegal drug that is medically less problematic than others, has some adverse health consequences for users: "the smoke produced . . . is approximately 50 percent more carcinogenic than that from tobacco. Lung capacity is reduced in chronic smokers and their airways have shown obstructions" (Fishbein & Pease, 1996:314).

In addition to medical problems, abusing some drugs can also lead to social and economic consequences for the users. There is little doubt that using hallucinogenic drugs on an extended basis makes functioning in an economic role difficult, if not impossible (Aronow, Miceli & Done, 1980). Similarly, heavy use of marijuana may lead to *amotivational syndrome* (although there is some evidence that this consequence may be culturally influenced):

> Users commonly become apathetic and lose their motivation
> to perform competently and achieve long-range goals. They
> have difficulty concentrating, learning new skills, coping
> with stressors and daily life events, and they become easily
> frustrated and develop certain deficits in verbal and writing
> abilities (Fishbein & Peace, 1996:315).

Any of these results are likely to be problematic for the users' economic and social roles. They may adversely affect interpersonal relationships and prevent regular participation in the economy.

The frequency of such adverse consequences is in dispute, partly as a result of the claimsmaking that has characterized the current war on drugs. Whereas some claim that there is an "epidemic" of drug use, and thus of negative health and social consequences, others, including the authors in this book, have maintained that there have been no dramatic increases in drug use in recent years. Nevertheless, whatever the actual rates may be, there is little doubt that *some* drug users, and their family members, experience problems as a result of the drug use itself (rather than the poorly conceived war on drugs). It is these users, and the consequences from which they suffer, that the current emphasis on law enforcement ignores.

The consequences of ill health and other negative effects are not likely to be distributed evenly throughout society. Relatively affluent users (and abusers) of illicit drugs are able to engage in their habits with impunity. They are likely to be able to insulate themselves from the criminal justice system. If they are in need of medical assistance, they are likely to arrange for private care and are likely to have health insurance that covers such treatment. Working- and under-class users, on the other hand, are less likely to be able to insulate themselves from the criminal justice system and are also less likely to have access to medical care if needed. The current war on drugs is thus likely to have more adverse consequences for some segments of society.

Finally, to the extent that there is a drug/crime connection, people in lower-class neighborhoods are more likely to be both offenders and victims of such crime. Middle- and upper-class people are not likely to have to resort to property crime to pay for a habit to the same extent as lower-class people. Furthermore, as most street crime is intraclass rather than interclass, the victims of drug-related property crime are likely to be the social peers of the offenders.

ALTERNATIVES TO THE WAR ON DRUGS

One alternative to the war on drugs, discussed by Erickson and Butters in the previous chapter, is provided by the harm reduction movement in various locations throughout the world. Whereas the specific assumptions, programs, and policies under this approach to dealing with drug use vary from society to society, the overall goal is the same:

> Harm reduction is a *framework* from which policy and program strategies are conceptualized, developed, and implemented with the outcome being the reduction or minimization of harm (without requiring user abstinence or less consumption) (Erickson & Butters, p. 179, this volume—emphasis in original).

Proponents of this approach have shown that it holds promise as an alternative to the law enforcement emphasis predominant in North America. In a program that involves the free medical dispensation of heroin in Zurich, Switzerland, 53 percent of participants had incomes from an illegal source during the 30 days preceding the initiation of the program, but only 13 percent of participants did during the 30 days prior to the follow-up interview six months later (Killias & Uchtenhagen, 1996). Perhaps even more dramatic, in an evaluation of a needle exchange program started in the early 1980s in Zurich, an average of 46.9 percent of addicts who began injecting hard drugs no later than 1981 were HIV-positive by 1990. Of those who started in 1985 or later, 4.8 percent were HIV-positive by 1990 (Killias & Uchtenhagen, 1996). In these two programs, the goal of reducing criminal and physical harm associated with drug use was achieved. As Erickson and Butters argued, such approaches might be used more effectively in North America than the current emphasis on law enforcement. Given the abysmal failure of the current war, any new tactic could not possibly be any less successful than the current one.

A second alternative to the war on drugs can be derived from the emerging perspective of *left realist criminology*. This school arose in the 1980s in England in response to the conservative policies of the Thatcher government. Conservatives in England, similar to what was occurring in the United States at the same time, argued for a return to "law and order" and called for ever-increasing sentences for criminals. Leftist criminologists felt compelled to respond to these demands but without "collapsing into the romanticism and idealism which has been evident in much of the radical and critical criminological literature of the 1970s" (Matthews & Young, 1992:6). Instead, they tried to develop a theory that takes into account the realities of the working- and under-classes, and thus their street-crime victimization, but without the heavy emphasis on the criminal justice system advocated by the *right realists*. In a nutshell, left realists maintain that street crime is caused by inequities in the political and economic systems, that some offenders are treated more harshly by the criminal justice system than others, but that the fear of crime in the inner cities must be taken seriously. As a result, the working-class victims of street crime, and preventing their victimization, play a prominent role in left realist criminology (for an overview, see MacLean & Milovanovic, 1991; Young & Matthews, 1992).

The left idealists of the 1960s and 1970s, and liberals and conservatives of all decades, are equally wrong in their approaches to crime:

> For some commentators, on the right, the [criminal justice system] is seen somewhat like a magic wand which, if waved more vigorously, will solve the problem of crime. For liberals, it is believed that if only the wand were waved in an impartial way, in time, with due process, the problems of crime would be greatly alleviated. And on the left, abolitionists . . . would seem to believe that if the wand ceased waving, crime itself would disappear and resolve itself into a series of rather minor "problematic situations." All of these notions are false (Young, 1992:42).

Returning to the war on drugs, similar conclusions can be drawn. Conservatives believe that using the criminal justice system "more" will get rid of the drug problem. Liberals maintain that using it "better" would greatly alleviate the problems (although they would also want resources devoted to the presumed underlying causes of drug use), while abolitionists believe that the system should disappear completely. None of these approaches are likely to work. The authors in this book argue that not only has the war approach been a complete failure, but that it has also led to adverse consequences for politically powerless segments of society. A criminal justice system that is *just*, and based on due process, is a goal worth pursuing, but unlikely to lead to a situation in which all negative consequences of drug use and abuse will disappear. Abolishing the role of the criminal justice system in controlling drugs, for instance by decriminalizing all drugs, may or may not be desirable. However, even if one were to do so, the problems that the war on drugs has created for the populations of inner cities would not disappear, at least not in the short run:

- The organized crime distribution systems fueled by the profits made possible by the war mentality would still be present. They would be based on something other than illegal drugs, but present nevertheless.

- The violence that accompanies the drug trade might still be present. Similar to the organized crime networks above, drugs would no longer be the focal point, but something else might be.

- Drug-related property crime would likely be reduced, as there would be less economic need for it, but not likely to disappear. If nothing else, there would always be new drugs that would not (yet) be available through legal channels. Thus, they would be expensive and generate new drug-related property crime.

- Prostitution, frequently associated with street level drug use/abuse, might be less prevalent, but would remain in existence for the same reasons as drug-related property crime.

- Because most solutions to any problem entail new problems, new forms of drug-related crime would likely emerge, even if strategies of harm reduction instead of war were pursued.

- The urban blight that contributes to the existence of inner-city drug use/abuse and crime would still be present. Residents of these areas would still be at disproportionate risks of being victimized by some forms of crime.

A long-term solution to the drug problem in North America is thus likely to involve multiple strategies and tactics. Whereas this book and this chapter are not focused primarily on solutions, at a minimum the following steps must be taken:

- The war mentality must be abolished.

- A strategy of harm reduction must be pursued. Included here is the need to establish on-demand treatment programs. Users who seek treatment should be afforded the opportunity to do so.

- In the short run, resources must continue to be devoted to the criminal justice system as a partial answer to public safety issues associated with illegal drugs.

- In the long run, resources devoted to the fighting of the drug problem through the criminal justice system must be reduced substantially.

- Perhaps most importantly, a more sophisticated understanding of the causes and distribution of drug use and abuse must emerge. Representing violence-prone, hedonistic, larceny-committing, prostituting, drive-by-shooting, gang-banging, juvenile crack heads as typical of today's drug problem may be politically popular, increase television viewership, and justify larger criminal justice budgets, but it does not provide the basis for sound policy.

Bibliography

Abramovsky, A. (1991). "Extraterritorial Abductions: America's 'Catch and Snatch' Policy Run Amok." *Virginia Journal of International Law*, 31:151-210.

Adams, L.P., II (1972). "China: The Historical Setting of Asia's Profitable Plague." In A.W. McCoy with C.B. Reed & L.P. Adams II *The Politics of Heroin in Southeast Asia*. New York, NY: Harper & Row.

Addiction Research Foundation (ARF) (1993). *A Response to Bill C-85, The Psychoactive Substance Control Act*. Standing House Committee on Health, May 26, 1993.

Adlaf, E.M., F. Ivis & R. Smart (1994). *Alcohol and Other Drug Use Among Ontario Adults in 1994 and Changes Since 1977*. Toronto, Canada: Addiction Research Foundation.

Adlaf, E.M., F. Ivis, R. Smart & G. Walsh (1995). *The Ontario Student Drug Use Survey, 1977-1995*. Toronto, Canada: Addiction Research Foundation.

Administrative Office of the United States Courts (1981). *1981 Annual Report of the Director*. Washington, DC: Administrative Office of the United States Courts.

Adoption Assistance and Child Welfare Act of 1980, 42 U.S. paragraph 420 et seq., as amended by the Omnibus Budget Reconciliation Act of 1987, Public Law 96-271.

Akers, R.L. (1985). *Deviant Behavior: A Social Learning Approach*, Third Edition. Belmont, CA: Wadsworth.

Aleinikoff, T.A. (1987). "Constitutional Law in the Age of Balancing." *Yale Law Journal*, 96:943-1005.

Alex, T. (1992). "Latest Shooting Reflects Trend Alot of People are Using Guns to Settle Disputes this Fall." *Newspaper A*, 1.

Altheide, D. & R.P. Snow (1991). *Media Worlds in the Era of Postjournalism*. Hawthorne, NY: Aldine de Gruyter.

American Federation of Government Employees v. Sullivan, 787 F. Supp. 255 (D.D.C. 1992).

Andreas, P.R., E.C. Bertram, M.J. Blackman & K.E. Sharp (1991-1992, Winter). "Dead-end Drug Wars." *Foreign Policy*, 85:106-128.

Anthony, J. & K. Petronis (1991). "Epidemiologic Evidence on Suspected Associations Between Cocaine Use and Psychiatric Disturbances." In S. Schober & C. Schade (eds.) *The Epidemiology of Cocaine Use and Abuse*, Research Monograph No. 110:71-94. Rockville, MD: National Institute on Drug Abuse.

Armstrong, A. (1995, August 15). "Crack Cocaine: Make the Sentencing Fair." *The Washington Post*, A17.

Aronow, R., J.N. Miceli & A.K. Done (1980). "A Therapeutic Approach to the Acutely Overdosed Patient." *Journal of Psychedelic Drugs*, 12:259-268.

Ashton, J. & H. Seymour (1988). *The New Public Health*. Bristol, PA: Open University Press.

Associated Press (1990). "Governor Vows to Support Dinkins." *Albany (New York) Times Union*, 12:B10.

Ball, J. & A. Ross (1991). *The Effectiveness of Methadone Maintenance Treatment: Patients, Programs, Services, and Outcome*. New York, NY: Springer-Verlag.

Ballard, L. (1991). "Evansdale Gang Stirs up Residents." *Newspaper B*, A4.

Barak, G. (1988). "Newsmaking Criminology: Reflections on the Media, Intellectuals, and Crime." *Justice Quarterly*, 5:565-587.

Barak, G. (ed.) (1994). *Media, Process and the Social Construction of Crime: Studies in Newsmaking Criminology*. New York, NY: Garland Publishing, Inc.

Barnes, S. (1995, September 23). "Bill C-7: The Controlled Drugs and Substance Act." Paper presented at the 9th annual Interdisciplinary Conference "Canadian Cannabis Policy," Student Legal Society, University of Western Ontario, Faculty of Law, London, Ontario, Canada.

Basis, M.S., R.J. Gelles & A. Levine (1982). *Social Problems*. New York, NY: Harcourt Brace Jovanovich.

Bassiouni, M.C. (1990). "Critical Reflections on International and National Control of Drugs." *Denver Journal of International Law and Policy*, 18:311-337.

Baum, D. (1996). *Smoke and Mirrors: The War on Drugs and the Politics of Failure*. Boston, MA: Little, Brown.

Beck, M., with G. Lubenow & M. Kasindorf (1981, February 2). "Nancy: Searching for a Role." *Newsweek*, 97:54.

Becker, H. (1967). "Whose Side Are We On?" *Social Problems*, 14:239-247.

Becker, H. (1963). *Outsiders: Studies in the Sociology of Deviance*. New York, NY: Free Press.

Beckett, K. (1997a). "Managing Motherhood: The Civil Regulation of Prenatal Drug Users." *Studies in Law, Politics and Society*, 16:295-321.

Beckett, K. (1997b). *Making Crime Pay: Law and Order in Contemporary American Politics*. New York, NY: Oxford University Press.

Beckett, K. (1995a). "Fetal Rights and 'Crack Moms': Pregnant Women in the War on Drugs." *Contemporary Drug Problems*, 22:587-612.

Beckett, K. (1995b). "Media Depictions of Drug Abuse: The Impact of Official Sources." *Journal of Research in Political Sociology*, 17:161-182.

Beckett, K. (1994). "Setting the Public Agenda: 'Street Crime' and Drug Use in American Politics." *Social Problems*, 41:425-447.

Belenko, S. (1990). "The Impact of Drug Offenders on the Criminal Justice System." In R. Weisheit (ed.) *Drugs, Crime and the Criminal Justice System*, 27-78. Cincinnati, OH: Anderson Publishing Co.

Belenko, S., J. Fagan & K.-L. Chin (1991). "Criminal Justice Responses to Crack." *Journal of Research in Crime and Delinquency*, 81(1):55-73.

Belenko, S.R. (1993). *Crack and the Evolution of Anti-Drug Policy*. Westport, CT: Greenwood Press.

Bennett, W.L. (1980). *Public Opinion in American Politics*. New York, NY: Harcourt Brace and Jovanovich.

Ben-Yehuda, N. (1990). *The Politics and Morality of Deviance: Moral Panics, Drug Abuse, Deviant Science and Reversed Stigmatization*. New York, NY: State University of New York Press.

Ben-Yehuda, N. (1986). "The Sociology of Moral Panics: Toward a New Synthesis." *Sociological Quarterly*, 27:495-513.

Berger, P.L. & T. Luckmann (1966). *The Social Construction of Reality*. Garden City, NY: Doubleday & Company, Inc.

Berridge, V. & G. Edwards (1981). *Opium for the People*. Opiate Use in the Nineteenth-Century England. Allen Lane, London/St. Martin's Press, New York.

Bertram, E., M. Blachman, K. Sharpe & P. Andreas (1996). *Drug War Politics: The Price of Denial*. Berkeley, CA: University of California Press.

Bertschy, G. (1995). "Methadone Maintenance Treatment: An Update." *European Archive of Psychiatry and Clinical Neurosis*, 245:114-124.

Best, J. (1990). *Threatened Children-Rhetoric and Concern About Child-Victims*. Chicago, IL: The University of Chicago Press.

Best, J. (1987). "Rhetoric as Claims-Making: Constructing the Missing Children Problem." *Social Problems*, 34:101-121.

Best, J. (ed.) (1989). *Images of Issues: Typifying Contemporary Social Problems*. New York, NY: Aldine de Gruyter.

Binder, H. (1994). "Syringe Exchange in Australia." *ICAA News*, 3(4).

Bingol, N., C. Schuster, C. Fuchs, M. Isosub, G. Turner, R. Stone & D. Gromisch (1987). "The Influence of Socioeconomic Factors on the Occurrence of Fetal Alcohol Syndrome." *Advances in Alcohol and Substance Abuse*, 6(4):105-118.

Blackwell, J. & P. Erickson (1988). "Concluding Remarks: A Risky Business." In J. Blackwell & P. Erickson (eds.) *Illicit Drugs in Canada: A Risky Business*. Scarborough, Ontario, Canada: Nelson Canada.

Blum, R.H. (1969). *Society and Drugs*. San Francisco, CA: Jossey-Bass, Inc.

Blumer, H. (1971). "Social Problems as Collective Behavior." *Social Problems*, 18:298-306.

Blumstein, A. (1996). *Youth Violence, Guns, and Illicit Drug Markets*. Washington, DC: National Institute of Justice, U.S. Department of Justice, Office of Justice Programs.

Blumstein, A. (1993). "Racial Disproportionality in U.S. Prisons Revisited." *University of Colorado Law Review*, 64:743-760.

Blumstein, A. (1982). "On the Disproportionality of United States' Prison Populations." *Journal of Criminal Law and Criminology*, 73:1259-1281.

Bonnie, R. & C. Whitebread (1974). *The Marijuana Connection*. Charlottesville, VA: University of Virginia Press.

Boston Globe. (1988, May 1), 4.

Bourdieu, P. (1990). *In Other Words: Essays Toward a Reflexive Sociology*. Stanford, CA: Stanford University Press.

Boyd, N. (1994, October). "The Liberals on Drugs: Ostriches in Search of More Sand." *Options Politiques*, 17-21.

Brecher, E. & the editors of *Consumer Reports*. (1972). *Licit and Illicit Drugs*. Boston, MA: Little, Brown.

Brownstein, H.H. (1995a). "The Social Construction of Crime Problems: Insiders and the Use of Official Statistics." *Journal of Crime & Justice*, 18:17-30.

Brownstein, H.H. (1995b). "The Media and the Construction of Random Drug Violence." In J. Ferrell & C. Sanders (eds.) *Cultural Criminology*, 45-65. Boston, MA: Northeastern University Press.

Brownstein, H.H. (1991). "The Social Construction of Public Policy: A Case for Participation by Researchers." *Sociological Practice Review*, 2:132-140.

Brownstein, H.H. & P.J. Goldstein (1990). "Research and the Development of Public Policy." *Journal of Applied Sociology*, 7:77-92.

Brownstein, H.H., P.J. Ryan & P. Goldstein (1992). "Drug-Related Homicide in New York City: 1984 and 1988." *Crime & Delinquency*, 38:459-476.

Bruun, K., L. Pan & I. Rexed (1975). *The Gentlemen's Club: International Control of Drugs and Alcohol*. Chicago, IL: University of Chicago Press.

Bryan, M. (1979). "Cannabis in Canada—A Decade of Indecision." *Contemporary Drug Problems*, 8:169-192.

Bullock, C.S., III, J.E. Anderson & D.W. Brady (1983). *Public Policy in the Eighties*. Monterey, CA: Brooks/Cole.

Bureau of Justice Statistics (1995). *Prisoners in 1994*. Washington, DC: U.S. Department of Justice.

Bureau of Justice Statistics (1981). *Prisoners at Midyear 1981*. Washington, DC: U.S. Department of Justice.

Cain, J.V. (1994). *Report of the Task Force into Illicit Narcotic Overdose Deaths in British Columbia*. Burnaby, BC, Canada: Office of the Chief Coroner, Province of British Columbia.

California v. Greenwood, 486 U.S. 35 (1987).

Camara v. Municipal Court, 387 U.S. 523 (1967).

Canadian Centre on Substance Abuse (CCSA) (1995a). *Action News*. Ottawa, Canada: CCSA.

Canadian Centre on Substance Abuse (CCSA) (1995b). *Canadian Profile: Alcohol, Tobacco & Other Drugs, 1995*. Toronto, Canada: Canadian Centre on Substance Abuse/Addiction Research Foundation.

Canadian Foundation for Drug Policy (1996). *Proposed Amendments to Bill C-7*. Ottawa, Canada: CFDP.

Canadian Police Association (1993, May). *Brief to Legislative Committee—Bill C-85 (Psychoactive Substances)*. Ottawa, Canada: Canadian Police Association.

Carr, R. (1975, December). "Oregon's Marijuana Decriminalization: One Year Later." *Intellect*, 104:235-236.

Carstairs, C. (1995). "Dope Fiends, Innocent Addicts and Nefarious Traffickers: Discourses of Illegal Drug Use in Canada, 1919-1939." Unpublished manuscript. Toronto, Canada: University of Toronto.

Carvell A. & G. Hart (1990). "Risk Behaviors for HIV Infection Among Drug Users in Prison." *British Medical Journal*, 26:1383-1384.

Cauchon, D. (1993, May 23). "Sentences for Crack Called Racist." *USA Today*, 1A-2A.

Chambliss, W. (1996). "Crime Control and Ethnic Minorities: Legitimizing Racial Opposition by Creating Moral Panics." In D.F. Hawkins (ed.) *Ethnicity, Race, and Crime*, 235-258. Albany, NY: State University of New York Press.

Chapelhorn J. & J. Bell (1991). "Methadone Dosage and Retention of Patients in Maintenance Treatment." *Medical Journal of Australia*, 154:195-199.

Chappell, D., T. Reitsma, D. O'Connell & H. Strang (1993). "Law Enforcement as a Harm Reduction Strategy in Rotterdam and Merseyside." In N. Heather, A. Wodak, E. Nadelmann & P. O'Hare (eds.) *Psychoactive Drugs and Harm Reduction: From Faith to Science*, 118-126. London, England: Whurr.

Chasnoff, I.J., W.J. Burns, S.H. Schnoff & K.A. Burns (1985). "Cocaine Use in Pregnancy." *New England Journal of Medicine*, 393-669.

Chasnoff, I.J., D.R. Griffith, C. Freier & C. Murray (1992). "Cocaine/polydrug Use in Pregnancy: Two-Year Follow-Up." *Pediatrics*, 89:337-339.

Chasnoff, I.J., D.R. Griffith, S. Gregor, K. Dirkes & K.A. Burns (1989, March 24/31). "Temporal Patterns of Cocaine Use in Pregnancy: Perinatal Outcome." *Journal of the American Medical Association*, 261(12):1741-1744.

Chasnoff, I.J., H.J. Landress & M.E. Barrett (1990). "The Prevalence of Illicit Drug or Alcohol During Pregnancy and Discrepancies in Mandatory Reporting in Pinellas County, Florida." *The New England Journal of Medicine*, 322(17):1202-1206.

Chauncey, R.L. (1980). "New Careers for Moral Entrepreneurs: Teenage Drinking." *Journal of Drug Issues*, 10:45-70.

Chavkin, W. (1991). Testimony presented to House Select Committees on Children, Youth and Families. U.S. House of Representatives. Columbia University School of Public Health.

Christie, N. (1994). *Crime Control as Industry: Towards GULAGS, Western Style*, Second Edition. London, England: Routledge.

Christie, P. (1991). "The Effects of Cannabis Legislation in South Australia on Levels of Cannabis Use." Adelaide, Australia: Drug and Alcohol Services Council.

Clark, H. (1993). "Koehrsen on Gang Activity: I Told You So." *Newspaper A*, A4.

Clinard, M. & R. Meier (1979). *Sociology of Deviant Behavior*, Fifth Edition. New York, NY: Holt, Rinehart and Winston.

Clymer, A. (1986, September 2). "Public Found Ready to Sacrifice in Drug Fight." *The New York Times*, 1.

Cochran, D. (1990). "The Privacy Expectation: A Comparison of Federal and California Constitutional Standards for Drug Testing in Amateur Athletics." *Hastings Constitutional Law Quarterly*, 17:533-565.

Cohen, S. (1980). *Folk Devils and Moral Panics*. New York, NY: St. Martin's Press.

Cohen, S. (1972). *Folk Devils and Moral Panics: The Creation of the Mods and Rockers*. London, England: MacGibbon and Kee.

Coles, C.D. (1992). "Effects of Cocaine and Alcohol Use in Pregnancy on Neonatal Growth and Neorobehavioral Status." *Neorotoxology and Teratology*, 14:23-33.

Comack, E. (1986). "We Will Get Some Good Out of This Riot Yet: The Canadian State, Drug Legislation and Class Conflict." In S. Brickey & E. Comack (eds.) *The Social Basis of Law*. Toronto, Canada: Garamond Press.

Comack, E. (1985). "The Origins of Canadian Drug Legislation—Labelling versus Class Analysis." In T. Fleming *The New Criminologies in Canada*, 65-86. Toronto, Canada: Oxford University Press.

Commission of Inquiry into the Non-Medical Use of Drugs (1973). *Final Report*. Ottawa, Canada: Information Canada.

Commission of Inquiry into the Non-Medical Use of Drugs (1972). *Cannabis*. Ottawa, Canada: Information Canada.

Committee on Education and Labor (1877). "The Social, Moral and Political Effect of Chinese Immigrants." A report of Public Hearings Conducted by the Committee of the Senate of California, House of Representatives, 45th Congress, 1st Session, Misc. Document 9.

Commonwealth of Kentucky v. Connie Welch, 864 S.W.2d 280 (1993).

Conrad, P. (1975). "The Discovery of Hyperkinesis: Notes on the Medicalization of Deviant Behavior." *Social Problems*, 23:12-21.

Conrad, P. & J.W. Schneider (1992). *Deviance and Medicalization: From Badness To Sickness*, Revised Edition. Philadelphia, PA: Temple University Press.

Cook, S. (1969). "Canadian Narcotics Legislation 1908-1923: A Conflict Model Interpretation." *Canadian Review of Sociology and Anthropology* (6), 1:36-46.

Crack Cocaine Crisis: Joint Hearing before the Select Committee on Narcotics Abuse and Control, and the Select committee on Children, Youth and Families, House of Representatives, 99th Cong., 2nd Sess., (1986).

Crack Cocaine: Hearing before the Subcommittee on Investigations of the Committee on Governmental Affairs, United States Senate, S. Hrg. 929, 99th Cong., 2nd Sess. (1986).

Crowley, D.W. (1995). "Student Athletes and Drug Testing." *Marquette Sports Law Journal*, 6:95-131.

Crowley, D.W. & J.L. Johnson (1988). "Balancing and the Legitimate Expectation of Privacy." *Public Law Review*, 7:337-358.

Culpepper, G. (1990). "UNI Professor Develops Plan to Fight Growing Gang Problem." *Newspaper B*, A4.

Cuomo, M.M. (1987). "Message to the Legislature." Albany, NY.

Currie, E. (1993). *Reckoning: Drugs, the Cities, and the American Future*. New York, NY: Hill and Wang.

Curry, G.D., R.J. Fox, R. Ball & D. Stone (1993). "National Assessment of Law Enforcement Anti-Gang Information Resources." *Report to the U.S. Department of Justice*. Washington, DC: National Institute of Justice.

Danielman, S.D. & L.H. Reese (1989). "Intermedia Influence and the Drug Issue: Converging on Cocaine." In P. Shoemaker (ed.) *Communication Campaigns About Drugs: Government, the Media and the Public*. Mahwah, NJ: Lawrence Erlbaum Associates, Publishers.

Daro, D. & K. McCurdy (1992, August). *Current Trends in Child Abuse Reporting and Fatalities: NCPCA's 1991 Annual Fifty State Survey*. Chicago, IL: National Committee for Prevention of Child Abuse.

Davis, J. (1973). "Crime News in Colorado Newspapers." In S. Cohen & J. Young (eds.) *The Manufacture of News*, 127-135. Beverly Hills, CA: Sage Publications.

Des Jarlais, D. (1995). "Editorial: Harm Reduction—A Framework for Incorporating Science into Drug Policy." *American Journal of Public Health*, 85:10-12.

Dickson, D.T. (1968). "Bureaucracy and Morality: An Organizational Perspective on a Moral Crusade." *Social Problems*, 16:143-156.

Disapproval of Certain Sentencing Guideline Amendments. Report from The Committee on the Judiciary, H.R. 272, 104th Cong., 1st Sess. (1995).

Dixon, S. (1989). "Effects of Transplantal Exposure to Cocaine and Methamphetamine on the Neonate." *Western Journal of Medicine*, 150:436-442.

Donnelly, J. (1992). "The United Nations and Global Drug Control Regimes." In P.H. Smith (ed.) *Drug Policy in the Americas*, 282-304. Boulder, CO: Westview Press.

Donnelly, N., W. Hall & P. Christie (1995). "The Effects of Partial Decriminalization on Cannabis Use in South Australia, 1985 to 1993." *Australian Journal of Public Health*, 19:281-287.

Drucker, E. (1995). "Harm Reduction: A Public Health Strategy." *Current Issues in Public Health*, 1:64-70.

Drucker, E. (1990). "Children of War: The Criminalization of Motherhood." *The International Journal on Drug Policy*, 1.

Drug Enforcement Enhancement Act of 1986. Report from The Committee on the Judiciary, H.R. 847, 99th Cong., Sess. (1986).

Drug Free Workplace Act (1988). Public Law 100-690.

Duke, S.B. & A.C. Gross (1993). *America's Longest War: Rethinking our Tragic Crusade Against Drugs.* New York, NY: Putnam.

Dupont, R. (1996). "Harm Reduction and Decriminalization in the United States: A Personal Perspective." *Substance Use & Misuse*, 31:1965-1970.

Dupont, R. & E. Voth (1995). "Drug Legalization, Harm Reduction, and Drug Policy." *Annals of Internal Medicine*, 123:461-465.

Edelman, M. (1988). *Constructing the Political Spectacle*. Chicago, IL: University of Chicago Press.

Edsall, T.B. & M.D. Edsall (1991). *Chain Reaction: The Impact of Rights, Race and Taxes on American Politics.* New York, NY: Norton.

Elden, J. (1995). "Drug Sentencing Frenzy." *The Progressive*, 59(4):25.

Epstein, E. (1973). *News from Nowhere: Television and the News.* New York, NY: Random House.

Erickson, P. (1996). "Commentary on Robert Dupont, Harm Reduction and Decriminalization in the United States: A Personal Perspective." *Substance Use & Misuse*, 31:1929-1945.

Erickson, P. (1995). "Harm Reduction: What It Is and Is Not." *Drug and Alcohol Review*, 14:283-285.

Erickson, P. (1993). "Prospects of Harm Reduction for Psychostimulants." In N. Heather, A. Wodak, E. Nadelmann & P. O'Hare (eds.) *Psychoactive Drugs and Harm Reduction: From Faith to Science*, 184-210. London, England: Whurr.

Erickson, P. (1992). "Recent Trends in Canadian Drug Policy: The Decline and Resurgence of Prohibition." *Daedalus: Journal of the American Academy of Arts and Sciences*, 121:239-267.

Erickson, P. (1991). "Past, Current and Future Directions in Canadian Drug Policy." *The International Journal of the Addictions*, (25)3A:247-266.

Erickson, P. (1989). "Living with Prohibition: Regular Cannabis Users, Legal Sanctions, and Informal Controls." *International Journal of the Addictions*, 3:175-188.

Erickson, P. (1980). *Cannabis Criminals: The Social Effects of Punishment on Drug Users*. Toronto, Canada: Addiction Research Foundation.

Erickson P. & B. Alexander (1989). "Cocaine and Addictive Liability." *Social Pharmacology*, 3:249-270.

Erickson, P. & B. Fischer (1997). "Canadian Cannabis Policy: The Impact of Criminalization, the Current Reality and Future Policy Options." In L. Boellinger (ed.) *Cannabis: From Crime to Human Right*. New York/Frankfurt: Peter Lang Verlag.

Erickson, P. & G. Murray (1989, Summer). "The Undeterred Cocaine User: Intention to Quit and Its Relationship to Perceived Legal and Health Threats." *Contemporary Drug Problems*, 141-156.

Erickson, P. & G. Murray (1986). "Cannabis Criminals Revisited." *British Journal of Addiction*, 81:81-85.

Erickson, P. & C. Ottaway (1994). "Policy—Alcohol and Other Drugs." In J. Langenbucher, B. McCrady, W. Frankenstein & P. Nathan (eds.) *Annual Review of Addictions and Treatment* 3:331-341. New York, NY: Pergamon Press.

Erickson, P., D. Riley, Y. Cheung & P. O'Hare (1997). *Harm Reduction: A New Direction in Drug Policies and Programs*. Toronto, Canada: University of Toronto Press.

Erickson, P., V. Watson & T. Weber (1992). "Cocaine Users' Perceptions of Their Health Status and the Risks of Drug Use." In P. O'Hare, R. Newcombe, A. Matthews & E. Buning (eds.) *The Reduction of Drug Related Harm*, 82-89. London, England: Routledge.

Erickson, R., P. Baranek & J.B.L. Chan (1991). *Representing Order: Crime, Law and Justice in the News Media*. Toronto, Canada: University of Toronto Press.

Esbensen, F. & D. Huizinga (1993). "Gangs, Drugs, and Delinquency in a Survey of Urban Youth." *Criminology*, 31:565-589.

Evans, S. & R. Lundman (1983). "Newspaper Coverage of Corporate Price-Fixing." *Criminology*, 21:529-541.

Ewoldt, J. (1992). "Three D.M. Men Injured in Gang-Related Shooting." *Newspaper A*, 7.

Executive Order 12564 (1986, September 15). *Federal Register*, 51, 32889.

Fagan, J. (1989). "The Social Organization of Drug Use and Drug Dealing Among Urban Gangs." *Criminology*, 27:633-669.

Falco, M. (1996, Spring). "U.S. Drug Policy: Addicted to Failure." *Foreign Policy*, 102:120-133.

Falco, M. (1989). *Winning the Drug War—A National Strategy*. New York, NY: Priority Press.

Farnhaen, M. (1993). "Kids Who Kill: Authorities Look for Reasons Why." *Newspaper B*, A1.

Farr, K.A. (1995). "Fetal Abuse and the Criminalization of Behavior During Pregnancy." *Crime & Delinquency*, 41(2):235-245.

Farrell, R. & V. Swigert (1982). *Deviance and Social Control*. Glenview, IL: Scott, Foresman.

Faupel, C. (1991). *Shooting Dope: Career Patterns of Hard-Core Heroin Users*. Gainesville, FL: University Press of Florida.

Feeley, M. & J. Simon (1992). "The New Penology: Notes on the Emerging Strategy of Corrections and Its Implications." *Criminology*, 30(4):449-474.

Feig, L. (1990). *Drug Exposed Infants and Children: Service Needs and Policy Questions*. Working paper. Office of Social services Policy, Division of Children, Youth and Family Policy, Office of the Assistant Secretary for Planning and Evaluation. Washington, DC: Department of Health and Human Services.

Felman, J. & C. Petrini (1988). "Drug Testing and Public Employment: Toward a Rational Application of the Fourth Amendment." *Law and Contemporary Problems*, 51:253-299.

Fine, C.R. (1992). "Video Tests are the New Frontier in Drug Detection." *Personnel Journal*, 76:148-161.

Fine, C.R., T.Z. Reeves & G.P. Harney (1996). "Employee Drug Testing: Are Cities Complying with the Courts?" *Public Administration Review*, 56:30-36.

Fischer, B. (1997). "The Battle for a New Canadian Drug Law: A Legal Basis for 'Harm Reduction' or New Rhetoric for Prohibition?" In P. Erickson, D. Riley, Y. Cheung & P. O'Hare (eds.) *New Policies and Programs for the Reduction of Drug-Related Harm*. Toronto, Canada: University of Toronto Press.

Fischer, B. (1996, March/April). "Drug Treaties Don't Require a War on Users." *The Journal*, 25:9. Addiction Research Foundation.

Fischer, B. (1995a). "Drugs, Communities, and 'Harm Reduction' in Germany: The New Relevance of 'Public Health' Principles in Local Responses." *Journal of Public Health Policy*, 16(4):389-411.

Fischer, B. (1995b). "Drugs, Power and Politics: Historical Phases of Narcotics Control in Canada." Unpublished manuscript.

Fischer, B. (1995c, November). "P.J Giffen's 'Saga of Promise, Hesitation and Retreat': Can the Cycle of Prohibition Be Broken This Time?" Paper presented at the American Society of Criminology Annual Meeting, Boston, MA.

Fischer, B. (1994a). "Maps and Moves—The Discrepancies Between Rhetoric and Realities of Canadian Drug Policy." *International Journal of Drug Policy*, 5(2):70-81.

Fischer, B. (1994b, November). "The Persistent Tale of Prohibition. A look at Canada's Failed Attempts for Drug Law Reform in the Past 25 Years." Paper presented at the American Society of Criminology Annual Meeting, Miami, FL.

Fischer, B., P.G. Erickson & R. Smart (1996). "The Proposed Canadian Bill C-7: One Step Forward, Two Steps Backward." *International Journal of Drug Policy*, 7(3):172-179.

Fishbein, D.H. & S.E. Pease (1996). *The Dynamics of Drug Abuse*. Boston, MA: Allyn and Bacon.

Fishman, M. (1978). "Crime Waves as Ideology." *Social Problems*, 29:31-43.

Flynn, S. (1993). *The Transnational Drug Challenge and the New World Order. The Report of the CSIS Project on the Global Drug Trade in the Post-Cold War Era.* Washington, DC: The Centre for Strategic and International Studies.

Forman, A. & S.B. Lachter (1989). "The National Institute on Drug Abuse Cocaine Prevention Campaign." In P. Shoemaker (ed.) *Communication Campaigns About Drugs: Government, the Media and the Public*. Mahwah, NJ: Lawrence Erlbaum Associates, Publishers.

Fox, R. (1994). "Drug Prohibition in Australia." In *Questioning Prohibition: 1994 International Report on Drugs*, 107-111. Brussels, Belgium: International Antiprohibitionist League.

Fraser, A. & M. George (1992). "The Role of the Police in Harm Reduction." In P. O'Hare, R. Newcombe, A. Matthews & E. Buning (eds.) *The Reduction of Drug Related Harm*, 162-171. London, England: Routledge.

Freedman, E.B. (1987). "Uncontrolled Desires: The Response to the Sexual Psychopath." *Journal of American History*, 74:83-106.

French, H.W. (1991, May 5). "Island-Hopping the Caribbean, Against Drugs." *The New York Times*, A11.

Fried, C. (1968). "Privacy." *Yale Law Journal*, 77:475-493.

Frisbie v. Collins, 342 U.S. 519 (1952).

Fromberg, E. (1994). "The Case of The Netherlands: Contradictions and Values." In *Questioning Prohibition: 1994 International Report on Drugs*, 113-124. Brussels, Belgium: International Antiprohibitionist League.

Gallup, A. (1986). "The 18th Annual Gallup Poll of the Public's Attitudes Toward the Public Schools." *Phi Delta Kappan*, 68:43-59.

Gallup Institute (1986, September). "Most Important Problem." *The Gallup Report,* Report Number 252:27-29.

Gallup Institute (1985, September 2). *The Gallup Report.* Toronto, Canada.

Gallup Institute (1984, July). "Most Important Problem." *The Gallup Report,* Report Number 226:17.

Gamson, W.A. (1992). *Talking Politics.* New York, NY: Cambridge University Press.

Gamson, W.A. (1988). "Political Discourse and Collective Action." *International Social Movement Research,* 1:219-244.

Gamson, W.A. & D. Stuart (1992). "Media Discourse as a Symbolic Contest: The Bomb in Political Cartoons." *Sociological Forum*, 7:55-86.

Gans, H. (1995). *The War Against the Poor.* New York, NY: Basic Books.

Gans, H. (1980). *Deciding What's News.* New York, NY: Vintage Books.

Gaughwin, M., R. Douglas, C. Liew, L. Davies, A. Mylvaganam, H. Treffke, H. Edwards & R. Ali (1991). "Human Immunodeficieny Virus (HIV) Prevalence and Risk Behaviors for its Transmission in South Australian Prisons." *AIDS*, 5:845-851.

Gaughwin, M., R. Douglas & A. Wodak (1991). "Behind Bars-Risk Behaviors for HIV Transmission in Prisons, a Review." In J. Norberry, M. Gaughwin & S. Gerull (eds.) *HIV/AIDS and Prisons Conference Proceeding No. 4.* Canberra, Australia: Australian Institute of Criminology.

Gerber, J., E.L. Jensen, M. Schreck & G.M. Babcock (1990). "Drug Testing and Social Control: Implications for State Theory." *Contemporary Crises*, 14:243-258.

Gest, T. (1995, November 6). "New War Over Crack: Racism Wasn't an Issue When Laws First Passed." *U.S. News and World Report*, 18, 81, 119.

Gibney, M. (1990). "Policing the World: The Long Reach of U.S. Law and the Short Arm of the Constitution." *Connecticut Journal of International Law*, 6:103-126.

Giffen, P., S. Endicott & S. Lambert (1991). *Panic and Indifference: The Politics of Canada's Drug Laws*. Ottawa, Canada: Canadian Centre on Substance Abuse.

Giffen, P.G. & S. Lambert (1988). "What Happened on the Way to Law Reform?" In J.C. Blackwell & P.G. Erickson (eds.) *Illicit Drugs in Canada: A Risky Business*, 345-369. Toronto, Canada: Nelson Canada.

Gillard, D. (1993). *Prisoners in 1992*. Washington, DC: U.S. Department of Justice, Bureau of Justice Statistics Bulletin.

Gilliom, J. (1994). *Surveillance, Privacy and the Law: Employee Drug Testing and the Politics of Social Control*. Ann Arbor, MI: University of Michigan Press.

Glaser, D. (1974). "Interlocking Dualities in Drug Use, Drug Control, and Crime." In J. Inciardi & C. Chambers (eds.) *Drugs and the Criminal Justice System*. Beverly Hills, CA: Sage Publications.

Goldstein, P.J. (1989). "Drugs and Violent Crime." In N.A. Weiner & M.E. Wolfgang (eds.) *Pathways to Criminal Violence*, 16-48. Beverly Hills, CA: Sage Publications.

Goldstein, P.J., H.H. Brownstein, P.J. Ryan & P.A. Bellucci (1990). "Most Drug-Related Murders Result from Crack Sales, Not Use." *The Drug Policy Letter*, 2:6-9.

Goldstein, P.J., H.H. Brownstein, P.J. Ryan & P.A. Bellucci (1989). "Crack and Homicide in New York City, 1988: A Conceptually-Based Event Analysis." *Contemporary Drug Problems*, 16:651-687.

Gomby, D. & P. Shiono (1991). "Estimating the Number of Substance-Exposed Infants." *The Future of Children*, 1(1):17-26.

Goode, E. (1994). *Drugs in America*, Fourth Edition. New York, NY: McGraw Hill.

Goode, E. (1989). "The American Drug Panic of the 1980s: Social Construction or Objective Threat?" *Violence, Aggression and Terrorism*, 3:327-348.

Goode, E. & N. Ben-Yehuda (1994). *Moral Panics: The Social Construction of Deviance*. New York, NY: Blackwell.

Gordon, D.R. (1994). *The Return of the Dangerous Classes: Drug Prohibition and Policy Politics*. New York, NY: W.W. Norton.

Gordon, D.R. (1990). *The Justice Juggernaut: Fighting Street Crime, Controlling Citizens*. New Brunswick, NJ: Rutgers University Press.

Government of Canada (1991). *Canada's Drug Strategy*. Ottawa, Canada: Minister of Supply and Services Canada.

Government of the Netherlands. (1995). *Drugs Policy in the Netherlands: Continuity and Change.* Netherlands: Ministry of Health, Welfare, and Sport.

Granfield, R. & K.F. Ryan (1996). "Drug Policy and Professional Conflict: The War Between the Docs and the Cops." Paper presented at the Law and Society Association Annual Meeting, Glasgow, Scotland.

Greenberg, J. (1990). "All About Crime." *New York Magazine*, 3:20-32.

Gusfield, J. (1985). *The Culture of Public Problems.* Chicago, IL: University of Chicago Press.

Gusfield, J.R. (1981). *The Culture of Public Problems: Drinking-Driving and the Symbolic Order.* Chicago, IL: University of Chicago Press.

Gusfield, J.R. (1963). *Symbolic Crusade: Status Politics and the American Temperance Movement.* Urbana, IL: University of Illinois Press.

Gustafson, N. (1991). "Pregnant Chemically Dependent Women: The New Criminals." *Affilia*, 6:61-73.

Hagedorn, J. (1994a). "Homeboys, Dope Fiends, Legits, and New Jacks." *Criminology*, 32(2):197-219.

Hagedorn, J. (1994b). "Neighborhoods, Markets, and Drug Organization." *Journal of Research in Crime and Delinquency*, 31(3):264-294.

Hagedorn, J. (1991). "Gangs, Neighborhoods, and Public Policy." *Social Problems*, 38(4):529-542.

Hagedorn, J. (1988). *People and Folks: Gangs, Crime and the Underclass in a Rustbelt City.* Chicago, IL: Lakeview Press.

Hall, S., C. Critcher, T. Jefferson, J. Clarke & B. Roberts (1978). *Policing the Crisis: Mugging, the State, and Law and Order.* New York, NY: Holmes and Meier.

Hallin, D. (1989). *The Uncensored War: The Media and Vietnam,* Berkeley, CA: University of California Press.

Hamid, A. (1990). "The Political Economy of Crack Related Violence." *Contemporary Drug Problems*, 17:31-78.

Hammett, T., S. Moini & A. Daugherty (1991). "HIV/AIDS in U.S. Prisons and Goals: Epidemiology, Policy, and Programs." In J. Norberry, M. Gaughwin & S. Gerull (eds.) *HIV/AIDS and Prisons. Conference Proceeding No. 4.* Canberra, Australia: Australian Institute of Criminology.

HANSARD (1995, October 30). *Debates of the House of Commons of Canada,* Ottawa, Canada.

Hartman, H. (1992). "Four D.M. Homes Hit in Drive-By Shootings Police Speculate That the Gunfire May Have Been Part of a Gang Initiation." *Newspaper A*, 1.

Health Canada (1995). *Canada's Alcohol and Other Drugs Survey*. Ottawa, Canada: Minister of Supply and Services.

Hearing Before the Committee on the Judiciary, United States Senate (1995). The U.S. Sentencing Commission and Cocaine Sentencing Policy. S. HRG. 154, 104th Cong., 1st Session.

Heather, N., A. Wodak, E. Nadelmann & P. O'Hare (eds.) (1993). *Psychoactive Drugs and Harm Reduction: From Faith to Science*. London, England: Whurr.

Hellawell, K. (1995). "The Role of Law Enforcement in Minimizing the Harm Resulting from Illicit Drugs." *Drug and Alcohol Review*, 14:317-322.

Helmer, J. (1975). *Drugs and Minority Oppression*. New York, NY: The Seabury Press.

Herman, E. & N. Chomsky (1988). *Manufacturing Consent*. New York, NY: Pantheon Books.

Hilgartner, S. & C.L. Bosk (1988). "The Rise and Fall of Social Problems: A Public Arenas Model." *American Journal of Sociology*, 94(1):53-78.

Himmelstein, J.L. (1983). *The Strange Career of Marihuana: Politics and Ideology of Drug Control in America*. Westport, CT: Greenwood Press.

Hoffman, P. (1993). "The Feds, Lies, and Video Tape." *Southern California Law Review*, 66:1453-1532.

Hogler, R. (1988). "Contractual and Tort Limitations on Employee Discipline for Substance Abuse." *Employee Relations Law Journal*, 13:480-500.

Horowitz, R. (1987). "Community Tolerance of Gang Violence." *Social Problems*, 34:437-450.

House of Commons Canada (1995). "Bill C-7" (as passed by the House of Commons on October 30, 1995). Ottawa, Canada: Canada Communication Group.

Hovelson, J. (1993). "Drug Gangs Wage War in Streets of Waterloo." *Newspaper A*, 19.

Hovelson, J. (1992). "Waterloo Fears Gang Wars Loom. Police Say the Groups are Involved in Drug Activity, and They Are Bracing for Fierce Fighting as Summer Approaches." *Newspaper A*, 3.

Howard, J., V. Kropenske & R. Tyler (1986). "The Long-Term Effects on Neurodevelopment in Infants Exposed Prenatally to PCP." *National Institute of Drug Abuse Monograph Series*, 64:237-251.

Howell, J. (1995). "Recent Gang Research: Program and Policy Implications." *Crime & Delinquency*, 40:495-515.

Huff, R. (1990). "Denial, Overreaction, and Misidentification: A Postscript on Public Policy." In C.R. Huff (ed.) *Gangs in America*, 310-317. Newbury Park, CA: Sage Publications.

Humphries, D. (1993). "Crack Mothers, Drug Wars, and the Politics of Resentment." In K.D. Tunnell (ed.) *Political Crime in Contemporary America: A Critical Approach*. New York, NY: Garland.

Hurt, H., N.L. Brodsleg, L.E. Braitman & G. Giannetta (1995, July/August). "Natal Status of Infants of Cocaine Users Comparison and Control Subjects: A Prospective." *Journal of Perinatology*, 15(4):297-305.

Husak, D. (1992). *Drugs and Rights*. New York, NY: Cambridge University Press.

In re Baby X, 97 Mich. App. 111, 293 N.W.2d 736 (1980).

In re Stevens S., 126 CA 3r 23, 178 Cal. Rptr. 525 (1981).

In re Troy D., 215 Cal. App. 3d 889, 263 Cal. Rptr. 868 (1989).

Inciardi, J. (1990). "The Crack-Violence Connection Within a Population of Hard-Core Adolescent Offenders." In M. de la Rosa, E. Lambert & B. Gropper (eds.) *Drugs and Violence: Causes, Correlates and Consequences*, 92-111.

Inciardi, J. (1990). *Handbook of Drug Control in the United States*. Westport, CT: Greenwood Publishing.

Inciardi, J. (1987). "Beyond Cocaine: Basuco, Crack, and Other Coca Products." *Contemporary Drug Problems*, 14:461-492.

Inciardi, J., D. Lockwood & A. Pottieger (1993). *Women and Crack Cocaine*. New York, NY: MacMillan Publishing Company.

Inciardi, J. & A. Pottieger (1991). "Kids, Crack and Crime." *Journal of Drug Issues*, 21:257-270.

Innis, D. (1990, March/April). "The UN Convention Against Illicit Traffic in Narcotic Substances and Psychotropic Substances." *Federal Bar News and Journal*, 37:118.

Institute of Medicine National Academy Sciences (IMNAS) (1988). *Confronting AIDS: Update 1988*. Washington, DC: National Academy Press.

Institute of Medicine National Academy of Sciences (IMNAS) (1986). *Confronting AIDS: Directions for Public Health, Health Care, and Research*. Washington, DC: National Academy Press.

International Narcotics Control Board (1994). *Report of the International Narcotics Control Board for 1994*. New York, NY: United Nations.

Irwin, J. & J. Austin (1994). *It's About Time: America's Imprisonment Binge*. Belmont, CA: Wadsworth.

Isikoff, M. (1991, August 14). "U.S. 'Power' on Abductions Detailed." *The Washington Post*, A14.

Iyengar, S. (1991). *Is Anyone Responsible?* Chicago, IL: University of Chicago Press.

Iyengar, S. & D. Kinder (1987). *News That Matters*. Chicago, IL: University of Chicago Press.

Iyengar, S., M.D. Peters & D. Kinder (1982). "Experimental Demonstrations of the 'Not-So-Minimal' Consequences of Television News Programs." *American Political Science Review*, 76:848-858.

Jensen, E.L. & J. Gerber (1996). "The Civil Forfeiture of Assets and the War on Drugs: Expanding Criminal Sanctions While Reducing Due Process Protections." *Crime & Delinquency*, 42:421-434.

Jensen, E.L. & J. Gerber (1993). "State Efforts to Construct a Social Problem: The 1986 War on Drugs in Canada." *Canadian Journal of Sociology*, 18:453-462.

Jensen, E.L., J. Gerber & G.M. Babcock (1991). "The New War on Drugs: Grass Roots Movement or Political Construction?" *The Journal of Drug Issues*, 21:651-667.

Johns, C.J. (1992). *Power, Ideology, and the War on Drugs*. New York, NY: Praeger.

Johnson v. Florida, 602 So.2d 1288 (Fla. 1992).

Johnson, B.D., A. Hamid & H. Sanabria (1992). "Emerging Models of Crack Distribution." In T. Mieczkowski (ed.) *Drugs, Crime, and Social Policy: Research, Issues, and Concerns*, 56-78. Boston, MA: Allyn and Bacon.

Johnson, J.L. & D.W. Crowley (1986). "T.L.O. and the Student's Right to Privacy." *Educational Theory*, 36:211-224.

Johnston, D. (1995, October 22). "Prisons Tighten Security After Uprisings." *The New York Times*, A12, A16.

Johnston, L.D., P. O'Malley & J.G Bachman (1996). *National Survey Results on Drug Use From the Monitoring the Future Study, 1975-1995*. U.S. Department of Health and Human Services, National Institute on Drug Abuse. Washington, DC: USGPO.

Jones, C. (1995, October 28). "Crack and Punishment: Is Race the Issue?" *The New York Times*, A1, A10.

Jos, P., M.F. Marshall & M. Perlmutter (1995). "The Charleston Policy on Cocaine Use During Pregnancy: A Cautionary Tale." *Journal of Law, Medicine and Ethics*, 23:120-128.

Joseph, P.R. (1987). "Fourth Amendment Implications of Public Sector Work Place Drug Testing." *Nova Law Review*, 11:605-645.

Justice Research (1994). *Drug Treatment Seven Times Cheaper Than Law Enforcement in Reducing Cocaine Consumption, Rand Study Finds*. Washington, DC: National Criminal Justice Association.

Kane, H.H. (1882). *Opium-Smoking in America and China*. New York, NY: G.P. Putnam's Sons.

Katz, M. (1989). *The Undeserving Poor*. New York, NY: Pantheon Books.

Katz v. United States, 389 U.S. 347 (1967).

Ker v. Illinois, 119 U.S. 436 (1886).

Kerr, P. (1993, June 27). "The Detoxing of Prisoner 88A0802." *The New York Times*, Section 6:22-27, 58-59.

Killias, M. & A. Uchtenhagen (1996). "Does Medical Heroin Prescription Reduce Delinquency Among Drug-Addicts? On the Evaluation of the Swiss Heroin Prescription Projects and its Methodology." *Studies on Crime & Crime Prevention*, 5:245-256.

Kleiman, M.A.R. (1992). *Against Excess: Drug Policy for Results*. New York, NY: Basic Books.

Klein, M.W. & C.L. Maxson (1989). "Street Gang Violence." In N. Weiner & M.E. Wolfgang (eds.) *Violent Crime, Violent Criminals*. Newbury Park, CA: Sage Publications.

Klingemann, H. (1993, October). "From Low-Threshold Intervention to Involuntary Commitment After the Closing of the Platzspitz 'Needle Park'? Drug Policy and Drug Treatment in Switzerland." Paper presented at the International Conference on Alcohol and Drug Treatment Systems Research, Toronto, Canada.

Koren, G., K. Graham, H. Shear & T. Einarson (1989, December 16). "Bias Against the Null Hypothesis: The Reproductive Hazards of Cocaine." *The Lancet*, 1440-1442.

Korthals, A.F. (1987). "Drug Policy in the Netherlands." Paper presented at the International Conference on Drug Abuse and Illicit Drug Trafficking, United Nations, Vienna, Austria.

Kraska, P. (1992). "The Processing of Drug Arrestees: Questioning the Assumption of an Ambivalent Reaction." *Journal of Criminal Justice*, 20:517-525.

Ladewig, D. (1996, March 13). "Heroin Substitution Trials in Switzerland: Context, Preliminary Data, and Findings from an Evaluation Perspective." Unpublished paper presented at the Addiction Research Foundation, Toronto, Canada.

Langan, P. (1985). "Racism on Trial: New Evidence to Explain Racial Composition of Prisons in the United States." *Journal of Criminal Law and Criminology*, 76:666-683.

Langel, A. (1993). "Charges Against Teenagers Continue to Mount." *Newspaper B*, A4.

Larson, C. (1991). "Overview of State Legislative and Judicial Responses." *The Future of Children*, (1):73-83.

Latessa, E.J., L.J. Travis & F.T. Cullen (1988). "Public Support for Mandatory Drug-Alcohol Testing in the Workplace." *Crime & Delinquency*, 34:379-392.

Latimer, D. & J. Goldberg (1981). *Flowers in the Blood: The Story of Opium*. New York, NY: Franklin Watts.

Lee, A.M. (1978). *Sociology for Whom?* New York, NY: Oxford University Press.

Lee, R.W. (1989). *The White Labyrinth: Cocaine and Political Power.* New Brunswick, NJ: Transaction Publishers.

Leff, D.R., D.L. Protess & S.C. Brooks (1986). "Crusading Journalism: Changing Public Attitudes and Policy-Making Agendas." *Public Opinion Quarterly*, 50:300-315.

Leiber, M., K.M. Jamieson & M. Krohn (1993). "Newspaper Reporting and the Production of Deviance: Drug Use Among Professional Athletes." *Deviant Behavior: An Interdisciplinary Journal*, 14:317-339.

Leslie, B. (1993). *Parental Crack Use: Demographic, Familial and Child Welfare Perspectives: A Toronto Study.* North York, Ontario, Canada: Children's Aid Society of Metropolitan Toronto, Canada.

Leuw, E. (1991). "Drugs and Drug Policy in the Netherlands." In M. Tonry & N. Morris (eds.) *Crime and Justice: A Review of Research*, 14:229-276. Chicago, IL: University of Chicago Press.

Levine, H. & C. Reinarman (1987, March 28). "What's Behind Jar Wars?" *The Nation*, 244:388-390.

Levine, H.G. (1984). "The Alcohol Problem in America: From Temperance to Alcoholism." *British Journal of Addiction*, 79:109-119.

Lindesmith, A. (1968). *Addiction and Opiates.* Chicago, IL: Aldine.

Lindesmith, A. (1965). *The Addict and the Law*. Bloomington, IN: University of Indiana Press.

Lindesmith, A. (1940). "Dope Fiend Mythology." *Journal of Criminal Law, Criminology, and Police Science*, 31:199-208.

Lockwood, D., A. Pottieger & J. Inciardi (1995). "Crack Use, Crime by Crack Users, and Ethnicity." In D.F. Hawkins (ed.) *Ethnicity, Race, and Crime*, 212-234. Albany, NY: State University of New York Press.

Lofquist, W.S. (1993). "Legislating Organizational Probation: State Capacity, Business Power, and Corporate Crime Control." *Law and Society Review*, 27(4):741-783.

The Los Angeles Times (1995, March 1). "Officials Urge Reduced U.S. Penalties for Crack Cocaine," A8.

Lowenfeld, A.F. (1990). "U.S. Law Enforcement Abroad: The Constitution and International Law, Continued." *American Journal of International Law*, 84:444-493.

Lowney, K.D. (1994). "Smoked Not Snorted: Is Racism Inherent in our Crack Cocaine Laws?" *Journal of Urban and Contemporary Law*, 45:121-171.

Lutiger, B., K. Graham, T.R. Einarson & G. Koren (1991). "The Relationship Between Gestational Cocaine Use and Pregnancy Outcome: A Meta-Analysis." *Teratology*, 44:405-414.

Lynch, M., M. Nalla & K. Miller (1989). "Cross-Cultural Perceptions of Deviance: The Case of Bopal." *Journal of Research in Crime and Delinquency*, 26:7-35.

MacLean, B. & D. Milovanovic (1990). *Racism, Empiricism and Criminal Justice*. Vancouver, Canada: The Collective Press.

MacLean, B.D. & D. Milovanovic (eds.) (1991). *New Directions in Critical Criminology*. Vancouver, Canada: The Collective Press.

Maguire, K. & T. Flanagan (eds.) (1990). *Sourcebook of Criminal Justice Statistics, 1990*. Washington, DC: Bureau of Justice Statistics.

Maguire, K. & A.L. Pastore (eds.) (1996). *Sourcebook of Criminal Justice Statistics, 1995*. U.S. Department of Justice, Bureau of Justice Statistics. Washington, DC: USGPO.

Maguire, K. & A.L. Pastore (eds.) (1995). *Sourcebook of Criminal Justice Statistics, 1994*. U.S. Department of Justice, Bureau of Justice Statistics. Washington, DC: USGPO.

Maher, L. (1992). "Punishment and Welfare: Crack Cocaine and the Regulation of Mothering." *Women and Criminal Justice*, 3(2):35-70.

Malamud-Goti, J. (1992a). "Reinforcing Poverty: The Bolivian War on Cocaine." In A.W. McCoy & A.A. Block (eds.) *War on Drugs: Studies in the Failure of U.S. Narcotics Policy*, 67-92. Boulder, CO: Westview Press.

Malamud-Goti, J. (1992b). *Smoke and Mirrors: The Paradox of the Drug Wars.* Boulder, CO: Westview Press.

Manning, P.K. (1996). "Dramaturgy, Politics and the Axial Media Event." *The Sociological Quarterly*, 37:261-278.

Marks, J. (1994). "The Paradox of Prohibition." In *Questioning Prohibition: 1994 International Report on Drugs*, 155-164. Brussels, Belgium: International Antiprohibitionist League.

Marshall, I., O. Anjewierden & H. Van Atteveld (1990). "Toward an 'Americanization' of Dutch Drug Policy?" *Justice Quarterly*, 7:391-420.

Marx, G. (1981). "Ironies of Social Control: Authorities as Contributors to Deviance Through Escalation, Nonenforcement, and Covert Facilitation." *Social Problems*, 28:221-246.

Massey, D. & N. Denton (1993). *American Apartheid: Segregation and the Making of the Underclass.* Cambridge, MA: Harvard University Press.

Mathias, R. (1992). "Developmental Effects of Prenatal Drug Exposure May Be Overcome by Post Natal Environment." *NIDA Notes*, 7(1):14-17.

Matthews, R. & J. Young (1992). "Reflections on Realism." In Y. Young & R. Matthews (eds.) *Rethinking Criminology: The Realist Debate*, 1-23. London, England: Sage Publications.

Mauer, M. (1990). *Young Black Men and the Criminal Justice System: A Growing National Concern.* Washington, DC: The Sentencing Project.

Mauss, A.L. (1989). "Beyond the Illusion of Social Problems Theory." *Perspectives on Social Problems*, 1:19-39.

Mauss, A.L. (1984). "The Myth of Social Problems Theory." *SSSP Theory Division Newsletter*, 15:12-13.

Mauss, A.L. (1975). *Social Problems as Social Movements.* Philadelphia, PA: J.B. Lippincott.

Mayer, R.R. & E. Greenwood (1980). *The Design of Social Policy Research.* Englewood Cliffs, NJ: Prentice-Hall.

Mayes, L. (1992). "The Problem of Prenatal Cocaine Exposure: A Rush to Judgment." *The Journal of the American Medical Association*, 267:406-408.

Mays, L., T. Winfree & S. Jackson (1993). "Youth Gangs in Southern New Mexico: A Qualitative Analysis." *Journal of Contemporary Criminal Justice*, 9:134-145.

McAllister, W.B. (1991). "Conflicts of Interest in the International Drug Control System." *Journal of Policy History*, 3:494-517.

McCarthy, J.D. & M.N. Zald (1977). "Resource Mobilization and Social Movements: A Partial Theory." *American Journal of Sociology*, 82:1212-1241.

McCarthy, J.D. & M.N. Zald (1973). *The Trend of Social Movements in America Professionalization and Resource Mobilization*. Morristown, NJ: General Learning.

McCloskey, H. & A. Brill (1983). *Dimensions of Tolerance: What Americans Believe About Civil Liberties*. New York, NY: Russell Sage Foundation.

McCombs, M. & D.L. Shaw (1972). "The Agenda-Setting Function of the Mass Media." *Public Opinion Quarterly*, 36.

McCoy, A.W. & A.A. Block (1992). "U.S. Narcotics Policy: An Anatomy of Failure." In A.W. McCoy & A.A. Block (eds.) *War on Drugs: Studies in the Failure of U.S. Narcotics Policy*, 1-18. Boulder, CO: Westview Press.

McCullough, C. (1991). "The Child Welfare Response." *The Future of Children*, 1(1):61-72.

McDonald, D., R. Moore, J. Norberry, G. Wardlaw & N. Ballenden (1995). *Legislative Options for Cannabis in Australia*, Monograph Series No. 26. Canberra, Australia: Australian Government Publishing Service.

McDonell v. Hunter, 612 F. Supp. 1122 (S.D. Iowa, 1985).

McNulty, N. (1987-1988). "Pregnancy Police: The Health Policy and Legal Implications of Punishing Pregnant Women for Harm to their Fetuses." *Review of Law and Social Change*, 16(2):277-319.

Merriam, J.E. (1989). "National Media Coverage of Drug Issues, 1983-1987." In P. Shoemaker (ed.) *Communication Campaigns About Drugs: Government, the Media and the Public*. Mahwah, NJ: Lawrence Erlbaum Associates, Publishers.

Merton, R.K. (1949). "The Role of Applied Social Science in the Formation of Policy: A Research Memorandum." *Philosophy of Science*, 16:161-181.

Merton, R.K. (1945). "Role of the Intellectual in Public Bureaucracy." *Social Forces*, 23:405-415.

Merton, R.K. & J.Z. Moss (1985). "Basic Research and its Potential for Relevance." *Mount Sinai Journal of Medicine*, 52:679-684.

Mieczkowski, T. (1990). "Crack Distribution in Detroit." *Contemporary Drug Problems*, 17:9-29.

Miller, W. (1982). "Crime by Youth Gangs and Groups in the United States." Washington, DC: U.S. Department of Justice, Office of Juvenile Justice and Delinquency Prevention, Rev. 1992.

Minister of Health (1994). *Bill C-7 'The Controlled Drugs and Substances Act'; An Act respecting the control of certain drugs, their precursors and other substances and to amend certain Acts and repeal the Narcotic Control Act in consequence thereof.* Ottawa, Canada: Department of Health.

Minnesota Statutes Annotated (1990). MN Stat. 626.5561.

Minnesota Statutes Annotated (1990). Section 626.6661. Subd. 1. (West Supp.).

Molotch, H. & M. Lester (1974). "News as Purposive Behavior: The Strategic Use of Routine Events, Accidents and Scandals." *American Sociological Review*, 39:101-112.

Moore, W. (1995, February 11). "Targeting Harlem, Not Hollywood." *National Journal*, 388.

Moreau, J. (1995). Adult Charges for Various Drug Offenses in Canada, 1971 1993. Unpublished Internal Document, Addiction Research Foundation, Toronto, Ontario. Tables based on data published in Canadian Crime Statistics, Statistics Canada Catalogue 85 215 Annual, Canadian Centre for Justice Statistics, Ottawa, Canada.

Morgan, D. (1986). *The Flacks of Washington: Government Information and the Public Agenda.* New York, NY: Greenwood Press.

Morgan, J., D. Riley & G. Chester (1993). "Cannabis: Legal Reform, Medical Use and Harm Reduction." In N. Heather, A. Wodak, E. Nadelmann & P. O'Hare (eds.) *Psychoactive Drugs and Harm Reduction: From Faith to Science*, 211-229. London, England: Whurr.

Morgan, J.P. (1988). "The Scientific Justification for Urine Drug Testing." *University of Kansas Law Review*, 36:683-697.

Morgan, P. (1978). "The Legislation of Drug Law: Economic Crisis and Social Control," *Journal of Drug Issues*, 8:53-62.

Morgan, P.A. (1990). "The Making of a Public Problem: Mexican Labor in California and the Marijuana Law of 1937." In R. Glick & J. Moore (eds.) *Drugs in Hispanic Communities*, 233-252. New Brunswick, NJ: Rutgers University Press.

Murphy, E. (1922/1973). *The Black Candle.* Toronto, Canada: Coles.

Musto, D.F. (1973). *The American Disease: Origins of Narcotics Control.* New Haven, CT: Yale University Press.

Nadelmann, E., P. Cohen, E. Drucker, U. Locher, G. Stimson & A. Wodak (1994, March). "The Harm Reduction Approach to Drug Control: International Progress." Paper presented at the 5th International Conference on the Reduction of Drug-Related Harm, Toronto, Canada.

Nadelmann, E. & J. McNeely (1996, Spring). "Doing Methadone Right." *The Public Interest*, 123:83-93.

Nadelmann, E.A. (1993). *Cops Across Borders: The Internationalization of U.S. Criminal Law Enforcement*. University Park, PA: Pennsylvania State University Press.

Nadelmann, E.A. (1992, Summer). "Thinking Seriously About Alternatives to Drug Prohibition." *Daedalus*, 121:85-132.

Nadelmann, E.A. (1990). "Global Prohibition Regimes: The Evolution of Norms in International Society." *International Organization*, 44:479-526.

Nadelmann, E.A. (1989). "Drug Prohibition in the United States: Costs, Consequences, and Alternatives." *Science*, 245:939-947.

Nadelmann, E.A. (1988). "U.S. Drug Policy: A Bad Export." *Foreign Policy*, 70:83-108.

Nanda, V.P. (1990). "The Validity of the United States Intervention in Panama Under International Law." *American Journal of International Law*, 84:494-503.

Narcotics Penalties and Enforcement Act of 1986. Report from The Committee on The Judiciary, H.R. 845, Part 1, 99th Cong., 2nd Sess. (1986).

National Institute on Drug Abuse (1991). *National Household Survey on Drug Abuse: Population Estimates*. Rockville, MD: National Institute on Drug Abuse.

National Institute on Drug Abuse (1988, April 11). "Enemy Within: Drug Money is Corrupting the Enforcers." *The New York Times*, A12.

National Institute on Drug Abuse (1988). *National Household Survey on Drug Abuse: Population Estimates*. Rockville, MD: National Institute on Drug Abuse.

National Institute on Drug Abuse (1986). *NIDA Capsules—Household Survey on Abuse, 1985*. Rockville, MD: Press Office of the National Institute on Drug Abuse.

National Treasury Employees Union v. Von Raab, 816 F.2d 170 (1989).

Neumayr, M.B. (1988). "Note, Maritime Drug Law Enforcement Act: An Analysis." *Hastings International and Comparative Law Review*, 11:487-508.

New Jersey v. T.L.O., 469 U.S. 325 (1985).

The New York Times (1995, November 5). "Cocaine Sentencing, Still Unjust," E14.

The New York Times (1995, October 28). "Crack and Punishment: Is Race the Issue?," A10.

The New York Times (1995, September 13). "Cocaine Terms Unchanged," A18.

Newspaper A (1994a). "Grandy: End Parole, Build More Prisons. The Challenger Accuses Branstad of Returning Guns to Felons and Allowing Violent Crime to Soar," 3.

Newspaper A (1994b). "Clinton Outlines Gun-Sarch Plan for Public Housing an Outright Ban on Guns in Federally Assisted Housing Units is Being Considered, the Housing Secretary Says," 9.

Newspaper A (1994c). "House Votes to Allow Random Locker Search. The 'Safe-Shools' Package Wins Approval After a Day-Long Debate Over Students' Rights," 4.

Newspaper A (1992a). "Gun Control Foes Give Legislature a Warning Lawmakers Say a Drive for Gun Control Sparked by the Shootings at the University of Iowa Will Likely Fade," 3.

Newspaper A (1992b). "Daily Briefing Nation," 3.

Newspaper A (1992c). "FBI Focuses on Street Gang Crime," 3.

Newspaper B (1991). "Youth Death Toll from Guns Still Rising," A10.

Newspaper B (1990). "Rural Areas War on Drugs," A4.

Nimmo, Dan (1964). *Newsgathering in Washington: A Study in Political Communication.* New York, NY: Atherton Press.

Note (1991). "Fighting the War on Drugs in the 'New World Order': The *Ker-Frisbie* Doctrine as a Product of Its Time." *Vanderbilt Journal of Transnational Law*, 24:535-570.

Note (1990). "Drug Diplomacy and the Supply-Side Strategy: A Survey of United States Practice." *Vanderbilt Law Review*, 43:1259-1309.

O'Connor v. Ortega, 480 U.S. 709 (1986).

Office of the Attorney General (1989). *Drug Trafficking—A Report to the President of the United States.* Washington, DC: U.S. Department of Justice.

Omaha World Herald (1993, April 17), 1.

Orcutt, J.D. & J.B. Turner (1993). "Shocking Numbers and Graphic Accounts: Quantified Images of Drug Problems in the Print Media." *Social Problems*, 40:190-206.

Padel, U., R. Twidale & J. Porter (1992). *HIV Education in Prisons: A Resource Book.* Hamilton House, Mabledon Place London, England: Health Education Authority.

Paltrow, L. (1993, August). "Winning Strategies: Defending the Rights of Pregnant Addicts." *The Champion.*

Paltrow, L. (1992). *Criminal Prosecutions of Women for Their Behavior During Pregnancy.* New York, NY: The Center for Reproductive Law and Policy.

Paltrow, L. (1990). "When Becoming Pregnant is a Crime." *Criminal Justice Ethics*, 9(1):41-47.

Pearson, G. (1990). "Drug-Control Policies in Britain." In M. Tonry & N. Morris (eds.) *Crime and Justice: A Review of Research*, vol. 14:167-227. Chicago, IL: University of Chicago Press.

Pearson, J. & N. Thoennes (1996). "What Happens to Pregnant Substance Abusers and Their Babies?" *Juvenile and Family Court Journal*, 1:15-28.

Peele, S. (1989). *Diseasing of America: Addiction Treatment Out of Control*. Lexington, MA: Lexington Books.

Peele, S. (1985). *The Meaning of Addiction: Compulsive Experience and Its Interpretation*. Lexington, MA: Lexington Books.

Perinatal Substance Abuse Act of 1990 (1991). California Senate, Sacramento, CA.

Perl, R.F. (1993-1994, Winter). "Clinton's Foreign Drug Policy." *Journal of Interamerican Studies and World Affairs*, 35:143-152.

Petitti, D. & M. Coleman (1990). "Cocaine and the Risk of Low Birth Weight." *American Journal of Public Health*, 80(1):25-28.

Pfohl, S.J. (1977). "The 'Discovery' of Child Abuse." *Social Problems*, 24:310-323.

Platt, A.M. (1994). "The Politics of Law and Order." *Social Justice*, 21:3-13.

Pollitt, K. (1990). "Fetal Rights: A New Assault on Feminism." *The Nation*, 247(12):455-460.

Portney, K.E. (1986). *Approaching Public Policy Analysis*. Englewood Cliffs, NJ: Prentice-Hall.

Powell, J. (1991a). "Guns For Sale." *Newspaper B*, A2.

Powell, J. (1991b). "Tri-County Force Taking Aim at Drug-Borders." *Newspaper B*, A.

Pryor, D. & E. McGarrell (1993). "Public Perceptions of Youth Gang Crime, An Exploratory Analysis." *Youth and Society*, 21:282-305.

Quindlen, A. (1990, October 7). "Hearing the Cries of Crack." *The New York Times*, E19.

Quinney, R.A. (1970). *The Social Reality of Crime*. Boston, MA: Little, Brown.

Railway Labor Executives Association v. Burnley, 839 F.2d 575 (1988).

Rana, S. (1996, March). "Harm Reduction in the Asian Context." Keynote address from the 7th International Conference on the Reduction of Drug Related Harm, Hobart, Tasmania, Australia.

Randall, D.M. & J.F. Short, Jr. (1983). "Women in Toxic Work Environments: A Case Study of Social Problems Development." *Social Problems*, 30:410-424.

Reeves, J.L. & R. Campbell (1994). *Cracked Coverage: Television News, the Anti-cocaine Crusade, and the Reagan Legacy.* Durham, NC: Duke University Press.

Reinarman, C. & H.G. Levine (1995). "Crack Attack: America's Latest Drug Scare, 1986-1992." In J. Best (ed.) *Images of Issues.* New York, NY: Aldine de Gruyter.

Reinarman, C. (1994a). "The Social Construction of Drug Scares." In P.A. Adler & P. Adler (eds.) *Constructions of Deviance: Social Power, Context, and Interaction*, 92-104. Belmont, CA: Wadsworth.

Reinarman, C. (1994b). "Unanticipated Consequences of Criminalization: Hypotheses on How Drug Laws Exacerbate Drug Problems." *Perspectives on Social Problems*, 6:217-232.

Reinarman, C. & H.G. Levine (1989, Winter). "Crack in Context: Politics and Media in the Making of a Drug Scare." *Contemporary Drug Problems*, 16(4):535-577.

Reinarman, C., S. Murphy & D. Waldorf (1994). "Pharmacology is Not Destiny: The Contingent Character of Cocaine Abuse and Addiction." *Addiction Research*, 2:1-16.

Reske, H.J. (1995, July, 30). "Congress Asked to Lower Crack Penalties." *ABA Journal.*

Reske, H.J. (1993, August 4). "Same Drug, Different Penalties." *The Washington Post.*

Restatement (Third) of Foreign Relations Law (1987). Washington, DC: American Law Institute.

Reuter, P. (1992). "The Limits and Consequences of U.S. Foreign Drug Control Efforts." *Annals of the American Academy of Political and Social Sciences*, 521:151-162.

Reuter, P., G. Crawford & J. Cave (1988). *Sealing the Borders.* Santa Monica, CA: The RAND Corporation.

Reuter, P. & R. MacCoun (1995). "Lessons From the Absence of Harm Reduction in American Drug Policy." *Tobacco Control: An International Journal*, 4(suppl. 2):28-32.

Reuter, P., R. MacCoun & P. Murphy (1990). *Money From Crime—A Study of the Economics of Drug Dealing in Washington, DC.* Santa Monica, CA: The RAND Corporation.

Richardson, G. & N. Day (1991, July-August). "Maternal and Neonatal Effects of Moderate Use of Cocaine During Pregnancy." *Neurotoxicology and Teratology*, 13:455-460.

Riley, D. (in press). "First Do No Harm: The Nature and Practice of Harm Reduction." *International Journal on Drug Policy.*

Riley, D. (1993). "The Policy and Practice of Harm Reduction: The Application of Harm Reduction Measures in a Prohibitionist Society." Ottawa, Canada: CCSA

Ritter, C. & J. Anthony (1991). "Factors Influencing Initiation of Cocaine Use Among Adults: Findings From the Epidemiological Catchment Area Program." In S. Schober & C. Schade (eds.) *The Epidemiology of Cocaine Use and Abuse*, Research Monograph No. 110:71-94. Rockville, MD: National Institute on Drug Abuse.

Rivard v. United States, 375 F.2d 882, *cert. denied,* 389 U.S. 884 (1967).

Roberts, D. (1991). "Punishing Drug Addicts Who Have Babies: Women of Color, Equality and the Rights of Privacy." *Harvard Law Review,* 104(7):1419-1482.

Roberts, J. & A. Doob (1990). "News Media Influence on Public Views on Sentencing." *Law and Human Behavior,* 14:451-468.

Roberts, J. & D. Edwards (1989). "Contextual Effects in Judgments of Crimes, Criminals and the Purpose of Sentencing." *Journal of Applied Social Psychology,* 19:902-917.

Roberts, J.V. (1992). "Public Opinion, Crime and Criminal Justice." In M. Toury (ed.) *Crime and Justice: A Review of Research,* 16. Chicago, IL: University of Chicago Press.

Robinson, C. & L. Powell (1996). "The Postmodern Politics of Context Definition: Competing Reality Frames in the Hill-Thomas Spectacle." *The Sociological Quarterly,* 37:279-305.

Robin-Vergeer, B.I. (1990). "The Problem of the Drug Exposed Newborn: A Return to Principled Intervention." *Stanford Law Review,* 42(3):745-809.

Roe v. Wade, 410 U.S. 113, (1973).

Rolleson Report (1926). *Report of the Developmental Committee on Morphine and Heroin Addiction.* London, England: HMSO.

Roos, J. (1992). "Bill Would Toughen Drug Laws." *Newspaper A,* 4.

Rosenbaum, M. (1997). "The De-Medicalization of Methadone Maintenance." In P. Erickson, D. Riley, Y. Cheung & P. O'Hare (eds.) *Harm Reduction: A New Direction for Drug Policies and Programs.* Toronto, Canada: University of Toronto Press.

Rosenberg, I.M. (1996). "Public School Drug Testing: The Impact of *Acton.*" *American Criminal Law Review,* 33:349-378.

Roshier, J. (1975). "The Selection of Crime News by the Press." In S. Cohen & J. Young (eds.) *The Manufacture of News,* 28-39. Beverly Hills, CA: Sage Publications.

Ross, J. (1992, September, 16). "Coming Down on Crack: Well-Intended Efforts Run the Risk of Becoming Racist in Nature." *L.A. Daily Journal,* col. 3:4.

Rouse, J.J. & B.D. Johnson (1991). "Hidden Paradigms of Morality in Debates About Drugs: Historical and Policy Shifts in British and American Drug Policies." In J.A. Inciardi (ed.) *The Drug Legalization Debate*, 183-214. Newbury Park, CA: Sage Publications.

Royal Canadian Mounted Police (RCMP) (1993). *Drug Intelligence Estimate 1990-1992.* Ottawa, Canada: RCMP.

Ruter, F. (1986). "Drugs and the Criminal Law in the Netherlands." In J. Van Dijk, C. Haffmans, F. Ruter, J Schutte & S. Stolwijk (eds.) *Criminal Law in Action.* Arnhem, The Netherlands: Gouda Quint.

Ryan, K.F. (1994). "How We Lost the War: Explorations of U.S. Drug Policy and Its Consequences." *Criminal Justice Review*, 19:79-99.

Sagatun, I. (1993). "Babies Born With Drug Addiction: Background and Legal Response." In R. Muraskin & T. Alleman (eds.) *It's a Crime: Women and Justice.* Englewood Cliffs, NJ: Regents/Prentice Hall.

Sagatun-Edwards, I. (1996). *Family Reunification for Drug-Exposed Infants: Interim Report.* Grant # 95-9239. Los Altos, CA: Packard Foundation.

Sagatun-Edwards, I., C. Saylor & B. Shifflett (1995). "Drug Exposed Infants in the Social Welfare System and the Juvenile Court." *Child Abuse and Neglect: The International Journal*, 19(1):83-91.

Samarasinghe, D. (1995). "Harm Reduction in the Developing World." *Drug and Alcohol Review*, 14:305-309.

Sanders, C.R. & E. Lyon (1995). "Repetitive Retribution: Media Images in the Cultural Construction of Criminal Justice." In C. Sanders (ed.) *Cultural Criminology.* Boston, MA: Northeastern University Press.

Sandor, R.S. (1995). "Legalizing/Decriminalizing Drug Use." In R.H. Coombs and D.M. Ziedonis (eds.) *Handbook on Drug Abuse Prevention: A Contemporary Strategy to Prevent the Abuse of Alcohol and Other Drugs,* 509-525. Needham Heights, MA: Allyn & Bacon.

Sasson, T. (1995). *Crime Talk: How Citizen's Construct a Social Problem.* New York, NY: Aldine de Gruyter.

Scheerer, S. (1978). "The New Dutch and German Drug Laws: Social and Political Conditions for Criminalization and Decriminalization." *Law and Society Review*, 12:585-606.

Scheingold, S.A. (1991). *The Politics of Street Crime: Criminal Process and Cultural Obsession.* Philadelphia, PA: Temple University Press.

Scheingold, S.A. (1984). *The Politics of Law and Order: Street Crime and Public Policy.* New York, NY: Longman.

Schivelbusch, W. (1981). *Paradiset, smaken og fornuften.* Pax, Oslo. Originally as: Das Paradis, der Geschmack und die Vernuft. Eine Geschichte der Genussmittel. München 1980.

Schmerber v. California, 384 U.S. 757 (1966).

Schneider, J.W. (1985). "Social Problems Theory: The Constructionist View." *Annual Review of Sociology,* 11:209-229.

Schram, M. (1994). "Crime Statistics are as Slippery as Wet Soap." *Newspaper B.*

Schudson, M. (1978). *Discovering the News: A Social History of America's Newspapers.* New York, NY: Basic Books.

Scientific American (1938). "Marihuana More Dangerous than Heroin or Cocaine," 293.

Shein, M.G. (1993). "Racial Disparity in 'Crack' Cocaine Sentencing." *Criminal Justice,* 8:2, 28-32, 61-62.

Sherizen, S. (1978). "Social Creation of Crime News: All the News That's Fitted to Print." In C. Winick (ed.) *Deviance and the Mass Media.* Beverly Hills, CA: Sage Publications.

Shoemaker, P. (ed.) (1989). *Communication Campaigns About Drugs: Government, the Media and the Public.* Mahwah, NJ: Lawrence Erlbaum Associates, Publishers.

Shoemaker, P., W. Wanta & D. Leggett (1989). "Drug Coverage and Public Opinion, 1976-1986." In P. Shoemaker (ed.) *Communication Campaigns About Drugs: Government, the Media and the Public.* Mahwah, NJ: Lawrence Erlbaum Associates, Publishers.

Sigal, L. (1973). *Reporters and Officials: The Organization and Politics of Newsmaking.* London, England: D.C. Heath.

Single, E. (1995). "Defining Harm Reduction." *Drug and Alcohol Review,* 14:287-290.

Single, E. (1989). "The Impact of Marijuana Decriminalization: An Update." *Journal of Public Health Policy,* 10:456-466.

Single, E.W., J. Skirrow, P.G. Erickson & R. Solomon (1991, December). "Policy Developments in Canada." Paper presented at the congress, "The Window of Opportunity," Adelaide, Australia.

Skinner v. Railway Labor Executives Association, 489 U.S. 602 (1989).

Smart, R. (1991). "AIDS and Drug Abuse in Canada: Current Status and Information Needs." *The Journal of Drug Issues,* 21:73-82.

Smith, A. (1994). "African-American Grandmothers' War Against the Crack-Cocaine Epidemic." *Arete*, 19(1):22-36.

Smith, G. (1993). "Officials: Drug Profits Will Fuel Gang Activity." *Newspaper B*.

Smith, P.H. (1996). *Talons of the Eagle: Dynamics of U.S.-Latin American Relations*. New York, NY: Oxford University Press.

Smith, P.H. (1992). "The Political Economy of Drugs: Conceptual Issues and Policy Options." In P.H. Smith (ed.) *Drug Policy in the Americas*, 1-21. Boulder, CO: Westview Press.

Smolowe, J. (1995, July 19). "One Drug, Two Sentences." *Time*, 44-45.

Sohn, L.B. (1984). "The Law of the Sea Crisis." *St. John's Law Review*, 58:237-266.

Solomon, R. & M. Green (1988). "The First Century: The History of Non-Medical Opiate Use and Control Policies in Canada, 1870-1970." In J.C. Blackwell & P.G. Erickson (eds.) *Illicit Drugs in Canada: A Risky Business*. Toronto, Canada: Nelson Canada.

Solomon, R. & T. Madison (1977). "The Evolution of Non-Medical Opiate Use in Canada—Part I: 1870 1929." *Drug Forum*, (5)3:52-60.

Spector, M. (1983-1984). "Spector on 'Social Problems.'" *Society for the Study of Social Problems Newsletter*, 15:11-12.

Spector, M. & J.I. Kitsuse (1987). *Constructing Social Problems*. Hawthorne, NY: Aldine de Gruyter.

Spector, M. & J.I. Kitsuse (1977). *Constructing Social Problems*. Menlo Park, CA: Cummings.

Spector, M. & J.I. Kitsuse (1974). "Social Problems: A Reformulation." *Social Problems*, 20:145-159.

Spergal, I. (1990). "Youth Gangs: Continuity and Change." *Crime and Justice*, 171-275.

Standing Senate Committee on Legal and Constitutional Affairs (1995, December 13). Evidence (Transcript), Ottawa, Canada.

Stares, P. (1996). *Global Habit: The Drug Problem in a Borderless World*. Washington, DC: Brookings Institution.

Stevens, J. (1987). *Storming Heaven: LSD and the American Dream*. New York, NY: Harper & Row.

Stewart, D.P. (1990). "Internationalizing the War on Drugs: The UN Convention Against Illicit Traffic in Narcotic Drugs and Psychotropic Substances." *Denver Journal of International Law and Policy*, 18:387-404.

Strandjord, T.P. & W.A. Hodson (1992). "Neonatology." *Journal of American Medical Association*, 268:377-378.

Stutman, R. (1992). *Dead on Delivery: Inside the Drug Wars, Straight From the Street.* Boston, MA: Little, Brown.

Suk, T. (1993). "Crack, Crime and Violence Follow as Gangs Gain a Foothold in Iowa." *Newspaper A*, 1.

Surette, R. (1992). *Media, Crime and Criminal Justice: Images and Realities.* Pacific Grove, CA: Brooks/Cole Publishing Co.

Takata, S. & R. Zevitz (1990). "Divergent Perceptions of Group Delinquency in a Midwestern Community: Racine's Gang Problem." *Youth and Society*, 21:282-305.

Tarazona-Sevillano, G. (1990). *Sendero Luminoso and the Threat of Narcoterrorism.* New York, NY: Praeger.

Taylor v. O'Grady, 888 F.2d 1189 (1989).

Taylor, A.H. (1969). *American Diplomacy and the Narcotics Traffic, 1900-1939.* Durham, NC: Duke University Press.

Taylor, M. (1995). "Parent's Use of Drugs as a Factor in Award of Custody of Children, Visitation Rights, or Termination of Parental Rights." *A.L.R. 5th*, 535-668.

Terry v. Ohio, 392 U.S. 1 (1968).

Thompson, D. & L. Jason (1988). "Street Gangs and Preventive Interventions." *Criminal Justice and Behavior*, 15:323-333.

Thompson, F.J., N.R. Riccucci & C. Ban (1991). "Drug Testing in the Federal Work-place: An Instrumental and Symbolic Assessment." *Public Administration Review*, 51:515-525.

Thornberry, T., M. Krohn, A. Lizotte & D. Chard-Wierschem (1993). "The Role of Juvenile Gangs in Facilitating Delinquent Behavior." *Journal of Research in Crime and Delinquency*, 20:55-87.

Tonry, M. (1995). *Malign Neglect: Race, Crime and Punishment.* New York, NY: Oxford University Press.

Tonry, M. (1988). "Structured Sentencing." In M. Tonry and N. Morris (eds.) *Crime and Justice*, 10:267-337. Chicago, IL: University of Chicago Press.

Toro, M.C. (1992). "Unilateralism and Bilateralism." In P.H. Smith (ed.) *Drug Policy in the Americas*, 314-328. Boulder, CO: Westview Press.

Trebach. A. (1988, September 29). *Testimony at the Hearings on Proposals to Legalize Drugs Held by the House Select Committee on Narcotics Abuse and Control.*

Trebach, A.S. (1987). *The Great Drug War*. New York, NY: MacMillan Publishing Company.

Tuchman, G. (1978). *Making News: A Study in the Construction of Reality*. New York, NY: Free Press.

U.S. Bureau of Justice Statistics (1991). *Federal Criminal Case Processing, 1980-1989*. Washington, DC: U.S. Department of Justice.

U.S. Bureau of Prisons (1987). *Statistical Report. Fiscal Year 1986*. Washington, DC: U.S. Department of Justice.

U.S. Department of Justice (1996). *Felony Sentences in the United States, 1992*. Bureau of Justice Statistics. Washington, DC: U.S. Department of Justice.

U.S. Department of Justice (1995). *Correctional Populations in the United States*. Bureau of Justice Statistics. Washington, DC: U.S. Department of Justice.

U.S. Department of Justice (1993). *Compendium of Federal Justice Statistics, 1990*. Bureau of Justice Statistics. Washington, DC: U.S. Department of Justice.

U.S. Law Week (1992). "United States v. Alvarez-Machain," 60:4523.

U.S. Law Week (1988). 57:3327.

U.S. News & World Report (1986, September 8). "What Americans Want," 14-16.

U.S. Sentencing Commission (1995). *Special Report to Congress: Cocaine and Federal Sentencing Policy*. Washington, DC: U.S. Sentencing Commission.

U.S. Sentencing Commission (1991). *Mandatory Minimum Penalties in the Federal Justice System: Special Report to Congress*. Washington, DC: U.S. Government Printing Office.

U.S.A. Today, June 28, 1995.

United Nations (1990a). A/S-17/PV.1.

United Nations (1990b). A/S-17/PV.2.

United Nations Convention Against Illicit Traffic in Narcotic Drugs and Psychotropic Substances (adopted 19 December 1988). New York, NY: United Nations.

United States General Accounting Office (April, 1994). *Foster Care: Parental Drug Use Has Alarming Impact on Young Children*. Washington, DC: Report to the Chairman, Subcommittee on Ways and Means, House of Representatives.

United States v. Behrman, 258 U.S. 280 (1922).

United States v. Davis, 905 F.2d 245, 1990 AMC 2289 (1990), *cert. denied,* 111 S. Ct. 753 (1991).

United States v. Errol MacDonald (1990). En Banc Brief for the United States of America. United States Court of Appeals. 89-1262, 89-1263.

United States v. Frazier, 981 F.2d 92 (3d Cir. 1992).

United States v. Lattimore, 974 F.2d 971 (8th Cir. 1992).

United States v. Martinez-Fuerte, 428 U.S. 543 (1976).

United States v. Thomas, 900 F.2d 37 (4th Cir. 1990).

United States v. Verdugo-Urquidez, 110 S. Ct. 1056-1064 (1990).

United States v. Villamonte-Marquez, 462 U.S. 579 (1983).

University of Colorado v. Derdeyn, 863 P.2d 929 (Colo. 1993).

Usprich, S.J. & R. Solomon (1993). "A Critique of the Proposed Psychoactive Substance Control Act." *Criminal Law Quarterly,* 35:211-240.

Vera Institute of Justice (1992). *The Neighborhood Effects of Street-level Drug Enforcement—Tactical Narcotics Teams in New York—An Evaluation of TNT.* New York, NY: Vera Institute of Justice.

Vernonia School District 47J v. Acton, 115 S. Ct. 2386 (1995).

Volpe, J.J. (1992). "Effects of Cocaine Use on the Fetus." *New England Journal of Medicine,* 327:399-407.

Waldorf, D., C. Reinarman & S. Murphy (1991). *Cocaine Changes: The Experience of Using and Quitting.* Philadelphia, PA: Temple University Press.

Walker, S., C. Spohn & M. Delone (1996). *The Color of Justice: Race, Ethnicity, and Crime in America.* Belmont, CA: Wadsworth.

Walker, W.O., III (1992). "International Collaboration in Historical Perspective." In P.H. Smith (ed.) *Drug Policy in the Americas,* 265-281. Boulder, CO: Westview Press.

Walker, W.O., III (1989). *Drug Control in the Americas,* Revised Edition. Albuquerque, NM: University of New Mexico Press.

Wardlaw, G. (1992). "Overview of National Drug Control Strategies." In *Comparative Analysis of Illicit Drug Strategy,* National Campaign Against Drug abuse Monograph Series No. 18. Canberra, Australia: AGPS.

The Washington Post (1995, November 2). "President Clinton and Crack," A30.

The Washington Post (1995, April 18). "Cocaine: Two Forms, Two Views," A16.

The Washington Post (1994, March 26). "Two Penny-Weights of Crack," A22.

The Washington Post (1993, August 4). "Same Drug, Different Penalties," A16.

Webster v. Reproductive Health Services, 492 U.S. 490 (1989).

Weisman, A. (1986, October 6). "I Was a Drug-Hype Junkie." *New Republic*, 195:14-17.

Wells, V., W. Helperin & M. Thun (1988). "The Estimated Predictive Value of Screening for Illicit Drugs in the Workplace." *American Journal of Public Health*, 78:817-819.

Weston, D.R., B. Ivens, B. Zuckerman, C. Jones & R. Lopez (1989). "Drug Exposed Babies: Research and Clinical Issues." *National Center for Clinical Infant Programs Bulletin*, 9(5):7.

White House Conference on Drug Abuse and Control Resolution of 1986. Report From The Committee on the Judiciary, H.R. 846, Part 1, 99th Cong., 2nd Sess. (1986).

Whitner v. State of South Carolina, 65 U.F.L.W. 2066 (7-15 1996).

Whitney, C.D., M. Fritzer, S. Jones, S. Mazzarella & L. Rakow (1989). "Source and Geographic Bias in Television News 1982-1984." *Journal of Electronic Broadcasting and Electronic Media*, 33:159-174.

Wilbanks, W. (1987). *The Myth of a Racist Criminal Justice System*. Monterey, CA: Wadsworth.

Wiley, D. (1993). "Second Killing in 2 Weeks Has People Edgy in Waterloo." *Newspaper A*, 1.

Wiley, D. (1992). "Gangs Gaining a Foothold in Iowa Cities." *Newspaper A*, p. 1.

Wilson, W.J. (1987). *The Truly Disadvantaged: The Inner City, the Underclass, and Public Policy*. Chicago, IL: The University of Chicago Press.

Winfree, T., K. Fuller, T. Vigil & G.L. Mays (1992). "The Definition and Measurement of Gang Status: Policy Implications for Juvenile Justice." *Juvenile and Family Court Journal*, 43:29-37.

Wisotsky, S. (1987). "The Ideology of Drug Testing." *Nova Law Review*, 11:763-778.

Woodhouse, B.B. (1994). "Poor Mothers, Poor Babies: Law, Medicine, and Crack." In S.R. Humm et al. (eds.) *Child, Parent and State: Law and Policy Reader.* Philadelphia, PA: Temple University Press.

Woods, I. (1996, March). "Minority Groups, Social Inequalities, Poverty, and the Reduction of Drug Related Harm." Keynote address from the 7th International Conference on the Reduction of Drug Related Harm, Hobart, Tasmania, Australia.

Woolson, E. (1991). "Gang Element Cause for Alarm, Area Leaders Tell States Panel." *Newspaper B*, A1.

World Health Organization (1995). "Cocaine Project: Programme on Substance Abuse."

Wright, J., F. Cullen & M. Blankenship (1995). "The Social Construction of Corporate Violence: Media Coverage of the Imperial Food Products Fire." *Crime & Delinquency*, 41:20-36.

Wright, L. (1990). "Fetus vs. Mother: Criminal Liability for Maternal Substance Abuse During Pregnancy." *Wayne Law Review*, 36:1285-1317.

Wright, P. (1995, March). "The Federal Crime Bill." *Z Magazine*, 36-40.

Wytsma, L.A. (1995). "Punishment For 'Just Us'—A Constitutional Analysis of the Crack Cocaine Sentencing Statutes." *George Mason Independent Law Review*, 3(2):473-513.

Yepsen, D. (1994). "Grandy: End Parole, Build More Prisons." *Newspaper A*, A1.

Young, J. (1992). "Ten Points of Realism." In J. Young & R. Matthews (eds.) *Rethinking Criminology: The Realist Debate*, 24-68. London, England: Sage Publications.

Young, J. (1971). "Drugs and the Mass Media." *Drugs and Society*, 1:14.

Young, J. & R. Matthews (1992). *Rethinking Criminology: The Realist Debate*. London, England: Sage Publications.

Zaal, L. (1992). "Police Policy in Amsterdam." In P. O'Hare, R. Newcombe, A. Matthews & E. Buning (eds.) *The Reduction of Drug Related Harm*, 90-94. London, England: Routledge.

Zatz, M. (1987). "Chicano Youth Gangs and Crime: The Creation of a Moral Panic." *Contemporary Crises*, 11:129-158.

Zimmer, L. (1991). "Proactive Policing Against Street-Level Drug Trafficking." *American Journal of Police*, 9:43-74.

Zimring, F. & G. Hawkins (1992). *The Search for a Rational Drug Control Policy*. Cambridge, England: Cambridge University Press.

Zimring, F.E. & G. Hawkins (1991). "What Kind of Drug War?" *Social Justice*, 18(4):104-121.

Zuckermann, B. & D.A. Frank (1992). "Crack Kids: Not Broken." *Pediatrics*, 89:337-339.

Index

About the Authors

Katherine Beckett is currently an Assistant Professor in the Department of Criminal Justice and an Adjunct Assistant Professor in the Department of Sociology at Indiana University. Beckett received her Ph.D. in Sociology from the University of California at Los Angeles in 1994. Her research focuses on the political and cultural dimensions of crime-related issues and policies, both of which are explored in her most recent publication, *Making Crime Pay: Law and Order in Contemporary American Politics* (1997). Her current research analyzes political-economic causes and consequences of the expansion of the social control apparatus in industrialized democracies.

Michael P. Brown is an Associate Professor of Criminal Justice and Criminology at Ball State University. His research interests include community corrections, juvenile justice, and delinquency.

Henry H. Brownstein is an Associate Professor in the Division of Criminology, Criminal Justice, and Social Policy and Director of the Graduate Program in Criminal Justice at the University of Baltimore. Prior to that, he was Chief of the Bureau of Statistical Services for the New York State Division of Criminal Justice Services. Brownstein earned his Ph.D. in Sociology in 1977 from Temple University. He has published numerous articles and book chapters on various subjects, including drug-related violence, homicide by women, and the social construction of public policy and social problems. His book titled *The Rise and Fall of a Violent Crime Wave—Crack Cocaine and the Social Construction of a Crime Problem* was published in 1996.

Jennifer Ellen Butters received her Masters in Sociology from the University of Western Ontario and is currently a Ph.D. candidate in Sociology at the University of Toronto. She has been working at the Addiction Research Foundation since 1995 as a Research Assistant and holds a Pre-Doctoral fellowship in the collaborative program: Alcohol, Tobacco, and Other Psychoactive Substances. Her work at the Addiction Research Foundation has focused on drug market violence and crack cocaine. Her research interests includes drug market violence, sociology of addiction, youth, drug policy, and mental health. She has co-authored two book chapters and has collaborated on several conference papers.

Donald W. Crowley is an Associate Professor of Political Science at the University of Idaho. He specializes in judicial decisionmaking and judicial impact. Much of his recent work has dealt with issues involving the right to privacy.

Tina Engstrom is a graduate student in Sociology at the University of Northern Iowa. She is working on the completion of her Master's thesis that focuses on gangs, delinquency, and drug use.

Patricia G. Erickson is a Senior Scientist with the Addiction Research Foundation in Toronto, Canada, where she has been conducting criminological research since 1973. She received her Ph.D. from the Glasgow University, Scotland in Criminology/Social Administration in 1983. She has published several books and many articles in the field of addictions, and has acted as an adviser to the World Health Organization Project on Cocaine. Erickson is also an Adjunct Professor in the Department of Sociology at the University of Toronto, and is just completing a term there as the Director of the Collaborative Program on Alcohol, Tobacco, and other Psychoactive Substances.

Ronald S. Everett is an Assistant Professor of Sociology and Crime and Justice Studies at the University of Idaho. Previously, Everett was an Assistant Professor of Sociology at Louisiana State University and for two years worked as a Senior Research Associate for the United States Sentencing Commission. Everett's most recent research explores the influence of expressions and perceptions of remorse on sentence severity and the continuing role of racial/ethnic bias in federal sentencing.

Benedikt Fischer (Dipl.-Verw.wiss) is a Ph.D. candidate at the Centre of Criminology at the University of Toronto, Canada, and is a Scientist in the Clinical, Social, and Evaluation Department (CSER) of the Addiction Research Foundation (ARF) of Ontario in Toronto. Educated in Europe and North America in the social sciences, his main fields of interest are policing and social control, international drug law and policy, and evaluative criminal justice and addictions studies. He has published and presented numerous articles and papers on drug law and policy development in Canada and Europe, as well as policing issues. He is currently working on an ethnographic study of community policing and local control, and on a field study on the harms and social costs of untreated opiate use in Toronto.

Jurg Gerber is an Associate Professor of Criminal Justice and Assistant Dean for Graduate Programs at the College of Criminal Justice, Sam Houston State University. Previously, he was Assistant Professor of Sociology at the University of Idaho. Gerber served as co-editor of *The Criminologist*, the official newsletter of the American Society of Criminology, from 1992 to 1995. He edited *Conflict Issues in Sociology: Introductory Readings* (1990), and a special issue of the *Journal of Criminal Justice Education* on "The Peripheral Core of Criminal Justice Education." He has conducted research and published on topics ranging from drug policy to corporate crime, women and crime, social movements, and prison education.

Eric L. Jensen is a Professor of Sociology at the University of Idaho. Jensen has published a number of articles on drug policy and the use of illegal drugs. In addition to his work on drugs, Jensen's recent research and publications have focused on the waiver of juveniles to criminal court juvenile sexual offenders, and the effectiveness of nonresidential treatment for high-risk juvenile offenders.

Michael J. Leiber is an Associate Professor at the University of Northern Iowa. His research interests and publications are in the areas of juvenile delinquency and juvenile justice, with a particular focus on race and decisionmaking.

Marlana Puls is a graduate student at Sam Houston State University. She is working on her thesis that compares subcultural theory with techniques of neutralization theory to account for delinquent behavior.

Kevin F. Ryan is an Associate Professor in the Department of Justice Studies and Sociology at Norwich University. Much of his published work focuses on drug policy, though he has also done work in the areas of deviance theory, international law, criminal justice ethics, and legal theory. He is currently at work on a book with Robert Grandfield on the origins of United States drug policy and their implications for contemporary policy debates.

Inger J. Sagatun-Edwards is the Chair of the Administration of Justice Department at San Jose State University. She received her B.A. from Whittier College in 1967, and her M.A. (1971) and Ph.D. (1972) from Stanford University. She is the co-author of *Child Abuse and the Legal System* (1995), and the author of several articles and reports on the legal and social welfare response to "fetal abuse" and drug exposed infants, and in the general area of child abuse and family violence. She is currently the Project Director on a coordinated agency partnership model intervention project for mothers with young drug exposed children, funded by the OCJP. She is the immediate Past-President of the Western Society of Criminology, and she recently received the President's Special Recognition Award for SJSU.

Kent L. Sandstrom is an Assistant Professor in the Department of Sociology, Anthropology, and Criminology at the University of Northern Iowa. His most recent publications focus on how men with HIV/AIDS negotiate intimate relationships, manage emotions, and sustain vital and valued identities. He is currently writing a book (with Gary Alan Fine) titled *Symbols, Selves, and Social Life: A Symbolic Interactionist Approach*.

Theodore Sasson is an Assistant Professor in the Department of Sociology at Middlebury College. He received his Ph.D. in 1994 from Boston College. His research analyzes the politics and history of crime; and his most recent publication is *Crime Talk: How Citizens Construct a Social Problem* (1995).

Gary L. Webb is an Associate Professor of Criminal Justice and Criminology at Ball State University. His research interests include criminology, victimology, and corrections.